Christleton

2000 Years of History

Published by Christleton Local History Group
25 Croft Close
Rowton
Chester
CH3 7QQ

First published 2000
Text copyright © The contributors 2000
Photography © The photographers 2000
Drawings © The artists 2000

All rights reserved. No part of this book may be reproduced in any form or by any means without permission in writing
from the publisher, except by a reviewer who may quote brief passages in a review.

ISBN 0-9538470-0-4

Printed and bound by Masons Design & Print, Chester, UK

Foreword

By The Right Worshipful the Lord Mayor of Chester
Councillor Eric Plenderleath

I am very pleased to have been invited to contribute this foreword to a history of the village of Christleton, and I congratulate all who have contributed to it in any way. Although a resident of Tarvin, I have always admired Christleton as an extremely picturesque village which quite rightly has, over the years, been awarded many accolades, for which the Parish Council and the residents should feel very proud.
This is not the first nor, I am sure, will it be the last book on your history, but it is very appropriate that in this, the Millennium year, you should have drawn together information of the village over the past 2000 years. The time spent on the research will have been stimulating, interesting and enlightening, and I am confident that this shows in the book.
I hope that you who are reading it will find something of interest and perhaps will now view the village through different eyes. Too many of us accept this heritage of ours too easily, and if this history of Christleton only makes us stop, think and appreciate its value, the book will have served its purpose. You, who are lucky enough to have resided in Christleton, have now shared with us a little of that heritage.
My thanks and congratulations to all those who have been involved in this venture, be they contributors, researchers or writers.

I wish *Christleton 2000 Years of History* every success.

Eric Plenderleath
Lord Mayor of Chester (1999–2000)

Subscribers

Simon & Margaret Ward
Alf & Margaret Croston
Roger Croston
The Cummings family
N P Skerrett
David Parry
Mr & Mrs John Roberts
Phil & Pat Hodges
Brian & Jean Nield
Mr & Mrs Ffrench-Lynch
Miss K Tilston
Rena Griffiths
John Huxley
Mr & Mrs A D G Lewis
Mr & Mrs M B Haswell
Margaret Renner
Susan Haywood
Geoff & Judith Butt
Mr & Mrs F McClelland
Mr & Mrs H Davies
Dorothy Checkley
Ian & Irene McDonald
Mr & Mrs D E Smith
Russ & Sylvia Kenyon
Mr & Mrs J Scott
The Nilssen family
Mr & Mrs G E Brocklesby
Mrs Jennie Davies
Don & Margaret Bass
Roy Clough
Mr & Mrs W J Stockdale
Nigel & Clare Hill
Mr & Mrs John Storey
Mrs R A Boothroyd
Dr & Mrs T Clarke
Mrs Avis Dean
Mr & Mrs E B Dentith
Mrs Brenda Clarke
Pam & Harry Evans
Jaqueline Evans
Mr & Mrs A Oxley
Mike & Gill Jenkins
Eric Skipper
Mr & Mrs Alec Barclay
Pauline & Phil Edwards
Lewis, Sue & Heather Rees
Tony Gardner
Mrs F M Heaps
Mrs Christine Turton
Mrs Frances Clague
Geoff & Helen Clifton

Chris & Pauline Goodwin
Bill & Lyn Malkin
Eleanor & Lydia Sowden
Tony & Beryl Shell
Humphrey Broad-Davies
Will & Hazel Edwards
Mr & Mrs L Shepherd
Eric Burton
Mr & Mrs Brian Davies
Dr & Mrs D R Jenkins
Mr & Mrs Brian Roscoe
Margaret Yorke
Mrs Gertrude Jones
Tim & Dorothy Colley
County Cllr Neil Fitton
Bernard & Barbara Airey
Helen & Andrew Newton
Pat & Ken Holding
John Addison
Mrs D Tyrell
Simon & Rosemary Ely
Joyce Parker
Martin & Margaret Wheeler
Ian & Sue Crossan
Dr & Mrs W Pollitt
The Donald family
Mr & Mrs D Morgan
Joan Webb
Eric Beech
Mr & Mrs R Gardener
Audrey Williams
Elizabeth Wilson
Mr & Mrs Catherall
John & June Pearson
Adele Pearson
Judith Tudor-Jones
Richard Nicholson
Don & Jane Hinde
Mrs Emma Hinde
Mr & Mrs Leo Carroll
Mr & Mrs Nigel Bromage
Ron & Ricky Bridges
Rodney & Sue Witter
Mike & June Bishop
Tom Bishop
Cathy Bishop
The Seddon family
Ben & Jean Williams
David & Jean Cresswell
Rev & Mrs G B Westwood
Miss P H Johnson

John C Jackson
Beryl Dimmer
Peter Dimmer
Jane Scott (Dimmer)
Gillian Tooley
Jim & Pat Hawkes
Eileen & Dennis George
Judy A Smith
Nick T Smith
Colin J Smith
Mrs R Wolfendale
Miss Celia Brierly
The Barrack family
Peter & Rachel Barnes
Mr & Mrs Ray Enticott
Mrs Joan Astley
Rev & Mrs K Peter Lee
Simon & Carina Moffat
Mr & Mrs M S Jowett
J Brian Roberts
The McGuicken family
Miss Anne Butterworth
The Smalls family
Barry Dixon Bate
D W Rutherford
G K Stratton
Mrs J Holloway
Mr & Mrs Len Vickers
Mr & Mrs G Bramhall
Eric & Alison Kenyon
Mr & Mrs C J Rydings
Gertrude Wright
Margaret Hogg
Martin & Kate Roberts
Jim & Cynthia Siddall
Donald & Joan Kidd
Mr & Mrs John Hughes
Mr & Mrs P McCloughlin
Rebecca & Susan Tall
Philip Hurst
Sian & James Walker
Steve & Chrissy Bowgen
Marjorie Stafford
Mr & Mrs C Boyce
Mr & Mrs Tom Dewhurst
Mr & Mrs D Stewart
The Musgrave family
The Goharriz family
Ian Jones
Bill & Dot Hughes
David Hughes

Stephen Hughes
Mr & Mrs P B Davies
Stuart & Helen Gillies
Andrew & Chris Thompson
Mrs C L Steward
Mr & Mrs G M Campbell
Mrs May Cummings
Mr & Mrs G A Smith
Miss R M Sunter
Eleanor & Derek Walker
Mrs M Bate
Sheila Pickervance
Sarah Evans
Jacob Evans White
Tim Hunt
Mr & Mrs T Freeman
Mr J Stephen Corkery
Mrs A Bedford
Mrs E A Brown
Bob & Alison Johnson & family
Mr & Mrs A N Hurst
David & Janet Bowden
Katherine Bowden
Sally Bowden
Lt Col P R Bridge
The Quick family
The Smith family
Mrs C M E Smith
Heather & Brian Sloan
Mr & Mrs K Vickers
Christine & Stephen Davies
Mr & Mrs Martin Rocke
Mr & Mrs R Handley
Richard & Sue Morris
Cliff & Sue Mallows
Mr & Mrs W H McLachan
Kim & Phil Hill
Vivienne & Alan Warne
Richard & Susan Hall
Liz & Dave Bramley
Kate Harland
Katie Heritage
Jonathan Heritage
Alex & Wendy Taylor
Charles & Jean Smeatham
Dave Ellis
Phillip & Edith Haywood
Mr & Mrs J M Ferns
Mr Cliff Boddy
Mrs Karin Tong
Nigel & Gill Allen

Contents

Introduction ... 9

1 The Shaping of the Parish ... 10
• Christleton before the Norman Conquest • The Lord of the Manor and the Old Hall • Common Land and the Enclosed Fields • The Parish Council and Vestry Meetings

2 The Churches of Christleton ... 39
• St James' Church • Ceremonies and Festivals • Christleton College Youths (the Bellringers) • The Methodist Chapel and Methodism • The Roman Catholics and the Salvatorian College • Churches Together in Christleton

3 Times Past and Present ... 53
• The Roman Bridges • Christleton in the Civil War • Life in Christleton in the late 17th century • Christleton: the self-contained village • Christleton 1927–1953 • Village Trades and Industries

4 Personalities and Memories ... 75
• The Mayers Family • The Dixons of Littleton • Lionel Garnett • William Huggins • Frank Poston • Cliff Boddy • Eric Beech • Jas Storrar, Vet and Fighter Pilot

5 Education ... 96
• John Sellers' Charity School • Dame Schools • Christleton Academy • Girls' School • Boys' School • Primary School • Secondary Education • Under-Fives Community Playgroup • Toddler Group • The College of Law

6 Social and Sporting Life ... 109
• Village Players • Wednesday Group • Football Club • Cricket Club • 1st Christleton Scouts • Guiding in Christleton • Village Fete • Village Show • Chester Flower Club • Pit Group • Millennium Group

7 Natural History ... 127
• Christleton Pit • Hockenhull Platts

Acknowledgements and Bibliography ... 134

Introduction

This new look at the history of the parish of Christleton is the culmination of a great deal of hard work and research by members of the Local History Group, who decided in 1997 that they wished to produce a new book to commemorate the start of the millennium. The Local History Group was formed in 1976 by Mr Frank Latham and others to research material for a book about Christleton, which was to take its place in a series of books about the history of Cheshire villages. We acknowledge here his special expertise and enthusiasm that enabled us to develop the research and writing skills needed to produce the first book in 1979. This was extremely successful and raised a great deal of money for worthy local charities. This new publication has similar aims and will follow its example in distributing funds. However, most of the material we've used is new information to the group, and a great deal of it from the private papers and documents of the late Rector A A Guest-Williams. Members of the group have spent many hours at the Cheshire County Record Office, Chester identifying and cataloguing this exciting material, which reveals a great deal more than was previously known about both the Guest-Williams family and the village itself. Unfortunately, like several other chapters that have been written for the book, it has had to be substantially edited to keep the publication within limits. However, some of this information will be published in separate articles or pamphlets at a later date. Details can be found, and information constantly updated, in the parish magazine and on our website www.christleton.org.uk.

Two of these books, *A Village Trail* and *A Child's History of Christleton*, will be published later in the year to join the existing publications, *Christleton Pit* and *Hockenhull Platts*. Funding for the first two publications comes from the Village Millennium Group under the Millennium Awards for All scheme, and all proceeds will go to the village appeal, A Well for Africa.

I would like to express my grateful thanks to all my colleagues in the group, but particularly for their work on this publication, to Simon & Margaret Ward, Phil & Pat Hodges, Eric Kenyon, Roy & the Rev David Fisher, David & Nora Wain, Jim & Lucy Partington, Ted & Mabel Kirk, Margaret Croston, Judy Smith, Charles Smeatham, Brian Smith, Eric Beech, Cliff Boddy, and the late Margaret Davies and her brother Frank Poston. Special thanks go to Phil Hodges for his superb watercolour painting for the cover and for the main illustrations, and to Eric Kenyon for his skilful research and meticulous drawing of local maps and artefacts. Also to the extremely efficient and professional editing team of Sarah Donald, Katherine Seddon and Pat Nilssen, and to colleagues at Masons of Chester, our printers.

We would also like to thank the many members of the community who have shared with us their family stories and loaned us their photographs and other family memorabilia. The majority of recent photographs are mine, but many of the older photographs are the work of Reg Morgan, who took and published a large number of village life between 1900 and 1914. They now form the basis of our village archive collection which numbers over 8,000 pictures. We also thank our many excellent subscribers who have helped the book to get off to a sound financial start.

We acknowledge the help, advice and support of the County Archivist Jonathan Peplar and his staff at the Cheshire County Record Office in Duke Street, particularly Marlene and Derek. Also the former County Archivist Mr Brian Redwood, and Miss Eileen Simpson, former Diocesan Archivist, who first made us aware of the existence of the papers of the A A Guest-Williams collection. We would also like to thank the Right Worshipful The Lord Mayor of Chester Councillor Eric Plenderleath for his words of encouragement and for writing our foreword. Although every effort has been made to check the accuracy of the work, we apologise if we have made any errors or omissions. I take full responsibility for any we have made. We do hope you enjoy reading the book about our beautiful village and its fascinating history. We dedicate it to the people of Christleton, past and present in this Millennium year 2000.

David Cummings
Chairman

1 The Shaping of the Parish

Christleton Before The Norman Conquest

The Roman period

The story of Roman Christleton must have been dominated by the great legionary fortress, which had been established by about 75 AD at Chester. The history of this fortress through the centuries has been much discussed. In contrast, the evidence for any Roman occupation of Christleton itself is sparse. Local myth has wrongly attributed Roman activity to three places in Christleton. First, the so-called Roman Bridges at Hockenhull Platts were constructed in the mediaeval period. Secondly, there is no evidence of Roman activity in the long-disused quarry, from which Quarry Lane derives its name. As late as the 4th century, the Romans were acquiring stone for the fortress from closer quarries, including that in Edgar's Field, Handbridge. Thirdly, the ancient aqueduct off Christleton Road was of mediaeval origin. The Abbots Well in Christleton only became a source of piped water supply to the abbey in Chester after 1282.

There is no historical record of any local opposition from the tribes of Cheshire, the greater part of whom were probably Cornovii, to the Roman conquest. By circa AD 75, the fortress at Chester had been founded by *Legio II Adiutrix*, a legion previously based at Lincoln but originally raised in AD 69 from the Adriatic fleet. By AD 88, that legion had moved to the Danube, and the Twentieth Legion, *Legio XX Valeria Victrix*, had moved to Chester. Within 20 years, the fortress boasted not only a port but also a thriving civil settlement through which the main road from the fortress ran east to Northwich, Manchester and York. This civilian settlement had sprung up outside the military base to supply the needs of around 6000 soldiers and their entourage. It has been estimated that the population in and around the fortress could have reached 20,000.

An extensive supply system would have been necessary to maintain the fortress as well as the civilian settlement. The legionary bathhouses and latrines alone would have required a considerable supply of water, and the Roman military certainly regarded a good water supply as essential for all its foundations (Stephens 1986, 59–61). At the source of the supply in Boughton, the Romans erected a shrine in honour of the sacred spring. In 1821, an altar dedicated by the Twentieth Legion to the nymphs and springs was found, along with the remains of a building, at what is now Cherry Road. From here, the Roman water supply was fed west to the fortress by means of an aqueduct of waterpipes along Foregate

The Roman Bridges at Hockenhull Platts

Street. The Romans knew that ceramic pipes were preferable to lead for their water supply and such pipes have been found in the area. However, lead service pipes were also used, some stamped with the consular date of AD 79, the year in which the bathhouse was dedicated. A lead ingot cast in AD 74 was found during construction of the railway line at Tarvin Road bridge, and this may have been associated in some way with the aqueduct and its lead pipes (*VCH 184*).

Roman cemeteries, containing cremation burials, have also been found in Boughton in an area approximately 1 km north to south. The Romans preferred to bury their dead outside their city limits. Burials have been found in the Cherry Orchard, Stocks Lane and Bachelor's Lane area (*VCH 184*). Many of the objects associated with these cremations date from the late 1st or early 2nd century.

It has been suggested that Boughton formed another separate civil settlement, nearly 2 km from that immediately beside the fortress. However, there is little other evidence of Roman occupation in this area, apart from the water source shrine and a few stray finds. A Samian ware bowl with moulded decoration, which was dated to the period c AD 80–110, was found west of Boughton Cross during the road-widening scheme, together with evidence of the Roman road leading out to the Littleton area (*CAB* 7, 1980–1, 37). The absence of any other buildings has suggested the likelihood that this whole area was regarded as a religious site which was not to be desecrated by occupation.

The legionaries would have required many other supplies to maintain their garrison. It is well-known that the Roman works depot at Holt, some 12 km upstream from Chester along the Dee, produced tiles and pottery for the army (Ward 1998). These works were probably installed on legionary land and run by the military.

The Roman army probably requisitioned a large area of land, known as the *prata legionis* (pastures of the legion), for its food and other supplies. Traces of buildings with painted wall plaster found at Tattenhall and Irby might represent farms run under a military licence (Carrington 1994, 39). The requisitioned area could have included the Wirral as well as part of the West Cheshire plain, an area estimated at perhaps 200 sq km. The bulk of this territory may have lain to the north and east of the Dee. The Central Cheshire Ridge could have been its eastern boundary, lying just to the west of the villa excavated at Eaton-by-Tarporley. The river Gowy may have been the Roman boundary of the legion's territory. Until mediaeval times the Gowy was known as the Tarvin. This name is the anglicised version of the Welsh *Terfyn*, which was derived from the British Latin *terminum* (Latin *terminus*, a boundary). David Mason (1998, 180) has suggested that the anglicised Latin name could reflect survival into the early mediaeval period of inscribed boundary markers referring to the *terminus* between the territory of the army and that of the local tribe or *civitas*. However, it is likely that the vicinity of modern Christleton lay within the requisitioned area.

A good supply chain needs a well-maintained infrastructure. The main Roman road passed close to the area in which Christleton now lies. This road has been known locally and traditionally, as many Roman roads are, as Watling Street. This is actually the Saxon name for the Roman road which ran north from London to Wroxeter (the former base of the Twentieth Legion, near Shrewsbury). The A51 now follows the route of this Roman road, which is known academically as Margary route 7a. The road crosses the river Gowy south-west of the village of Stamford Bridge. (A road surface 6 m wide was recorded during fieldwork east of this crossing {*Britannia* **15**, 1984, 258}.) It then headed north-east up Kelsall Hill (Williams 1997, 25).

The line of the Roman road to the west of Littleton was examined by Simon Ward for Chester Archaeological Service in 1991, when it was cut during the construction of the new M53/A55 Link Road (*Cheshire Past* **1**, 1992, 13). Two successive surfaces were found. The lower one consisted of a substantial layer of river cobbles, about 3 m wide, set in a hollow in the soft sand subsoil. This was sealed by a clay dump on which lay a much more scattered and sporadic upper surface of cobbles. This in turn was sealed by the substantial make-up of the modern road. No direct dating evidence for the two roads was forthcoming from the site. However, the lower surface is thought to be the Roman road and the upper one the 18th century turnpike, which succeeded it. (The route of the link road was walked after the soil had been stripped mechanically, in case any spreads of finds or building debris might be found to indicate ancient settlement sites. However, only finds from the last two centuries were picked up, namely pottery and claypipe fragments. These are thought to be the results of manuring and kitchen midden spreading on the fields after they were enclosed early in the 18th century.)

South of Christleton, at Saighton, an ancient road, known in mediaeval times as the Blakestrete, may have been of Roman origin; this runs east of Ridges Lane from Ridgway Farm along the line followed by the township boundary. Kenneth Jermy has pointed out (*Britannia* **24**, 1993, 257) that ridge-and-furrow ploughing on both sides respects its line, and that its metalling and other features could indicate Roman origin. If so, this may have been a minor road linking an agricultural site with its market.

The fact that the legionary fortress was so well-established within 20 years of its foundation could infer well-developed building skills. The construction of Roman camps and fortresses involved great skill and must have needed considerable practice. Aerial photographic reconnaissance has revealed a group of practice camps, apparently of Roman origin, to the east of the fortress, including the area around modern Christleton. The group extends as far north as Fox Covert Lane in Picton and as far south as Waverton. To date (1999), aerial reconnaissance has revealed 13–15 camps to the one of which is the most easterly in the group. Recent examination of the photographs taken by the RAF in 1947 above Stamford Heath revealed two rectangular earthwork enclosures in the north-east of Christleton parish, north and east of Chester. Three of these camps have been noted within the modern parish of Christleton, lying immediately south of the A51. The full report (Ainsworth *et al* 1990) is summarised here.

The two enclosures lie only 450 m apart within the former area of Stamford Heath, which was enclosed in 1794. Their survival as earthworks may owe much to their location on what had been long-term heathland. The more westerly of the two appeared in the 1947 aerial photographs principally as a crop- or grass-mark. Now listed as a scheduled monument, it lies south-east of Stamford Lodge on a very slight north-facing slope on boulder clay.

Ground inspection in 1985 showed it to have survived as a severely degraded earthwork, 110 m by 83 m, rectangular in shape and with rounded corners. It lay in two arable fields, Commons Field and Hallows Field, which are regularly under the plough. The enclosure is defined by a low bank which has been spread by ploughing on the north and south sides. A break in the centre of the east arm probably represents an entrance. A surrounding ditch is best preserved along the south and east sides. There may be traces of an outer bank spread by ploughing on the south side. No internal

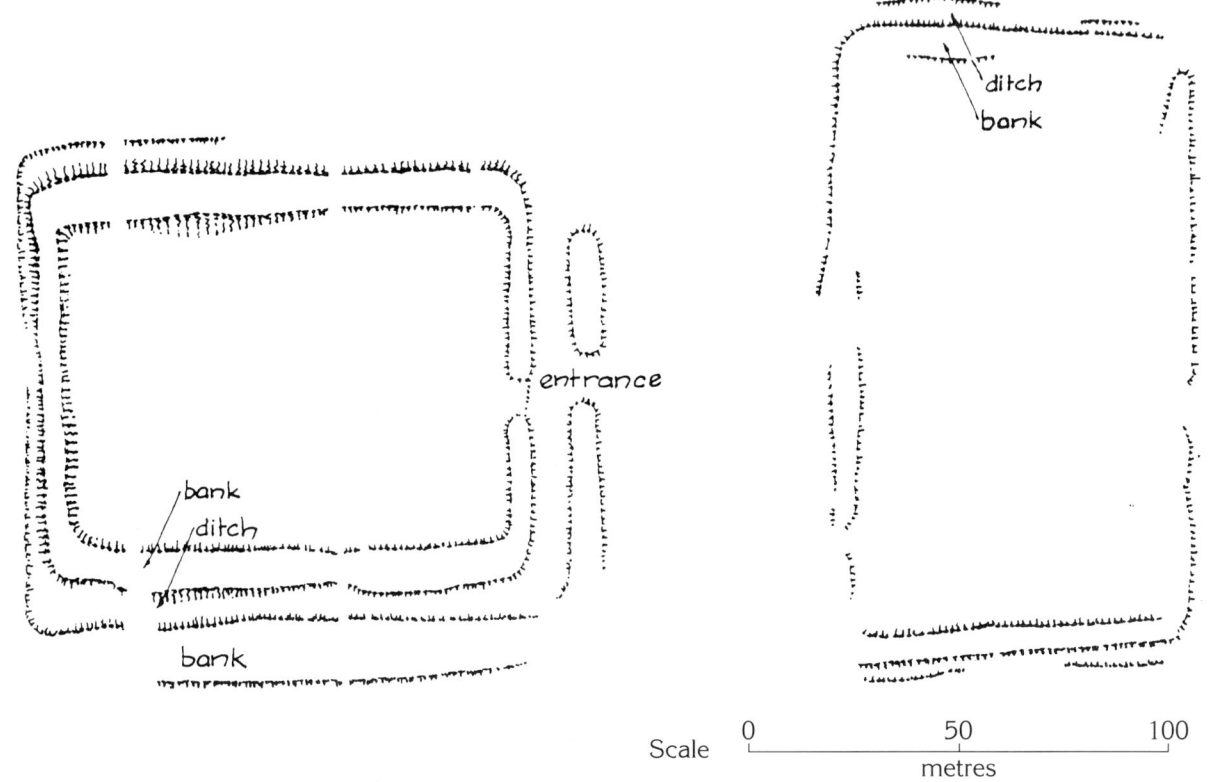

The remains of two Roman enclosures on Stamford Heath

features were noted within the enclosure. The site is overlain by ridge and furrow, one phase running north-south and another east-west. The aerial photographs alone show traces of a possible network of drains north and north-east of the enclosure and linked into its ditch at the north-east corner. There is no firm dating evidence for this enclosure, although it obviously predates the ridge-and-furrow ploughing and the enclosed fields. However, its proximity and orientation to the Roman road, together with its rectangular shape, rounded corners and narrow ditch, suggest a Roman military origin.

The eastern enclosure appeared nearby in the aerial photographs of 1947 as a rectangular earthwork. It lies in two modern hedged fields, known in 1844 as Mrs Townsend's Fields, to the east of Stamford Lane. The enclosure has been over-ploughed by narrow ridge and furrow in its southern half, with striations which suggest modern ploughing or drainage overlying the northern half. The corners appear to have been angular. The south-west corner has been partly destroyed by a hedge, but the remains are best preserved on the south and south-west side where there is a slight bank and ditch. Originally the enclosure would have measured 120 m by 85 m, with a possible entrance on the east side. No internal features were visible. A modern pond has been cut through the ridge and furrow which overlies the earthwork. Although the site lies close to the first enclosure, there are differences in the angularity of corners and the narrowness of bank and ditch. Since this site lies in the centre of what was Stamford Heath, it might represent a compound or enclosed paddock associated with mediaeval or post-mediaeval use. However, given the further discoveries made since 1986, the likelihood of a Roman origin cannot be dismissed.

In July 1996, during the recent series of discoveries, aerial photography revealed a third enclosure in Littleton, within the parish of Christleton. It was discovered in a field, formerly known as Isles Moor Field, where it has survived as a slight earthwork measuring 90 m by 58 m. The earthwork was sufficiently prominent in the mediaeval period to have been incorporated into the open field, with broad ridge-and-furrow butting against the exterior on the eastern side but running parallel to the long sides in the interior (Philpott 1998, 343). This enclosure is the smallest in the series of the three in the parish lying in a line immediately south of Tarvin Road, and it represents by far the smallest of all the examples observed to date.

The first in the recent series of discoveries was made in Upton-by-Chester during aerial reconnaissance by Manchester University in 1986 (Williams 1997, 23). Two enclosures had already been observed prior to 1986 at Upton-by-Chester. One of these, at Upton High School, was observed in 1964, but it had been interpreted as a Civil War redoubt (Philpott 1998, 341–2). Since 1989 several new sites have been discovered (J Collens in Nevell 1999, 36).

Most of the camps were observed as cropmarks or parchmarks, which are most obvious during periods of drought. Cropmarks do not form easily in Cheshire because of the clay subsoil and because of the extensive areas of pasture. Observations are therefore required over several seasons and the long dry summers of 1994 and 1995 were particularly productive from this archaeological viewpoint. (Subsequent trial-trenching of the first site revealed a V-shaped ditch, and although a Roman date was thought probable, no dating evidence was found.)

That some of these enclosures have been considered as mediaeval compounds or Civil War redoubts demonstrates the difficulty encountered in dating such earthworks. Aerial photography only provides a record of a feature that becomes evident as a result of the particular circumstances on a particular day. Excavation of these earthworks can reveal no date when no other structural evidence or

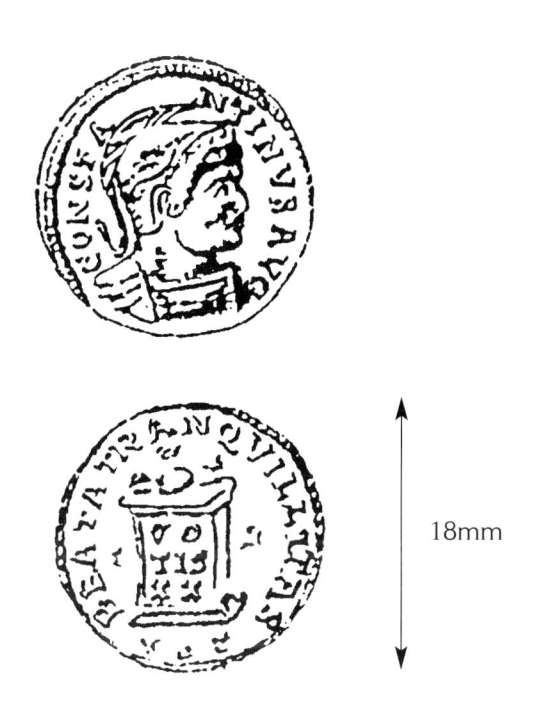

A Roman coin of Constantine the Great, minted AD 321

18mm

finds are recovered. All the available evidence of size, shape and details of construction indicate a Roman origin for these enclosures. Evaluation excavations at Upton have produced interesting environmental samples and charcoal from the lowest fill of the ditch, which gave a radiocarbon date lying within the Roman period.

As a result of the new discoveries, the pairs of enclosures at Upton and at Stamford Heath now seem to form part of a larger series of similar sites running in an arc 3–5 km from the legionary fortress. Of the 13–15 instances, six have been noted at Upton and at least three lie between Hoole and Guilden Sutton, including one at Belle Vue Farm. All have parallel sides and rounded corners but they are of differing size and orientation and have different types of entrance. Most, including the Christleton examples, are merely interrupted on their long sides. Only two, one at Waverton and one south of Hoole Hall (Philpott 1998, pl 28.A–B), display the additional earthworks known as *claviculae*, which the Roman army sometimes employed to defend fort entrances. These curved extensions of the ramparts, projected either inside or outside the entrance, would have caused any attackers to expose their unshielded side to the defenders. These defensive devices, when applied to rectangular enclosures, are indicative of their Roman origin, as they were used in the Flavian to Hadrianic period (AD 69–138).

The Hoole Hall example displays external *claviculae* at its entrances, and the Waverton enclosure shows evidence of an internal *clavicula* at an entrance on the south side. The latter's connection, therefore, with the main group is uncertain in the light of its apparently narrower plan, the use of internal *claviculae* and its remote situation (3 km away from any other example).

Roman military dispositions in the Chester area were clearly complex. More of these enclosures may yet be detected, and another might have been constructed to the west of that in Littleton. Their positioning seems closely related to the road system because all, except that at Waverton, lie close to the major Roman roads out of Chester. The Christleton examples seem to follow the alignment of the main Roman road to Manchester (A51) at a distance of a few metres. Philpott notes that since the road was probably built in the Flavian period (AD 69–96), these two groups of sites were unlikely to have been constructed earlier than this.

The positioning of several of the sites near Chester is on level clayland, which was recorded as heath in the Middle Ages. The environmental evidence gathered from excavating at Upton suggests that in the Roman period the area was already heathland. It may be that the Romans avoided placing these camps on land that was under cultivation, choosing instead areas of marginal agricultural value. Evidence from Bootham Stray, Clifton, c 2.5 km north of the fortress at York, provides an interesting parallel. Only two of seven or eight enclosures noted in the 18th century now survive, but they are comparable in size to the Chester examples. Their Roman origin is attested by their use of *claviculae*, and it is suspected that they too were situated on poor land in Roman times. The Chester series now represents the largest known complex of camps close to a legionary fortress in England. Their importance has been recognised in the recent scheduling of several of these sites, including the two on Stamford Heath, as ancient monuments.

This region's presumed marginal status as a remote backwater on the edge of the Roman Empire has been questioned recently by the late Professor Barri Jones (in Nevell 1999). Although it is true that rural settlement in this area is little known or understood, scholastic knowledge increases as research takes more interest in the subject. Occupation debris has long been found throughout western Cheshire. Some derives from small settlements or individual farmsteads, such as that at Tattenhall and the villa excavated at Eaton-by-Tarporley (*VCH* 210; Williams 1997, 26). Military diplomas, like that of a cavalry officer found at Malpas, may suggest that veterans

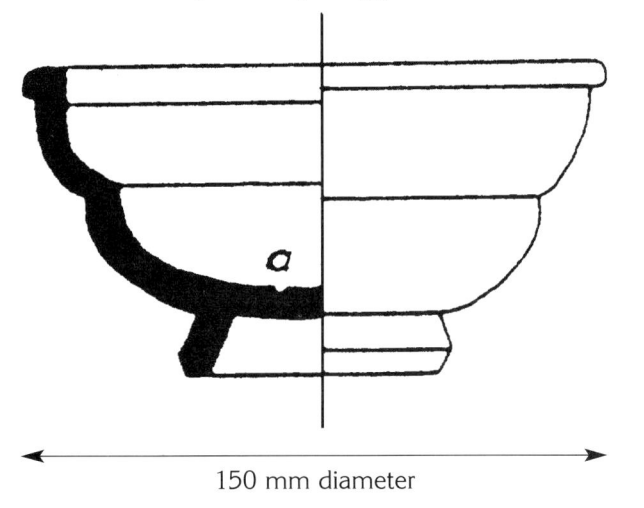

150 mm diameter

Roman Samian ware cup similar to the fragment found at the Law College. 'a' - the position of the potter's stamp

retired from the army to the surrounding countryside (Thompson 1965, 106ff), unless, of course, such items had been lost by their owners. Much of the evidence for rural activity of any sort in the Roman period consists of scatters of pottery or tiles, such as those found at Kelsall, Frodsham and Tarvin. Sporadic finds have been noted in Christleton and its immediate vicinity, including those listed below. They do not prove Roman occupation and all of them could represent stray losses. However, pottery is less likely to represent casual loss than is coinage. More finds of tableware, such as the Samian ware cup (5), would provide firmer evidence of Roman occupation.

Roman finds noted locally

The Sites and Monuments Record for Cheshire holds a list of the following finds from Christleton and its vicinity, ranging from the area of Vicar's Cross to Waverton, and has provided information incorporated in the following catalogue.

1. A bronze coin of Constantine I as Augustus (*VCH* 232), of the *BEATA TRANQVILLITAS* (Blessed Tranquillity) type, found in 1958 in a garden in Hawthorn Road. The inscription *VOTIS XX* is a standard legend on coins of the time and is unrelated to *Legio XX Valeria Victrix* and Chester; Roman coins were not minted in Chester. Dr David Shotter of Lancaster University has dated this coin to AD 321. (Now in the Grosvenor Museum, Chester.)

2. A lead weight, again found in 1958 in a garden in Rowton Bridge Road. This was punched with digits indicating two *unciae* (Roman ounces), but in fact was in deficiency of 2.6% less than that. (Now in the Grosvenor Museum.)

3. A barbarous radiate bronze coin of the 3rd century, reported to the Grosvenor Museum in 1992 along with a hoard of mediaeval silver coins, found in a field off Rake Lane.

4. A damaged fragment of the upper section of a dolphin-type bronze brooch, found off Skips Lane and reported to the Grosvenor Museum in 1988.

5. The finding in 1978 of the footring of a red-gloss (Samian ware) cup of form Dragendorf 27 in a trench by the entrance door to the Law College was recorded in Latham, *Christleton* 1979 16. It is stamped with the potter's name, Secundus, inside the base. Although the potter's stamp has not been identified precisely, a date in the 1st century is presumed (Grimes 1930, 124 no 30 from Holt). The vessel was reported to Manchester Museum by its finder, but the museum keeps no record of material handed in for identification and therefore has no information on the find.

6. A coin of Geta (c AD 208) of unknown provenance. This was drawn by John Speed on his map of Chester of c 1610 in the area of the Earl's Eye, illustrated likewise by Wenceslaus Hollar on his plan dated 1653 and mentioned by Ormerod in his *History of Cheshire* in 1882. It was supposedly inscribed *COL. DEVANA LEG. XX VICTRIX*. Ormerod does not suggest a provenance, but Latham, *Christleton*, 1979 15 gives details of this coin with reference to the much later coin of Constantine found at Christleton (1). The reverse of the latter bears no relation to Chester. Nor can the coin of Geta be taken as evidence for the colonial status of Chester. Its very existence is uncertain.

7. A silver coin, a *denarius* of Lucius Verus of AD 163–4, bearing the figure of Mars on the reverse. This has been identified precisely by David Shotter as *RIC* (Marcus) 514. It was found on Rowton Moor in the late 19th century, along with the following and other unspecified coins. It was recorded in *JCAS* 24, 1922, 151, 153. (Now in the Grosvenor Museum.)

8. An illegible bronze coin, also found on Rowton Moor. (Now in the Grosvenor Museum; see 7.)

9. A bronze coin, an orichalcum *dupondius* of Vespasian, with the goddess Fortuna on the reverse, minted at Lyons AD 77–78. This was found in a garden at Fir Tree Lane, Littleton in 1979.

10. A bronze knobbed terret ring: a horse-trapping with three clusters of knobs evenly spaced on the upper section. This was found in the river-bank at the time of straightening the river Gowy and building of the new bridge. It is of a type which was first produced in the 1st century, probably reaching the peak of production in the earlier 2nd century (*CAB* 10, 1984/5, 95). (Now in the Grosvenor Museum.)

11. A bronze bell, 8 cm high, 12.2 cm in diameter and with linear decoration. It was found just south of Stamford Bridge over the river Gowy on the bank in about 1957, but was reported to the Grosvenor Museum in 1987.

12. A bronze coin, a heavily worn *as* of Trajan, bearing the personification of Salus, the goddess of safety, on the reverse and minted in Rome in the period AD 103–111. This was found in a field near the Abbot's Well and was reported to the Grosvenor Museum in 1989.

13. A lead weight of eight *unciae* found at Vicar's Cross in 1885 on the line of the Roman road

running east from Chester. (Now in the Grosvenor Museum.)
14. A sherd from an amphora, possibly Dressel type 20, stamped *SALS*, found at Watling Court in Vicar's Cross. (Now in the Grosvenor Museum.)
15. A fragment of a bronze trumpet-brooch, found before 1978 south of Waverton.
16. A lead weight of four *unciae* found by the canal south of Waverton in 1977.

The *VCH* also notes that in 1870 a gold coin of Galba, Emperor in AD 68–69, was found at Huxley. At Saighton, recorded finds include a coin of Constantine II, a lead weight of one *uncia* and a bronze figurine probably representing an athlete (*CAB* **6**, 1978–9, fig 7.)

The Site and Monuments Record Office for Cheshire at the County Council's Commerce House, Chester maintains a database of all discoveries reported there and welcomes notification of any ancient find in the county. For many years the Archaeological Officer at the Grosvenor Museum in Chester has provided an identification service for antiquities. Recently, as a consequence of the Treasure Act, a national Portable Antiquities scheme has been set up to record and identify all finds. Its local officer can be contacted at Liverpool Museum.

The Dark Ages
The term *Dark Age* is used to refer to the period when coinage was no longer reaching Britain to pay the Roman army and the Emperor Honorius in AD 410 had instructed Britain to defend itself. The political system disintegrated, manufacturing industries (including pottery) collapsed, the written record largely disappeared and the archaeological record becomes obscure. The Dark Ages are so-called because of the gradual collapse of Roman civilisation and also because there is very little known about the post-Roman period. Throughout England material evidence of the Saxons and the Vikings is far less conspicuous than that of the Romans, and the area of Christleton is no exception. Other sources of evidence for contemporary activity in the locality must be sought.
Literary sources, including the great 8th century Northumbrian scholar Bede and the later Anglo-Saxon Chronicle, record events in the Chester area. In the 6th century the monk Gildas, possibly living at the monastery of Bangor-on-Dee, wrote of a massacre of martyrs at the *legionum urbs* (the city of the legions), which may have been Chester. Later, in his *Ecclesiastical History of the English People*, Bede wrote about St Augustine's second synod of c 603, at which Augustine, Archbishop of Canterbury, met with seven British bishops and many learned monks from Bangor-on-Dee. There has been speculation that this synod could have taken place in St Peter's basilica in Chester (T J Strickland in Ward 1994, 11).

Mediaeval coin found in Christleton in the 1990s

None of these literary sources contributes specifically to knowledge of the Christleton area. More helpful is the evidence of Old English that can be found in modern place names. While it is general knowledge that the Romans' name for Chester was *Deva*, few would recognise the Anglo-Saxon transliteration of the Latin *castra* (fort) into the Mercian form of Old English, *Ceaster*, from which the modern pronunciation of Chester is derived. Even more obscure is the reference in the Anglo-Saxon Chronicle for 980 to *Legeceaster scir*, which, by the time of Domesday in 1086, had become *Cestrescir* (Cheshire).

The name Christleton derives from the Old English *Cristentun*, meaning the Christian, or the Christians', enclosure, farm, or village (Dodgson **iv**, 1972, 107). The suffix *-tun* represents an enclosure, farmstead, estate or village, a suffix which is very common in Anglo-Saxon place names such as this. Apart from Christleton, the suffix is found in Waverton (the farm by the swaying tree) and Saighton (willow-tree farm). Names with this suffix appear to have evolved before the 8th century, and in this particular area the date is considered to be between 600 and 750. However, although the identification of the elements within place names requires linguistic skill, great caution must be taken in dating settlements from their modern names. For example, some place names ending in -ham could have developed from either of the suffixes -*ham* or -*hamm* (Gelling 1984, 48). Place names with the suffix -*ham* (meaning a village or estate) may also be among the earliest evidence, dating perhaps before the 7th century. However, -*hamm* can mean land in a river bend or a promontory into marshland, and these derivatives may represent much later developments (*VCH* 244). Indeed, those records referring to Christleton as Ham Christleton (meaning the home, or main, village of Christleton) belong to the 13th century onwards, when the subsidiary villages of Littleton and Rowton had already developed.

It seems that the Roman roads, which were still in use in the early Saxon period, dictated the pattern of distribution of early English place names and settlements. Names with the suffix -*ton* seemed to occur most frequently in the open landscape where Romano-British settlement had been most dense. This distribution suggests that these names occupied territory that had been cultivated by farming communities in the Roman period.

It seems that *British* Cheshire was being infiltrated by small groups of Mercian *English* from the later 6th century onwards. At first, this would have been an unobtrusive social infiltration, but it must have escalated later until the *British* or, as they became known, *Welsh* settlements became the minority. There are Welsh place names in Cheshire, together with English names referring to the Welsh, reflecting the fact that these minority communities still survived in the 7th century. Bede recorded that Chester lay within Welsh territory at the time of the Battle of Chester (probably in 616), when the Northumbrian king briefly defeated the king of Powys. However, it had fallen within English territory by 689 when the church of St John's was founded under Aethelred I, king of Mercia. It has been suggested that the river Gowy formed a political (not an ethnic) boundary between the Welsh and English until it became obsolete after c 616 (Dodgson 1997, 303).

The reference in the name Christleton to the Christianity of its inhabitants indicates that it was originally the pagan Saxons who named the settlement at an early date before the general conversion to Christianity. The religion of the inhabitants of this village must have been a distinguishing characteristic. It is unlikely that the first English people in Cheshire were Christians, and Christleton may be presumed to have been a British settlement. There is some evidence of late Roman Christianity in Cheshire. In 1993 and 1998, two inscribed lead salt pans were found on farmland at Shavington, near Crewe. Stephen Penney and David Shotter noted (*Cheshire Past* **4**, 1995, 6) that the inscription gives the name Viventius, a 4th century name with Christian connotations, followed by a fragment of a word which may represent *episcopus*, the Latin for bishop.

It seems that Christianity did not become popular as a rural religion in this region until as late as the 10th century. The settlement at Eccleston must have been similarly outstanding as a Christian community. The Old English element *eccles* derives from the Old Welsh *egles*, which is itself derived from the Latin *ecclesia*, meaning a church. The dedications of several local churches also indicate that some Christian settlements here may have been early. There are, for instance, dedications to St Chad (the Lindisfarne missionary who became bishop of the Mercians in 669), including the church at Farndon with its curvilinear churchyard.

The curvilinear, or oval, shape of churchyards is taken generally to be evidence for early Christianity. The churchyard at St James' Christleton is reputed to have been curvilinear (*VCH* 288), but at some later date it must have been enlarged to a rectangular shape (cf *VCH* 240). Several oval churchyards are known in the area, including Eccleston, Farndon, Dodleston and Pulford. These oval churchyards originate from the enclosures around sub-Roman or Celtic churches. In Wales they are considered to belong to foundations of the 5th and 6th centuries. It is possible that the church in Christleton existed before the arrival of pagan Saxons in the 7th century, but there is no documentary reference to it before 1093, and nothing is known of the early church building.

The absence of Anglo-Saxon finds is not unexpected for a small Dark Age settlement. In fact, curvilinear churchyards are the most common evidence of contemporary activity in rural Cheshire. Many of the Anglo-Saxon crosses in the county were associated with curvilinear churchyards. In Christleton there

St James' Church tower and graveyard

was once a large sculptured cross, which may have been pre-Norman, but this is now lost (*VCH* 275–6, 288). In 1614 it was noted along with six other instances, all reputedly 24 ft high. The three at Christleton, Barrow and Eccleston were clearly decorated monuments; four more including those at Tarvin, Delamere Forest and Vicar's Cross appear to have been plain pillars. Part of the Vicar's Cross pillar is reputed to have survived in Littleton. Fragments of sculptured stonework have been observed in Christleton, and one of uncertain, though probably later, date was formerly visible in the garden wall of Whitegates in Rowton Bridge Road. At Bruera, carved stones thought possibly to be Anglo-Scandinavian were built into the inside arch of the south doorway of the Norman church of St Mary's. This was originally a chapelry of St Oswald's parish in Chester (Williams 1997, 50; cf *VCH* 288). Amongst the Anglo-Saxon crosses in Cheshire, the grandest are the famous late Anglian examples at Sandbach, which have been dated to the 9th century (*VCH* 276 ff).

At the beginning of the 10th century, one of the Archbishops of Canterbury was St Plegmund, a Mercian scholar. The late 12th century writer, Gervase of Canterbury, records that Plegmund had lived as a hermit on an island which is presumed to have been Plemstall (Plegmundestowe—Plegmund's holy place) on the Gowy. An impression of this hermitage on an isle in the once extensive marshes can be seen from aerial photography around the modern church of St Peter's (Williams 1997, 36). Plegmund became one of Alfred the Great's advisers during his troubles with the Danes. (He was appointed Archbishop in 890, nine years before Alfred's death in 899.) Plegmund died in 923 during the time when Alfred's children were pushing back the tide of Viking incursions. West Cheshire had been suffering raids from the Vikings at the end of the 9th century. A Danish army had spent the winter of 893–4 encamped in Chester's deserted Roman fortress. A decade later the Norse, expelled from Ireland, had attempted to seize Chester. In 907, in order to secure it for the Saxons, it was refortified as a *burh* (a fortified enclosure or defended settlement) by Aethelflaed, the daughter of Alfred the Great and sister of Edward the Elder. (As part of their campaign against the raids, the Iron Age hill fort at Eddisbury in 914 became one of Edward's *burhs*, as its name indicates.)

It is unclear what effect the Viking settlement had on the population of Christleton. In the surrounding region, Viking finds have been made in various locations including Chester and Neston. A few Cheshire place names betray Viking influence, such as Caldy, the Norse for a cold place. The name Tarporley, which contains the Saxon element *leah* (wooded glade), may have seen the attachment of the Old Norse *porpari* (one who lives in a hamlet). This would suggest that an ethnic minority of Scandinavians had been given a nickname, presumably by their English neighbours (Dodgson **iii**, 1971, 295). In Chester, two church dedications are of Hiberno-Norse origin, namely those to St Bridget and to St Olave, the Norwegian king who was killed in 1030. Documentary evidence suggests that the Scandinavians occupied the southern part of the *burh*. The archaeological evidence from excavations in Chester indicates that the Saxons and the Scandinavians lived side by side (Ward 1994, 121). Reconquest of the Danelaw, the parts of the country under Danish control, was gradually achieved. After the deaths of Aethelflaed in 918 and Edward in 924 on the royal estate of Farndon, perhaps at Aldford, Chester prospered as a result of Irish

Sea trade with Dublin and the Norse, including a slave trade. By the reign of Athelstan (924–939), Chester was so prosperous that its mint was for a while the most prolific in England. However, this prosperity did not last through the 11th century.

The Domesday period
In 1086 William the Conqueror commissioned the Domesday survey, which included a record of the state of the country on the eve of the Norman invasion in 1066. Chester was the only town of any size in the county, with 508 houses, and it was the only borough with burgesses. After the arrival of William and his army in Chester in 1070, the city in 1086 was described as greatly wasted and half of its houses were unoccupied. Domesday lists the *manerium* of Christleton in the Hundred of Dudestan (Broxton) as one of the richer and larger 'manors,' being of the fiscal value of seven hides and including a mill and an extensive wood. Its recorded population was 23, of whom the two reeves and two radmen (probably riding men) appear to have been freemen. In 1066 it was held by Edwin, Earl of Mercia, and was worth £6. By 1086, although still one of the more valuable manors, it was worth only £3. Hugh Lupus, the first Norman Earl of Chester and nephew of William the Conqueror, had found Christleton 'wasted' in 1071, when he passed it on to Robert FitzHugh, the favoured Baron of Malpas. Domesday records that 'of this manor Rannulfus [Ranulf] holds of Robert two hides and renders him twelve pence.' Ranulf, or Randle, was a Norman under-tenant who also had holdings elsewhere. The origins of FitzHugh himself are obscure, but the manors which Earl Hugh gave him in Cheshire, most of them in Dudestan, outnumbered all except the Earl's own. He may indeed have been Hugh's illegitimate son. It appears that Christleton, like Chester and many other settlements in Cheshire, was wasted during the Norman Conquest. The village then became part of the barony of Malpas. It is documented that FitzHugh went on to donate the church, or *capella,* and its land to the Abbey of St Werburgh on its foundation in 1093. After his death, his daughter Letitia was to extend the grant by giving the whole manor of Christleton to the abbey. The Dark Ages had ended, and the Normanisation of England was under way.

The Lord of the Manor

The Manor of Christleton
The Manor of Christleton originally formed part of the Norman barony of Malpas and came into the hands of the Bermingham family in the time of Henry II. William de Bermingham is said to have sided with Simon de Montfort and was killed at the Battle of Evesham in 1265. By the dictum of Kenilworth in 1266, ransoms were made payable by the rebels, and they and their heirs were allowed to redeem their lands. As late as 1285 the ransom for Bermingham's land had not been fully paid, and Isabel his wife only held

The Manor House

Portrait of King Charles II on a Christleton property deed

between a third and fourth part of the lands. An order was issued that the lands in Buckinghamshire should be taken into the King's hands, and a similar order applied to the Christleton property.

By 1400 it had become the property of Sir Hugh Browe (Broome). Sir Hugh was originally a supporter of King Henry IV, but was one of the Cheshire Knights who fought on the losing side at the Battle of Shrewsbury. The lands and possessions of Sir Hugh were then granted to a John Mainwaring who had earned fame together with Thomas le Grosvenor by raising a troop of soldiers to invade Ireland in 1399. He was then made an attendant to the Prince of Wales, later Henry V. John Mainwaring had no children and he bestowed the Manor on Thomas le Grosvenor. By 1422 it appears to be in the ownership of John de Macclesfield, and passed by him to Humphrey, later Duke of Buckingham. The Buckinghams sold the Manor to Sir William Sneyde of Keele, who in turn sold it to Sir John Harpur of Calke Abbey in Derbyshire. (The Sneydes are also recorded as being owners of the Windmill at Christleton.) The ownership of the Manor remained in the hands of the Harpurs until 1782, although there were several attempts in the 1700s at selling it to the Townsends, who had by then acquired the Old Hall. Robert Townsend offered £4,200 and later, in April 1765 in a joint bid with William Widdens, £5,900 was offered and turned down. It was then sold to Thomas Brock, Town Clerk of Chester, for £9,529 3s 4d. The family, who later became known as the Brock-Woods, retained it for many years. It then passed on to Joseph Cooper and later to John Williams.

The Old Hall

The Old Hall would seem to be the natural place for the Lord of the Manor of Christleton to live, but this was not the case. It was built soon after 1603 by a member of the Egerton family, who had their main family seat at Tatton Park, Knutsford. It was a half-timbered building later enclosed in brick by the Rector Canon Lionel Garnett in the 1890s. John Egerton was described as a husbandman in a will of 1667 and possessed a coat of arms of six quarterings. The building was purchased by Gerard Townsend, a Merchant of Chester, around 1710, and he was succeeded by his son Robert Townsend, a Lawyer and Recorder of Chester. Although the Old Hall itself was built in 1603, there is some evidence of buildings of an earlier period on the site. Above the Tudor-looking fireplace in the main hall, the original grate for which is still preserved, there are two ovals of plaster. The right panel shows the emblems of the English Rose, the Unicorn and the Thistle of Scotland, representing the Stuart dynasty. On the left oval panel is a curious device of a crest or badge of an oak tree, with an eagle preying upon an infant. There is no doubt the house was originally built in black and white timber frame style, but was encased in 1890 in red Ruabon brick by Lionel Garnett, possibly to help preserve it from decay.

The main doorway and its jambs are carved, and there is similar decoration on the doorposts of the library. The staircase is Elizabethan in style. The ceilings in the hall, dining room and library are good examples of early 17th century plasterwork. The dining room has warm Jacobean oak panelling and a charming closet in the south-east corner. The Oak Room above has lost its original panelling; however, it still has a powdering closet. All the floors of the main rooms are of solid oak. There are still traces of the old arrangement of buttery screens. Reconstruction has taken place in the drawing room according to the fashions of different periods, and pillars shaped like mahogany bedposts have been introduced to strengthen the main beam in order to preserve the Georgian ceiling. A tunnel surrounds the whole building; much of it is comparatively modern, but there are portions of the older work at the south-east angle and under the drawing room. This connected the house with a passage of ashlar-work (masonry of squared stone), now mainly uncovered, but originally roofed over. A local tradition links this tunnel with the Manor House and the church, and this would make sense if the house had been part of the Christleton Parliamentarian garrison during the Civil War, but the remains now visible run in the opposite direction. It is possible that a hideout existed at the back of the library reaching up to the roof. A concealed staircase may also have existed by the fireplace in the hall, which connected with the tunnel. Behind the house there is evidence of six bread ovens and a lawn that may have been an archery court. The garden slopes gently to the east between yew, holly, oak, ash and acacia trees with rhododendrons behind on both sides, and golden elms, cypresses, a cedar and a magnolia beyond.

The Townsends

Towards the end of the 17th century the Old Hall was purchased by Gerard Townsend, a rising and wealthy merchant in Chester. He was named after his maternal grandfather, Gerard Jones, a Goldsmith and Mayor of Chester in 1658, who was the youngest son of Owen Jones of Gworton and Dorothy, daughter and co-heiress of John Titteley of Tittley in the County of Chester. He also married a co-heiress, Katherine, daughter of Humphrey Dymocke of Willington, and brought into the ancient Jones family the blood of the Eytons, Grosvenors, Hanmers, Breretons and many other names of note in Cheshire, Shropshire and the Principality. All this can be seen in an illuminated pedigree drawn up by Randle Holme in 1648. Gerard Jones married Priscilla, daughter of John Brerwood of Chester, and it was their daughter Priscilla who married Robert Townsend, Ironmonger and Sheriff of Chester in 1672 (the year in which he died). A memorial brass to Robert can be found in St Peter's Church at the Cross, Chester. He was the son of Richard Townsend, also an Ironmonger in the City and Sheriff in 1652. His wife, Dorothy, was the daughter of Robert Selsby, a Butcher and Freeman of Chester in 1639.

Gerard, the son of Robert Townsend, married Sarah Stratford, widowed daughter of Randle Vause. They had many children, all baptised in Christleton. The eldest son, another Gerard, whose son predeceased him at the age of nine months, was succeeded at Christleton by his brother Robert Townsend, a very shrewd Lawyer and Recorder of the City of Chester 1754–1787. He was evidently a grasping and ambitious man of affairs who married three times for profit: first to Elizabeth, daughter of William Farrington of Eardshaw, by whom he had two surviving daughters, Anne and Elizabeth; secondly to Anne, younger daughter of John Myddleton of Chirk Castle; and thirdly to Betty, widow of Thomas Farrington, but there is no record of any more children. His eldest daughter Anne made a favourable marriage to Mr Cecil Forester, and their son, the first Lord Forester, married the daughter of the Duke of Rutland. Elizabeth married Thomas Ince, an ensign in the Army and son of the Reverend Thomas Ince, a minor Canon of Chester Cathedral and later a much loved Rector of Handley. His wife Susan Robinson was the daughter of Hugh Clough of Plas Clough and 'lady of distinguished parentage from Denbighshire.'

The Ince family

The Inces were another family of Chester merchants and thriving tradesmen, and they too possessed a pedigree by Randle Holme, connecting them with the Inces of Ince,

Part of the illuminated pedigree drawn up by Randle Holme in 1648

The Seal of Robert Dudley, Lord Leicester, from a parchment deed of 1585 (part of the Guest-Williams collection)

Lancashire. However the Townsends, though of similar origin and status, because they were Councillors and Aldermen of Chester disapproved of this alliance. To satisfy his wife's vanity Thomas Ince was forced to give up his career in the Army and live in Christleton. All might have been well, for he had an estate of his own called The Beachin at Coddington, which was left to him by his father, but this was not grand enough for his wife. She compelled him to build a house on the Stoneydale property in Christleton, which had been acquired by the family, to rival the Old Hall where her father lived.

This new mansion, known as Christleton Hall and now the College of Law, was typical of a house built in the late Georgian period, with large rooms and grounds laid out in the approved style of the day. In order to erect this mansion, Thomas Ince was obliged to sell his commission in the Army and gradually mortgage every acre of his own land to enable his wife to live in style. Elizabeth repeatedly promised that he would be reimbursed, and that all would be well when the 'Old Rascal', her father, died, but although she outlived her father, she did nothing to compensate her husband for her extravagance. On the contrary, she heaped insults upon his head to the end of her life and compelled him to live in penury, while she and her daughters wanted for nothing.

(When Elizabeth died Thomas married again, seemingly very happily to a Margaret Adams of Christleton, although not for money this time. According to his own record he would have sacrificed his life in order to secure his widow and her child a sufficient income. Their son was also named Thomas.)

Thomas Ince and Elizabeth Townsend married in 1744 and had four children: Elizabeth who married Robert Passingham; Emma who married Hugh Webb; a younger son Bell Ince who died unmarried; and an elder son Townsend Ince, who married Miss Mary Catherine Currie, daughter of Dr William Currie of Boughton Hall. (Mary Catherine's grandmother, Elizabeth, had married John Williams of Gwersylt Hall near Wrexham, and from this line the Rev Guest-Williams is descended.)

During his marriage to Elizabeth, Thomas Ince was in such despair over his financial affairs that he threatened to commit suicide, and among the papers found at the Old Hall is a very detailed suicide letter written by Thomas to Townsend, his elder son, explaining his problems and asking for help. At the end of this long and desperate letter he asks for forgiveness and that Robert should give the news to Bell and his youngest son Tom. He threatens to 'weight himself down and jump off a boat in the Irish Channel.' It is unclear whether or not he actually took his life, but a Thomas Ince of the right age was buried in the churchyard at St James' Christleton in 1805, but significantly not in the family vault.

The Townsend Ince family

Townsend Ince and his wife Mary had a son, also called Townsend, who married Lucy Anne, daughter of Augustus Fuller of Rose Hill. They both devoted themselves to the welfare of Christleton, and Lucy Anne in particular had a great influence on village life during the rectorship of Lionel Garnett. The latter often said that without her great moral and financial support he would have not been able to carry out his many plans and ideas for the people of Christleton. In dying without surviving issue, Townsend and Lucy Anne's property came by will to Major William Townsend Currie, grandson of Bishop Graham and great-grandson of Dr Currie. Major Currie came to live at the Old Hall in Christleton in preference to his ancestral home at Boughton, and the impressive Christleton Hall was sold. Major and Mrs Townsend Currie lived in Christleton and did much to make the Old Hall a centre of hospitality and good causes in the neighbourhood. Major

Currie was particularly interested in the work of the Boy Scout movement, and entertained the Chief Scout, Lord Baden-Powell, in Christleton. Major Currie died at Amlwch, Anglesey in 1942.

A.A. GUEST-WILLIAMS, F.S.A.
Christleton Old Hall

The Guest-Williams coat of arms

The Reverend Alyn Arthur Guest-Williams

The Rev Alyn Arthur Guest-Williams claimed descent from the Currie family pedigree, which also involved the Davenport, Gardner, Smith and Gerard families. In his records there is a family pedigree of the Davenport and Hand families dated 1665, and Dr Currie's descent continues from them through the Foulkes of Llechred. Elizabeth Currie married John Williams of Gwersylt Park near Wrexham and, from this marriage, comes another family line of the Rev Alyn Arthur Guest-Williams. Samuel their son married Elizabeth Guest, the daughter of John Guest of Preston Brook, in 1815. (Elizabeth's grandfather was William Sellers, Mayor of Chester in 1778, who was born in Christleton in 1732. John Sellers, his son, founded the Charity School in Christleton in 1779.)

Samuel Williams and Elizabeth had a son in 1818 named John Guest-Williams, who married Elizabeth Kirkham in 1849. Their son Samuel Blackwell Guest-Williams became Canon of Norwich Cathedral and later married Catherine Gray. They had four sons: Captain Warren Guest-Williams and Captain Wynne, who both died in the First World War, Captain Richard and the Rev Alyn Arthur.

The Rev Alyn Arthur was a renowned genealogist, and his personal papers show his numerous attempts to create a family pedigree. One document shows a descent from an alliance between Llewellyn the Great, the last Prince of Wales, and Joan, the daughter of King John, in 1206. Their daughter Princess Margaret married John de Blaon in 1232, and then Sir Walter de Clifford in 1263. The line continues through Faulk, Lord Straryn and Brian de Cornwall to Sir John Blount of Kinlet, 1382. From the Blounts, the line follows through Oteley of Pickford to John Bruyn of Stapleford, a local family. It continues through the Bruyn line to Griffith Dicas and the marriage of his daughter to Richard Pulford of Rowton. A daughter, Ann Pulford, married John Sellers of Littleton in 1641, and the line continues in the Sellers family through William who married in 1689, another William who married in 1717, to Alderman William Sellers (Mayor of Chester in 1756) who died in 1790. (The line continues as described in the paragraph above until the death of Rev Alyn Arthur in 1974.)

After graduating from St John's College, Cambridge where he was a student of Classics and a Choral Scholar, Alyn Arthur Guest-Williams was ordained in 1911 and went to the Parish of Binfield. After a short time there he became the Precentor (leader of the music) at Norwich Cathedral, where he married Harriet Beaching, the eldest daughter of the Dean. On the death of his father-in-law he accepted the living at Trowell in Nottingham, and came to Christleton in 1926 after exchanging parishes with the Rev Hickey. He was an enthusiastic antiquarian and was elected a Fellow of the Society of Antiquaries in 1943. He also edited the Registers of Christleton for the *Cheshire Sheaf* for many years. An avid collector of Georgian silver, it was one of his pleasures to present small pieces from his silver collection to brides, at whose wedding he officiated, and to babies on their baptism. Some of these pieces are now extremely valuable and a baptism spoon, believed to be from his collection and found in a village garden, was sold in the late 20th century for a very large sum to a collector. He was also a keen supporter of the St James' Church Bellringers, of village Fetes and other festivities including the Agricultural and Flower Shows, many of which took place at the Old Hall under his patronage.

The Rev Alyn Arthur, or Mr Guest-Williams as he was sometimes called, was described as a real gentleman by local people who knew him, and he regularly hosted parties for parishioners at the Old Hall. He was said to have been extremely kind to anyone in need and regularly made long journeys to hospitals to see parishioners. His wife died in 1949 and after he retired in 1966, the Rev Alyn Arthur lived the remainder of his life at the Old Hall with his rather eccentric brother Richard. The Rev Alyn Arthur Guest-Williams died in 1974, the year after his brother, and his remains were buried in the family grave at Gresford Church.

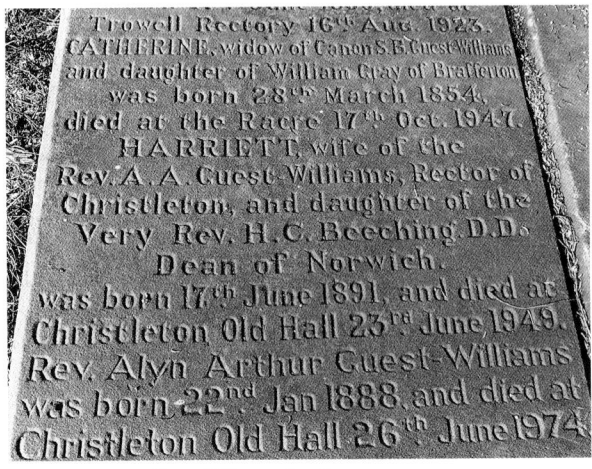

Detail from the Guest-Williams family gravestone

Life in the Old Hall

One of the benefits of having a lawyer living at the Old Hall was that he kept good accounts, particularly receipts. Like many families of the period, the Townsends often acquired land and money by making good marriages for their children and several of these are described earlier. However, Robert Townsend was also a very astute businessman, and there are several instances of money and land being acquired by his skills as a lawyer. The inheritance of land and property occurred fairly frequently, but there were also frequent disputes, many of which ended up in the law courts. Robert seems to have been the beneficiary of many such battles.

For example in 1738, deeds exist showing that 'properties including new river works in London, lands in Guilden Sutton, Christleton and a dwelling house in Bridge Street Chester', transfer to Robert Townsend. Following the settlement of the Adams Estate, fields in Christleton, The Meadows, Long Croft, Streetaway Hill, Caldy Shoot and Finney's Field were acquired by Robert Townsend. Valuable land on the edge of the City of London at Muswell Hill, which had been part of the Mottershead and Hardy Estates, was sold and the finances were eventually acquired by the Townsend Ince family who were related by marriage to the former. This was prime land and is described in the sale as:

Lot 2. All those messuages, barns, and other buildings with gardens and having the most excellent grazing and mowing lands adjoining there, and held therewith by Mrs Sarah and Mr John Upton and their undertenants. Situated on that delightful spot Muswell Hill near Highgate in Middlesex, about four miles from London with plenty of fine spring water in every field and commanding the most beautiful and extensive views over London. These last premises are most admirably adapted for building upon, and will be sold in one or more lots etc.

Other land in London also came their way. In 1793, land in his cousin Nathaniel Hardy's estate in Queen Street Cheapside, Stepney and Aldgate was transferred to the Townsend estate in Waverton, Christleton and Guilden Sutton. Nathaniel's son, also Nathaniel, was later committed to a lunatic asylum, and Robert became involved in the case both as lawyer and next of kin.

The family also invested heavily, and details from their shares and investments can be seen in the various annual accounts, for example: Flintshire Oil & Canal Co £8,000 stock; Chester River Dee Navigation Co; Great Western Railway Company £4,500; Chester Canal Company; Columbia & Spanish Stock £47,000; Western Bank of Scotland; land in Brymbo containing coal £18,000; and South Sea Annuities £500.

Involvement with the Military

From the 18th century, the Townsend, Ince and Currie families had a strong involvement with the military, starting with Thomas Ince who resigned as an ensign in the Army in order to build Christleton Hall. Bell Ince, his son, became Lieutenant Colonel of the Royal Cheshire Militia of Stockport in 1809 and was closely followed in this by his brother

Townsend. Their letters of approval were personally signed by Lord Palmerston and Hugh Walpole, who had both been Secretary-at-War. As Lt Col of the Stockport Militia, Robert is asked to raise 988 men, 865 from Macclesfield and 123 from Stockport. The family records contain details of the clothing needed for the regiment, as well as details of how it was to be organised. A later directive in 1814 requires the regiment to reach a strength of 3,500 men.

During the 1850s the Currie branch of the family become more prominent, and they fought in significant battles. Richard Henry Currie was appointed to serve as a young soldier in the 6th Inniskillen Dragoons, and by 1853 he had been promoted to Lieutenant. He experienced the horrors of war at Varna and Sebastopol, and in a letter of 1854 there are references to the Light Cavalry being cut up at Balaclava. Another letter refers to the death of his brother-in-law, Captain Robert Campbell, in the Crimea. In 1846 a captaincy in the Horse Guards was purchased for the sum of £450 for William Ferguson Currie and by 1854 he had been made a Captain in the 81st Regiment of Foot. His son William became a 2nd Lieutenant in the 5th Battalion Royal Fusiliers (City of London Regiment) and in 1902 he fought in Rangoon with the 1st Battalion Royal Fusiliers.

The Church connection

Whilst many of the family served their country through the Army, others joined the Church. The Reverend Thomas Ince was the first known family member to do so and he became Rector of Handley in the 1730s. Thomas was clearly well respected by the people of his parish, and this is reflected in a poem written by Samuel Hopley, a farm labourer, as Thomas was about to leave Handley to become a Canon at Chester Cathedral.

> *With gales of sighs each tender breast does heave,*
> *That pious Ince he soon will Handley leave.*
> *He that with scripture did their hearts enstil,*
> *And did each day some hungry belly's fill.*
> *Wayfaring vagrants did not need to want*
> *But soon found plenty when laid at his gate.*
> *His charities to strangers did not stop,*
> *But neighbouring poor fed from the butcher's shop.*
> *A friend to all, for by him we were fed,*
> *The rich with counsel, and the poor with bread.*
> *Denying none, that were in deep distress,*
> *The mournful widow, or the fatherless.*
> *Where now alas, will they such comfort find,*
> *When he's at Chester and leaves them behind.*

Currie family members also became ministers in the church, and in 1823 the Bishop issued a license for William Currie to serve as a Curate in Christleton Church, and to live at £100 a year in the parsonage house. In 1832 William became the Rector of Adderley on the Cheshire/Shropshire border. The family continued to have great influence on the village of Christleton as owners of the Old Hall, and successive members of the family were heavily involved in important church decisions. This can be seen in the way the village church revolved around the family who lived in the Hall. They had their own chapel within the church, complete with fireplace and pews for all their servants, and their own burial place or oratory, initially beneath the chancel, and later in the churchyard where their large family mausoleum still exists today. The Rev Lionel Garnett stated that he could not have done anything to change the village without the help of Lucy Anne Ince and there are many letters documenting this. Amongst other things, he asked her to provide 'coal for the poor', 'instruments for the village band' and 'money for the rebuilding of both schools'. He particularly relied upon her for support during the rebuilding of the church in 1876, even asking for her help in building a new bridge into the village across the canal. Lucy Anne purchased the new font made from Derbyshire limestone with money she had collected in the village, and she insisted that the best oak furniture should be supplied during the refurbishment of the church after the Butterfield rebuilding in 1876.

The following letter from the Rector shows the great influence she had.

'Christleton Rectory 26th October 1883

Dear Mrs Ince

Thank you, Tuesday seems to suit me very well, and I hold myself engaged for that morning at 7.30 am. I have received a letter from Mr Barker [solicitor] regarding your subscription to the proposed new school. I am very grateful for your kind and literal support. I am afraid I could hardly have ventured on another large undertaking if I had not thought you would help me, and with the help which you have now promised through Mr Barker, I have good hopes of raising the money required. I think I shall wait just a few days before writing to the Duke*. He has just lost a great match on the Race Course. His horse the Duke of Richmond has been beaten by the Duke of Portland's Sir Simon and he may

possibly be a little out of temper. I shall remember to put before him the Public House Argument. I shall be satisfied if he gives us £100, delighted if he gives £200. I wrote to Parry yesterday regarding the Ring o'Bells. I expect his answer tomorrow, and shall then know how to act.
Yours sincerely
Lionel Garnett.
P.S. Important and perhaps you may think impertinent. You promised earlier this year to give £30 towards buying instruments for a brass band. The scheme has now come to a head. The band is formed and has begun music. The Instruments are purchased and cash is now needed for that purpose. May I call in your subscription. The band is 15 in number including most of our best young men. I've drawn up the rules very carefully, and think all has been done for the proper conduct of the thing. The instruments will be the property of the Rector and Churchwardens in trust for the parish.'

Other letters exist to show that their working relationship ensured that village opinion followed their ideas and not those of others. Some situations were manipulated at public meetings to make sure that they had their way, particularly during a dispute about where the new church should be. The Dixons of Littleton had offered £1000 towards a new church providing it was on a greenfield site. However, the Rector with the support of Lucy Anne Ince, made sure that villagers preferred to retain the old Tower and to build a new nave and chancel on the present site.

The Duke mentioned was the Duke of Westminster. The Ring o'Bells was a pub standing on the site of the present Parish Hall. The Rector and churchwardens were trying to purchase the site to allow the John Sellers' Charity School, then situated in the churchyard, to move across the road to a new building

Common Land And The Enclosed Fields

The three areas of community land in Christleton, the Village Green, Little Heath and Birch Heath, are now mainly amenity areas but, in earlier times, common lands were essential elements in the life of the community. Little Heath, better known as the Pit and its surrounds, was one of several areas in the township of Christleton recorded 200 years ago as sources of sand and other minerals. The other recorded areas were small parts of four unfenced 'wastelands' or heaths (Stamford Heath, Birch Heath, Gibbet Heath and Brown Heath) that were enclosed and taken into private ownership as a result of the Christleton Inclosure Act of 1794. The heaths had probably been used for centuries for grazing cattle, pigs and poultry, and had been part of the extensive area of woodland in Christleton mentioned in

Servants at the Old Hall, circa 1900

the Domesday Book. The original trees would have been gradually felled to supply wood for building and tool making, or would have been burnt as firewood; most new saplings would have been eaten by the livestock with the result that more hardy plants such as bramble or gorse probably became widespread. Regular burning of these newer plants was probably necessary to allow more nutritious plants to develop. Birch trees often spread on areas of ungrazed common, and these were a particularly useful source of wood for cottage furniture and for small turned items such as cotton reels and tool handles.

In mediaeval times the heaths were called wastelands, but in practice they were by no means wasted as the grazing they provided was vital to the many small-scale farmers who had very little enclosed land of their own. The late 18th century was a time of changing fashions, including the desire for personal ownership of all land. It was also a time when the quality of grazing on many heaths had deteriorated and when improved farming techniques had made it possible to cultivate marginal land successfully, provided it was carefully controlled, usually within enclosing hedges. These factors led to the enclosure of most commons across the country.

There are no precise details of the status of each area of common land in Christleton, but commons were usually the property of the Lord of the Manor. The right to use them belonged to the tenants of 'ancient enclosures' within the manor, in proportion to the size or value of that enclosure. The same proportional basis was used to divide up common land when it was enclosed. In feudal times the Lord

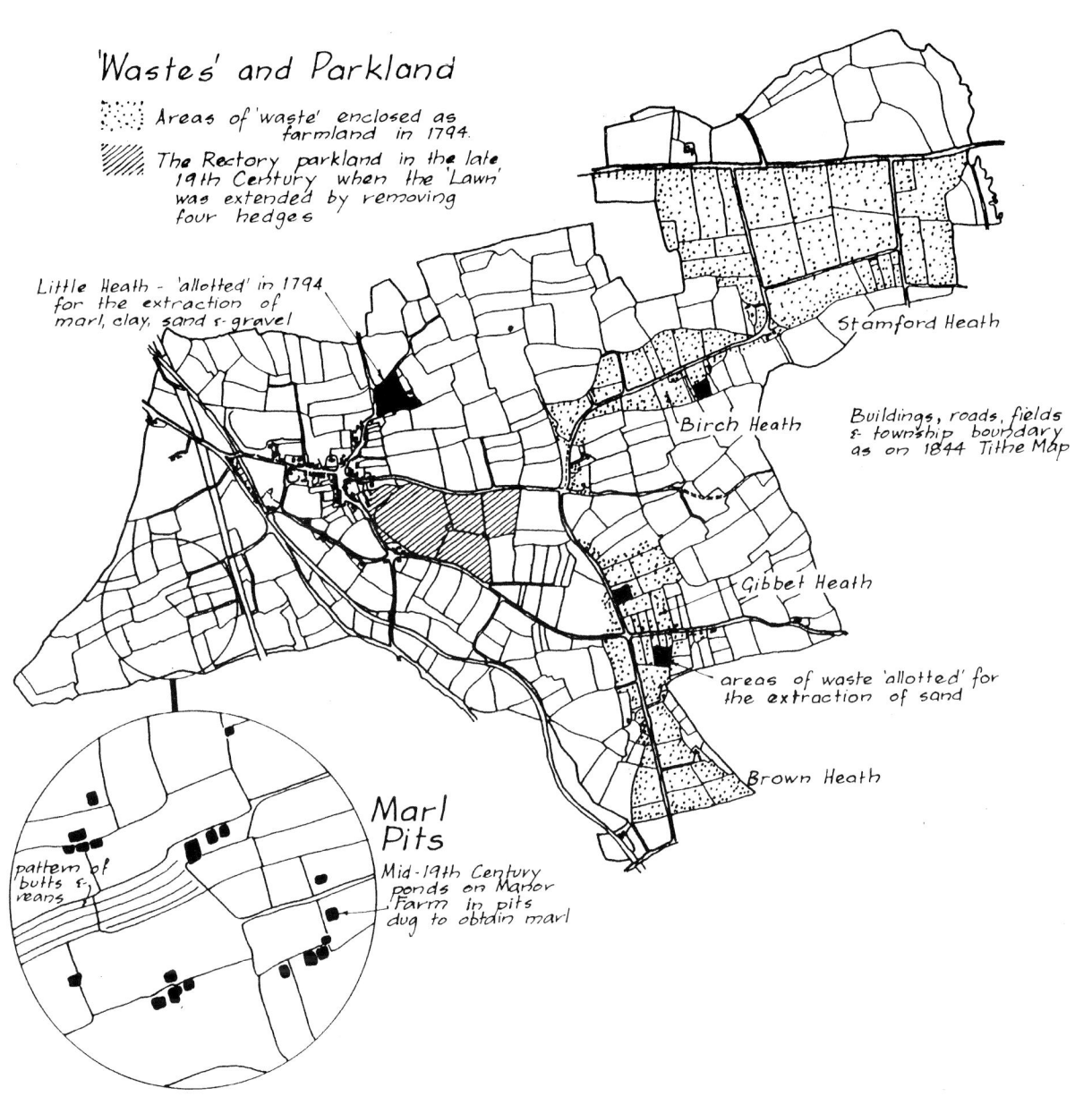

Wastes and parkland around Christleton in 1794

of the Manor would effectively be the owner of all the land in the Township, although officially all land was ultimately owned by the Crown. The Lord would farm part of the land himself; other areas were either farmed by tenants or were common land and waste. Many of the tenants became freemen, owning the land themselves. In addition to land ownership, the Lord would also have legal or social responsibilities, such as the upholding of law and order and the maintenance of highways, which over the centuries were transferred to the local community, the courts and local authorities.

In Christleton the four heaths, totalling about 270 acres, were enclosed in 1794; of this total, 35 acres were sold to Robert Townsend to pay the enclosure commissioners' and surveyors' expenses, 78 acres were allotted to Thomas Brock, the Lord of the Manor, 43 acres were allotted to Robert Townsend and 10 to the Rector. The remaining 104 acres were divided among 31 claimants, 11 of whom received less than half an acre. The cottages in Rake Lane, adjacent to the Plough Lane crossroads, are on land that formed part of the smallest allocations.

After enclosure, a considerable amount of effort must have been necessary to turn the wastelands into good, workable farmland. The enclosure coincided with a period of renewed interest in spreading marl (a fine-grained sedimentary rock used as a fertiliser) over fields, and at least eight large new pits were dug in the centre of the new fields. The Tithe map produced in 1844 shows 44 other ponds in the enclosed area, which probably resulted from marl digging. However, these ponds are nearer to roads or are adjacent to previously enclosed fields and may have been created before 1794, when farmers regarded the wastes as a normal source of marl.

Due to the weight and the cost of moving marl around, most pits were dug in, or very near to, the fields that needed improving. The greatest density of pits shown on the Tithe map is on what is now Manor Farm, the spacing suggesting that they were to provide successive applications to the fields. The total number of marl pits in the parish is uncertain but, if the effect of marling only lasted about 12 years, there must have been many pits, which would have considerably reduced the useful field areas. To reduce this loss many pits were filled in with rubbish or other cheap material and re-covered with soil. An early map of part of Brown Heath Farm shows three pits that had been filled in at some time before 1844. The Tithe map also shows instances, particularly on other farms, of wide offsets in hedge lines, which probably mark the position of pairs of former ponds. The filling in of old pits or ponds is by no means a recent practice. In addition to the creation of farmland, there were many smaller encroachments into the commons to meet the needs of working people, who would be permitted to build a cottage and enclose a garden, or small croft, in return for a small rent paid to the Lord of the Manor. Vegetables, such as beans, would probably have been grown in the garden and some poultry kept. The tenants of these cottages would graze small numbers of cattle or other animals on the common, but they did not have any formal right to do so and, therefore, would be unlikely to receive any compensation for the loss of the grazing rights when the common was enclosed. In Christleton there were 'diverse cottages' of this type, which caused difficulties in 1770 when it was discovered that the title to some parts of the estate was not clear. The result was that, until legal matters had taken their course, the new owner, Mr Brock, Town Clerk of Chester, was unable to take possession of his property. The properties offered for sale had included '25 cottages and encroachers' paying rent from 1s 5d per week. (At that time in Christleton a ploughman was paid 1s 2d per day.)

One problematic enclosure was on Brick Heath, an area of land to the north of the present Birch Heath common and presumably the site of small-scale brickmaking (unless the word *Brick* was an error on the surviving legal document). Another encroachment, which had to be investigated in 1770 (and is referred to in

Shorthorn cattle at Little Heath marl pit, circa 1900

more detail elsewhere), was on Little Heath where, in 1710, Gerard Townsend had enclosed part of the common without, it was claimed, any formal approval and for which he had never paid any rent. Another enclosure by the Townsends that caused legal difficulty, despite having a much clearer basis, was on part of Brown Heath. In 1733 the Lord of the Manor, Sir John Harpur, and 27 freeholders agreed that Robert Townsend could enclose six acres of Brown Heath. These were of poor quality, only being used by the adjacent cottagers to cut turf for their fires, and were considered to be worth a rent of only 5s per acre. In consideration for the agreement, Mr. Townsend paid £37 10s, the equivalent of 25 years' rent for the land, the money being used for the improvement of the highway between Christleton and Chester, which was at that time in very poor condition.

Alongside the wastelands and individually enclosed fields, the other land in Christleton was farmed as communal strip fields. This well-known system was probably invented by the Saxons and consisted of large fields (usually three in number) divided into many narrow strips, each one controlled by a different individual but usually worked by communal effort. The standard strip was, in theory, one furlong (220 yards) long by 22 yards wide, but in Christleton there is only evidence of much narrower strips. The number of strips controlled by each individual varied and strips could be bought or exchanged, but in each field all the strips were planted with the same crop at the same time. Each area of ownership, irrespective of its number of strips, was known in Christleton as a loon.

At first, a limited range of crops was grown on the strips, with grain, particularly wheat and oats, alternating with the field being left fallow for a year. Later many variations of crop rotations developed covering two, three or even four years. Each farmer might have strips in several fields and might also have the right to graze livestock on the stubble left after each harvest and on the plants that developed during the fallow years. The division of fields into strips and the regular ploughing of the same, each time turning the earth towards the centre of the strip, produced a regular undulating pattern across the field known nationally as ridge and furrow, but in Cheshire as butts and reans. The pattern of butts and reans was usually irregular in Christleton, varying in both width and direction. It is still visible in some places, most obviously to the east of Rake Lane on Tony Mitchell's land near the path towards Cotton Hall, although it may be that these butts and reans are evidence of ploughing by oxen in individually owned fields. The pattern of surviving butts and reans throughout Christleton was more clearly and extensively shown on the aerial photographs taken by the RAF in 1947.

The wooden ploughs had a single board, or ploughshare, that was pulled by oxen, usually four in a team. The teams were not very agile but could be turned more easily in less space if they approached the end of a field, or headland, at a slight angle. The teams were normally turned to the left at each end of the furrow and this produced a slight reverse S shape to each butt, the average width of each butt being about 10 metres in Christleton. This pattern should not be confused with the very regular straight patterns produced by the later horse-drawn ploughs, which resulted in the low butts and shallow reans at about five metres spacing still visible on many fields in Christleton. Horses gradually replaced oxen from the 16th century onwards.

The butt and rean pattern in both strip and ploughed fields had the practical advantage in clay areas of preventing water from standing around growing plants in wet weather. Instead, the water would run into the reans, which formed minor watercourses on sloping ground, or it collected and was gradually absorbed into more level ground. Sometimes the butt and rean pattern was deliberately introduced onto later pastureland to improve drainage; this may be the explanation for the exceptionally wide and deep patterning still visible on some land to the east of Stamford Lane that was enclosed from waste in 1794. During the last 50 years, many of the older ploughing patterns have been obliterated by the more intensive use of machinery and heavier cropping on both grassland and arable fields.

There are no records of the conversion of most of the strips in Christleton into square or rectangular fields but, by the mid 18th century, there may only have been four areas of strip (or flatt or butty) field remaining in Christleton. These were Townfield (Birch Heath Lane), Long Loons (Bricky Lane), Finneys Field or Finisfield (Plough Lane), and Cross Flatt, which is now almost obliterated by houses, the railway, the canal and the A55. In 1752, a scheme was agreed under which, 'ye

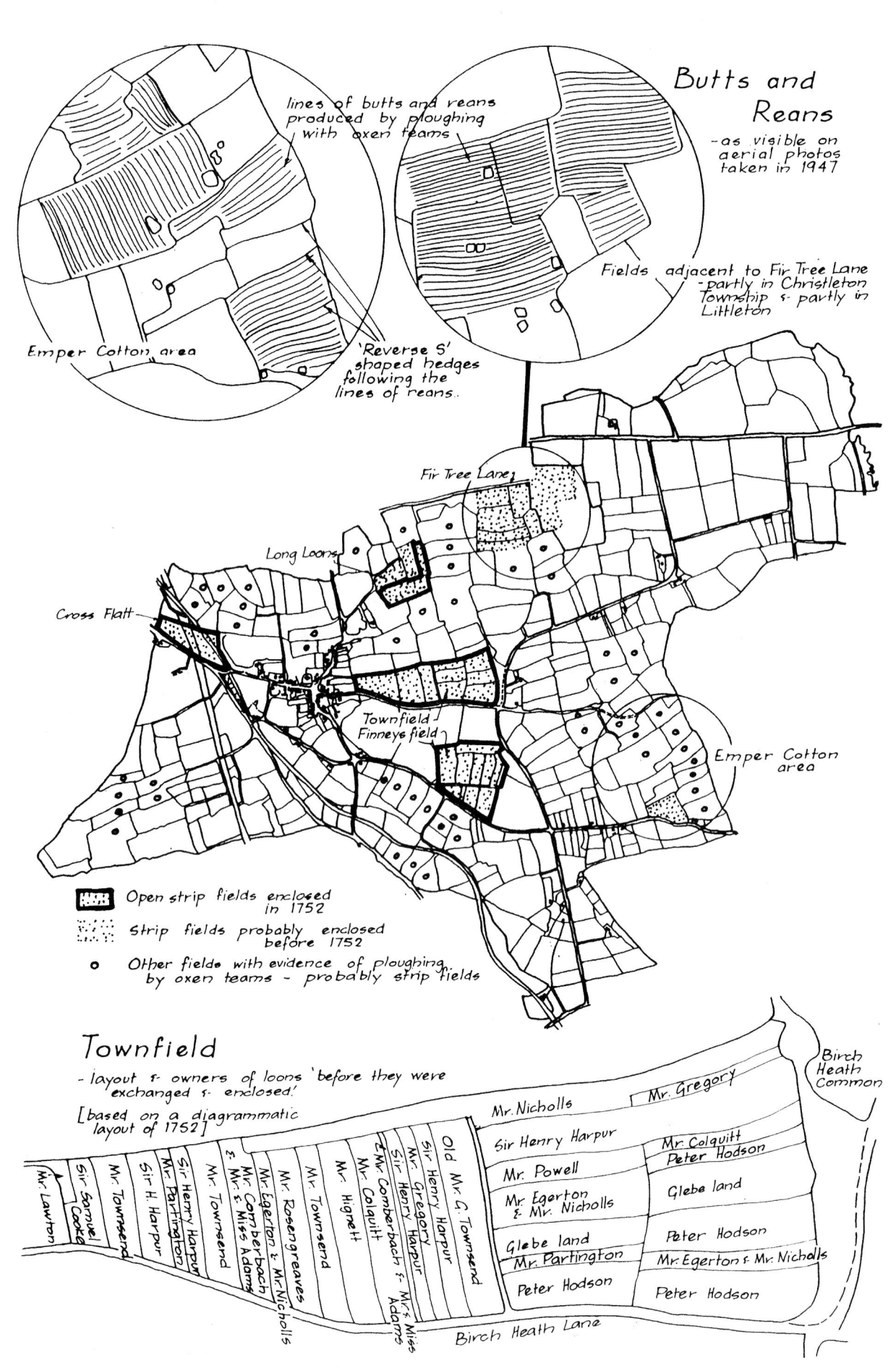

Division of common lands around Christleton in 1752

whole quantity of every owner's ground in ye said three fields being ascertained each such owner shall have his whole quantity as his share in one place therein.' A fourth field was added later. Within the four fields, there were 81 parcels of land, or loons, divided between 19 owners. Robert and Gerard Townsend together had the greatest number, 12, followed by Peter Hodson with 10 and Sir Henry Harpur, the Lord of the Manor, with nine. The area of each loon was measured in sowings, roods and yards. The term *sowing*, as a measurement of area, is unknown to the Cheshire County Archivists. From the few fields that are readily identifiable, the following calculations can be made.

A Christleton yard of area is probably equal to eight or nine standard square yards.
Eight Christleton yards of area make a Christleton rood.
Twenty Christleton roods make a sowing.
Twenty Christleton roods were probably slightly larger than one standard rood, and a sowing was slightly larger than a standard quarter acre.

Henry VIII had, in theory, standardised systems of measuring areas, but even in the early 19th century, Cheshire surveyors still used an acre that was more than twice the national standard area.

It was the duty of each landowner to provide hedges around his or her property after the revised layout of the open fields was agreed. Some of the hedges were on new straight lines, but others followed the reverse S curves of the reans. Despite the recent removal of many hedges, these slightly curved shapes are still evident in a few places in the parish. However, they were more clearly and widely shown on the 1844 Tithe map, suggesting that the strip field system was once in use throughout much of Christleton and that, before the 1744 enclosure, the other areas had been taken out of communal use and were reorganised as privately controlled farmland.

In addition to evidence of ploughing, the 1947 aerial photographs show many field markings, probably derived from recent cropping or fertilising. In Long Loons, at the end of Bricky Lane near the Pit, there are two marks that appear to relate more to buildings or some man-made structure, suggesting that after the field was enclosed in 1752 it was used in part for drying bricks prior to firing. The marks are no longer visible and no evidence of buildings has come to light during recent ploughing.

The map of Christleton produced in 1844 by the Tithe Commissioners was part of a national programme to rationalise the financial rights of landowners and the Church of England. Instead of contributions to the Church being based on a tenth of the value of crops or goods, landowners were, to begin with, to make cash payments to the Rector of £320 per year. This was based on a complex calculation that related property values to the price of a bushel of wheat (7s $1/4$d), barley (3s $11\frac{1}{2}$d), and oats (2s 9d). As the values of grain changed, so did the Rector's income. The payment of the tithe was phased out early in the 20th century. Surprisingly, the Tithe documents do not show any evidence of there ever having been a Tithe barn for the storage of grain or other contributions received in kind by the Rector. The map, however, does show unidentified buildings on Little Heath Road adjacent to the Rectory and near the house now called Tithebarn, which may have served this purpose. Both buildings were demolished before 1881.

The Tithe map and its supporting documents give the name of each field, many of which give insights into the use, or former uses, of each one. For example, Sand hole field, Old common piece, and Horse pasture, but what does Bath field (the field between the Pit and the cricket field) mean? Unfortunately for those looking at old documents, field names often change and few legal documents include maps, so there are many references to fields, or part fields, which cannot be traced now; for example, Stackyard, Sandy Townfield and Jenkins Butt. Road names have also changed: Plough Lane was formerly Wick Way and the road over Quarry Bridge was Coopers Lane.

The ownership of farmland in Christleton in 1844 was following a pattern of change that had been gradually developing in most places for 300 years or more, with fewer owners, many of whom were involved in diverse professions or businesses elsewhere. Half of the farmland in Christleton in 1844 was in the hands of three owners: Townsend Ince (341acres), John Brock Wood (312 acres), and the trustees of the late Thomas Hodson (113 acres); the Rector also held 56 acres as his glebe-land. Very little of the land was farmed by the owners, although Townsend Ince did keep some land under his own control. The

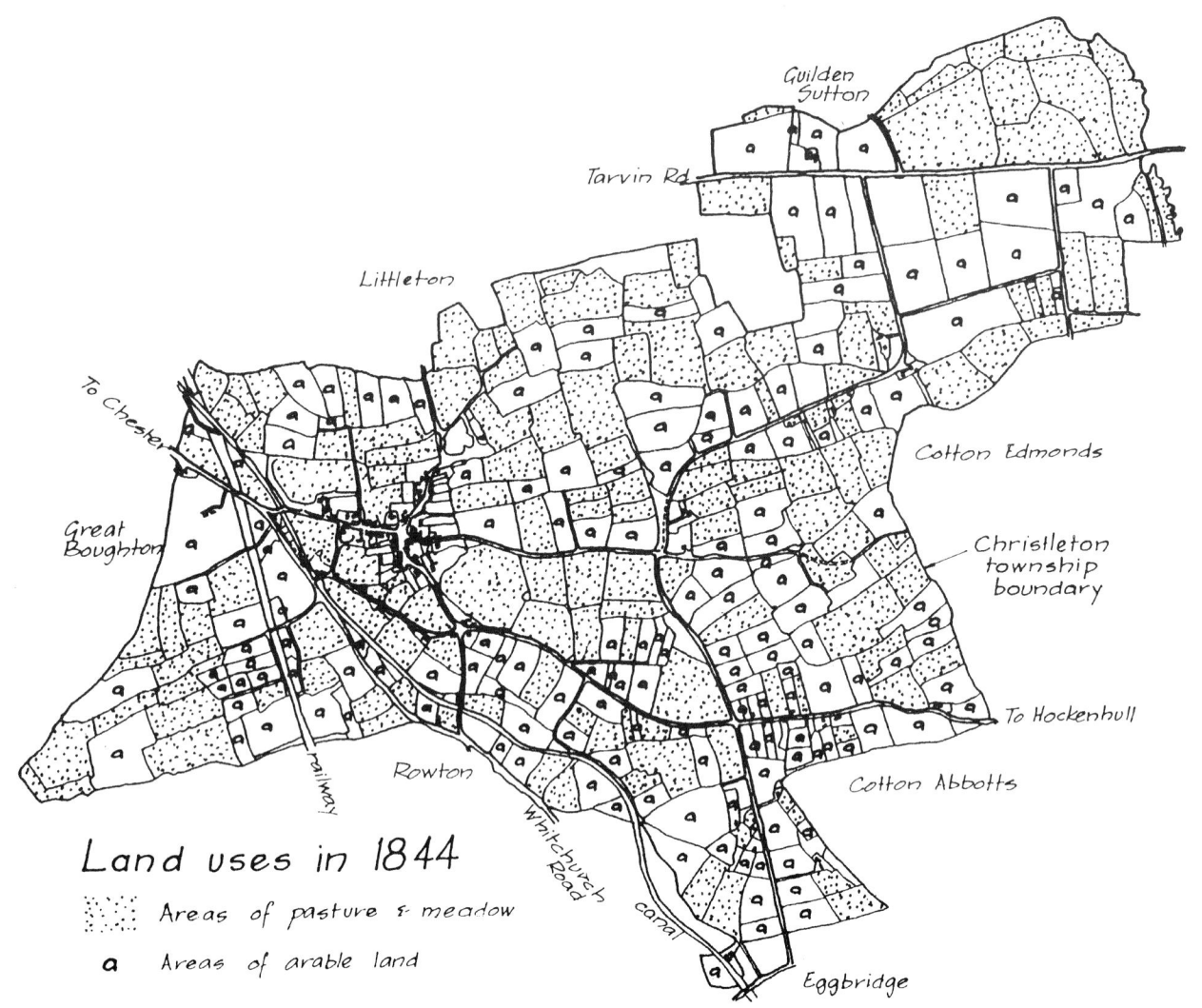

Land uses in 1844

Tithe documents also give the use of each field in 1844, showing large areas of arable, meadow and pasture—livestock rearing was the main priority but not to the total exclusion of planted crops. Many of the arable fields were quite small and isolated and could be successfully worked with manual labour—an extreme contrast to the scale of modern fields and the use of machinery. The varying uses of the arable fields are rarely referred to in the documents, but it is likely that vegetable growing was increasing and that oats were significant as food for both people and horses. There was an increasing demand for hay and oats at that time to meet the needs of the growing number of horse owners in both the expanding towns and the countryside.

Following developments in farming techniques in the 18th century, it was no longer necessary to slaughter most animals in the autumn as it had been in the past because of the difficulties in providing appropriate winter-feed. Many crops were tried as winter-feeds, the best known being turnips, and several areas in Christleton are noted as growing them. However, whilst 19th century Cheshire was noted for its dairy products, feeding cows on turnips tainted the taste of the resulting milk and cheese, which not surprisingly was unpopular. The turnip crop in Christleton was probably fed to sheep, either those bred in the area or those brought down from hilly areas for the more gentle winter climate and improved feeding. Vetches, clover and cabbages were used more successfully as winter-feeds for cattle, allowing calving periods to be spread over the year and making the year-round supply of milk and cheese to urban areas a practical possibility. Several of the fields were listed as growing potatoes, which had been introduced as a general crop in the 18th century: before that they were regarded as unusual and exotic.

The four fields behind the Grange (formerly the Rectory) were part of the Rector's glebe-land and are described in the Tithe records as being pastureland. By 1872, however, the Ordnance maps described the areas as *Parkland*

and showed that the hedges had been removed and that there were many free-standing trees. Presumably this was the type of farmed parkland now associated on a larger scale with places such as Tatton Park, Knutsford. The largest part of the Parkland was the field near the Rectory known as the Lawn, on which W G Grace is believed to have played cricket. It seems that the Lawn must have been the Rector's parkland for many years, as recent research by the County Council foresters has shown that the large sweet chestnut tree (growing in close proximity to the High School buildings) is probably about 470 years old. It was planted about 100 years before the 17th century rectory (the predecessor of the Grange) was built in 1634. More tree planting took place around the Lawn about 1800, resulting in the many fine trees still surviving. (Eric Beech and a group of other schoolboys many years ago had to write out a number of times, 'In getting conkers, I must not do wanton damage,' after collecting conkers from a large horse chestnut tree!) Before the High School took over most of the Parkland, it was known as a ley (a meadow) and was let out each year between May and October as grazing for cattle.

Over the centuries, there have been many ways in which governments have collected taxes; many of these have related, in one form or another, to land or property ownership. Tithes were effectively a form of tax on land agreed by the state and church. In 1692, the British government first imposed a land tax 'for granting an aid to His Majesty.' The detailed records of the tax for Christleton, 1784–1831, cover a period when, as an alternative to paying the tax on a regular basis, property owners were allowed to redeem the requirement by paying a single lump sum in lieu. As a result of this, the tax collected in Christleton decreased from £104 in 1800 to £81 in 1821, but it does seem that it was only the larger landowners who considered the redemption appropriate or, more probably, were able to afford the payment. In 1784, 84 properties were liable to tax, the largest payments of £9 19s 0d and £9 18s 0d were made by the Rector, Thomas Mostyn, for his tithe and part of the glebe, and Robert Townsend, respectively. At the other end of the tax-paying scale, William Rosingreave, Jacob Adams and William Hickson each paid one shilling. By 1831, there were 149 properties liable to tax. The highest single amount was again paid by the Rector, now Griffith Lloyd, £5 1s 7d, for his tithe, the lowest was paid by Elizabeth Thomas, who had to pay three pence for 'a bit of land at Birch Heath'. The Tax Assessors and Collectors were the churchwardens. In more recent years, farmers' income tax was based on the rental value of the farm, however large or small that might happen to be, but since 1940 they have had to produce business accounts.

Planting potatoes, Birch Heath Lane in the 1990s

Over the past few years farming in Christleton has changed in many ways, as it has done in most parts of the country. Many hedges have been removed, most grassland has been improved by reseeding with fewer, more productive, grass species, and most arable areas are worked very intensively. Yet agriculture in the parish still retains the basic diversity which seems always to have existed, being partly dependent on arable farming and partly dependent on cattle rearing for either dairy or beef purposes. For centuries Cheshire has had a reputation for dairy farming, but from the evidence available it does seem that in Christleton there has always been a significant element of arable farming. It has been stated that 'the use of the plough in Cheshire was to feed the cows', but the extent of the ploughing must have varied significantly over the years to meet changing demands, probably peaking during the periods of war since the Napoleonic era. Now, in 2000, the proportion of arable fields in Christleton is probably not dissimilar to that recorded in the 1844 Tithe documents and it may not be so very different to the areas that were included in the mediaeval strip fields.

The Parish Council And Vestry Meetings

The Local Government Act of 1894 established the present system of Parish Councils and Parish Meetings, but previously the churchwardens had dealt with parish matters, and decisions were made at Vestry Meetings. Even today, at the annual Vestry Meeting, wardens can be elected from the parish and not merely from those on the church electoral roll. The Vestry Meetings used to take place at about 11 am around Easter time and were attended by the local ratepayers who then nominated their chairman. The Vestry Meetings were responsible for: 'Surveying of the Highways and keeping roads in repair. Overseeing of the Poor and giving help when needed. Attending to Local Education. Assessing the local rates to be paid by parishioners.'

Each parish also had the responsibility for policing its own area, and the Vestry Meetings nominated one of the ratepayers to be Village Constable. The very first Parish Council Meeting was held on 17th December 1894 when John Cullimore was elected Chairman, the Rev Lionel Garnett Vice Chairman, and Mr C J Owen appointed Clerk. Mr Owen eventually retired having served for 41years at an unaltered salary of £5 a year. Both the Vestry Meetings and the Parish Council had to deal with a wide range of issues. The minutes are full of interesting details about all these matters, important and trivial. A flavour of some of those issues is provided in this section, concentrating on the church, the roads, the pump, parish festivities, and policing in the village.

Church

One of the earliest records of the Vestry Meetings includes a letter dated August 1841 from the Rural Dean, the Reverend Henry Raikes, complaining about the state of the church and the churchyard. 'The Churchyard ought to be mown or kept in a neater state; the ivy has grown into the roof of the North side of the Chancel and is doing harm. The key of the Belfry is not kept with the Minister or Church Wardens—these points must be attended to immediately. I likewise point out that four square pews near the Pulpit have had their sides raised. This ought not to be done without

View of Christleton village from St James' bell tower, 1907

the authority of the Wardens in any case, and ought not to have been permitted here. Large tombs likewise have been formed in the Churchyard and without Faculties—this is wrong and must not be repeated. The Churchyard is already too small and cannot bear these encroachments.'

The Vestry Meeting was also involved with the rebuilding of the church. The parishioners approved Mr Butterfield's plans in January 1875 for the partial rebuilding and enlargement of the parish church and authorised the Rector and churchwardens to apply for a Faculty to carry out the same. A couple of months later Mr Ambrose Dixon offered £1,000 on condition that a church was built on a new site. After a full discussion the committee came to a unanimous conclusion that 'everything considered it was desirable to adhere to the present plans and a letter was read from Mr Butterfield strongly advising that course.'

The wardens were in charge of financial matters. They had to collect land tax each year from the citizens of the village. They were then responsible for paying for Easter and Visitation dinners, the bread for the sacraments, wine, and soap and oil for the bells. Other duties included moving snow, cleaning paths, paying for sparrow heads and eggs, washing the surplices and linen, and cleaning the plate.

Roads

The state of the roads and footpaths in the parish has always been a topical issue, and road repairs, safety, and protests have all been discussed at the Vestry and Parish Council meetings. Originally, road repairs were the province of the wardens and later the council. In May 1851 Rowton Bridge was to be repaired and the road leading to the village from Chester repaired with broken stones. It was also resolved that the roads at Birch Heath and Stamford Heath should be repaired with cinders, and the ruts in the pavements should be mended. In 1896 the Parish Council strongly supported the requisition by a householder to substitute the pavement in the village with macadam, and repairs to the stile ways and footpaths off Village Road were undertaken in September 1897. By 1933 the county council had taken over responsibility for road matters, and in this year the County Surveyor had white lines painted at several places in the village.

Road safety appears to have been of great importance even at the turn of the 19th century. In April 1906 the Clerk was requested to write to Cheshire County Council (CCC) and Chester Rural District Council about 'the great nuisance and danger to the public, and loss to roadside farmers and owners due to the dust from traffic on the roads.' Less than a year later, in February 1907, the Clerk wrote to the Corporation of Chester about the 'very serious danger to traffic on Christleton Road because of trams being allowed to stand so long at the Cherry Orchard terminus and in such close proximity to the electric light standard.'As a sign of the changing times in 1907, a request was made to CCC for a 'motor car danger' post at the corner of Littleton village, and in October 1908 the Clerk protested against the County Council taking away the bridle path leading from Christleton to Chester. The motor car was well established in the village by 1937: the County Council were asked to provide a 30 mph speed limit because of the 'terrible speed of some motor vehicles and motor cycles through the Village.' In 1999 the Council identified safer pedestrian and cycle routes as a top priority for the village.

Road protests appear to be nothing new. Twenty four rate payers signed a petition in September 1867 calling for a meeting to object to pavements being taken up in Plough Lane and being used to repair Christleton Bridge against the majority of the township's wishes. A week later, 'It was the unanimous wish of the rate payers that a Vote of Censure be passed, which was done, upon the Way Warden for his conduct in removing the said pavement.' One hundred years later, in July 1984 the Parish Council objected to a proposed link road to join the M53 and A55. This objection was sent to the Secretary of State for

Building of the A55 Link, 1990

Transport and the local Member of Parliament. The then Chairman Mr E A Gardener and Councillor Mrs M Croston attended a London meeting with the Department of Transport. Joint meetings with Littleton and Guilden Sutton Parish Councils were set up, and later, links were established with Great Boughton Parish Council and Cheshire County Council. All was to no avail. After a public enquiry lasting one month, permission was given for the road.

The Pump House

The Pump House was built in 1886 in memory of Augusta Maria Fuller, sister of Lucy Anne Ince, and it served the village until the 1950s when the water supply was modernised. In fact, water was last drawn from the well during the severe winter of 1963.

The responsibility for the upkeep of the pump fell to the Way Warden. In 1863 he was requested 'to make arrangements with the firm of Gates of Chester or some other Pump Maker to keep the town pump in repair at a stated sum per annum.'

The Pump was obviously very important to all the villagers. The same Mrs Ince who built the pump house wanted her own pump. In March 1885 the records say that 'permission be granted to Mrs. Townsend Ince to connect Holly Bank and the Old Hall with the Parish Well by means of a separate pump fitted with a nozzle and tapped a yard from the bottom, at her own expense, on the condition she pay the Church wardens the sum of five shillings per year; that Mrs Townsend Ince allow the parishioners the use of her pump when the Parish pump is out of order.'

In 1984 the Pump House and Parish Boundary Stone on Whitchurch Road were included on Cheshire County Council's list of buildings of special architectural or historic interest. After over a century of exposure to the elements, the original oak shingles, which had lasted since the Pump House was built, were replaced in March 1995. Councillor Charles Smeatham made an oak lid for the well and County Council lighting officials provided a quartz-halogen spotlight. Councillor Eric Kenyon attended a ceremony to receive a commendation award for the Pump House.

Festivities

Christleton has always celebrated great events, and the Parish Council has always played an important role in village festivities. The parishioners met in April 1887 to consider Queen Victoria's Silver Jubilee. It was decided to hold village festivities on Tuesday 21 June. Rejoicing at Christleton began at 7 am on a beautifully fine day. The ringers started at that hour and a special thanksgiving service was held in church at 11 am. At 1.30 pm a dinner of cold beef, bread, pickles and beer was provided for 125 men in the Boys' School. At 3 pm, also in the Boys' School, a tea was provided for about 270 Day and Sunday Scholars, who had each previously been given a medal and a special Jubilee mug. After this, at 4.30 pm, a general tea was provided,

The Pump House

Celebration of the Coronation of Edward VII, 1902

including ham sandwiches, to some 300 people. During the afternoon sports of different kinds were held and the prizes were presented at 8 pm by Mrs Garnett. The Christleton Brass Band played for dancing until 10 pm, when the top of the church tower was lit up with coloured Bengal lights. Beacon fires could be seen all around, on the Roodee, Moel Fammau, and Helsby Crag, and at Barrow and Delamere.

Since then jubilees, coronations, the end of the Second World War, and the start of the European Union have all been commemorated in some way or another in Christleton. In April 1935, a joint Jubilee Celebration Committee of Christleton, Rowton, Littleton, and Cotton was formed to celebrate George V's Silver Jubilee. Two years later in 1937, a charge of 5d in the pound was paid to the Coronation Celebration Committee, which was set up to commemorate the coronation of George VI, for the parish celebration. After the end of the Second World War, in the summer of 1946, an allowance of 1s 6d per head was accepted from CCC for Victory Celebrations for children of the parish. The coronation of Elizabeth II in June 1953 was also celebrated jointly by Christleton and Littleton Parish Councils. In 1992, the Parish Council planted 62 trees at the King George V Playing Fields one Sunday in December to commemorate the formation of the European Union. Lyndon Harrison, Member of the European Parliament, donated two of the trees and helped with the planting. The Wednesday Group donated two rowan trees in memory of Mrs Muriel Neate and Mrs Alex Skipper. The Parish Council bought some trees and 40 were donated by the Cheshire Landscape Trust in celebration of the Queen's 40th Anniversary.

For the Millennium celebrations, the Parish Council decided to give each village child under 16 a specially designed cover, post marked Christleton 01.01.2000. Inside the cover there was a short piece about Christleton. Mr Phil Hodges, a former headmaster at Christleton High School, provided the design and wrote out each child's name and address in script.

Local village festivities have also been important for Parish Councils. A sub-committee was formed in January 1992 to resurrect the Village Show, and this has gone from strength to strength over recent years. As the show grows in status and success, several local businesses and parishioners have donated cups and shields and there are now 18 trophies to be won. The Hanging Basket Competitions and Garden Trails have proved very popular and have enhanced the appearance of the village. After a lapse of several years, Christleton again won the Best

Kept Village Award in Cheshire in 1998 and was runner up in 1999. In 2000 the village was also awarded a Silver Award in the National Green Apple Conservation & Heritage Award Scheme.

Police

Prior to the establishment of the present police force, each parish had the responsibility for policing its own area and nominating its own constable. The Vestry Meetings were attended by the local ratepayers who, having nominated their chairman, would then nominate one of their number to be Village Constable; he would then be sworn into office by a Justice of the Peace (JP) at the Quarter Sessions. It was the duty of the Constable to obey the orders of the JPs, execute their warrants and serve summonses. The Constable ensured the necessary taxes were collected and saw that the parish accounts were kept in order. His other duties included ensuring shops were closed on Sunday during church services, and acting as a peace officer. An Assistant Overseer, who had some interesting duties of his own, assisted the Constable. In 1863, for example, the minutes record that 'the Assistant Overseer obtain the consent of the farmers for moles to be caught at the rate of a penny per acre.' Four local men called Burleymen were elected annually to assist the Constable in his duties. Twelve jurymen were also elected. Messrs Hollywell, Swindley, Holland and Beech were the last Burleymen to be elected and Mr Sam Broster was the last foreman of the jury.

The Constable did not wear a uniform but carried a Staff of Office. The Staff of Office is now displayed in the church and would have been used on ceremonial occasions. The Christleton Staff bears the Royal Arms of 1801–1816. It was in the possession of the Mayers family of Christleton for many years and was purchased by Mr W Cullimore at a family sale. He presented it to the church in 1935.

Policing matters were as varied as all village matters. The Parishioners assembled in April 1885 to consider the matter of the swing boats, hobby horses, and booths that had been erected on the village green. They considered they were a public nuisance and dangerous to passers by, and they requested the Chief Constable of the County to take steps as he thought best to abate the nuisance. In 1895 the Clerk was requested to write to PC Davies to stop 'nuisance committed in and around the parish pump.' But, as village life changed, the need for a local policeman gradually disappeared. On 15th August 1969 the Chief Constable appointed a mobile police constable whose area was to include the parish of Christleton. However, the Parish Council has continued to take an active role in crime prevention, and in May 1984 a sub-committee was formed to meet the Cheshire Police Force to consider a Home Watch scheme. This was successful and one of the aims of the present Council is to reduce crime by setting up more such schemes.

The continuity of village life in Christleton has always been enhanced by the number of people willing to give their services to the community, first by serving at the Vestry Meetings and later on the Parish Councils. Serving on the current (1999–2000) Parish Council are John Pearson, Chairman, Susan Haywood, Clerk, Janet Brown, Geoffrey Butt, Colin Crawford, Margaret Croston, Pam Evans, Eric Kenyon, Jim Partington, Steve Henson and Margaret Renner.

2 The Churches of Christleton

St James' Church

Recent investigations suggest that a church existed on this site soon after the Roman occupation of Chester. The evidence for this comes from the fact that early churches of this period were built with a circular churchyard, and Christleton, like several others in the Chester area, followed this pattern. The balance of probability is that the church was in existence before the arrival of the pagan Saxons during the 7th century. The name Christetone in the Domesday Book of 1086 suggests the existence of a Christian settlement. The name Christleton means *the village or place of Christ*, or alternatively Cristentum *the enclosed farm of the Christians*. Local names of this type are thought to date back to AD 600–750. Other sources state that the name Christleton comes from *farmstead with a cross* or the *Township of Christ*.

It is likely that this early meeting place was in the vicinity of the Manor House Farm or on the present church site. The church sits on a broad expanse of underlying old red sandstone on the top of a ridge, which runs from Helsby to Waverton, and overlooks the Cheshire Plain and the city of Chester and the river Dee. The fact that the farm inhabitants were sufficiently unusual to be noted as Christians suggests pagan Saxons coined the name. Another indicator for the early origins of the church is that it stood originally in an oval churchyard. It is not apparent today from the enlarged rectangular shape, although old maps do perhaps show it in an oval form. It is one of a group of churches around Chester that shared the same feature. They are also quite common in nearby Wales and usually associated with the fourth or fifth centuries.

Christleton, Christetone, Christlington, Ham cristleton (the main hamlet near the church), Magna Cristleton, Kirkecristleton, Kysterton and Kryrsylton are all variations of the village name. Littleton, an abbreviation of little or *parva* Christleton, appears in the 12th century, as does *rogh* or rough Christleton, now Rowton. The name Cotton Abbots comes from the Abbots of Chester who owned the land in about 1096, and Cotton Edmunds comes from *parva* Cotton, the land which belonged to William de Cotton who lived at Cotton Hall in the 14th century, and who had a son called Edmund. Hence the name Cotton Edmunds. The five townships of Christleton, Littleton, Rowton, Cotton Abbots and Cotton Edmunds make up the ecclesiastical parish of Christleton.

It is almost certain that a more substantial wooden building existed by the 14th century, and the present tower is thought to be from the second church built in the time of Rector Thomas in 1484. The timber for the church building would have come from local forests, and there is evidence of timber from Christleton being sold for building purposes as late as the 18th century. There are no formal records of the building of this first stone church, but local stone from the nearby Christleton and Waverton quarries was used. The earliest recorded clergyman was Robert, Parson of Christleton in 1215, but as the church was in the patronage of the monks of the Abbey in Chester, there might have been a

St James' Church interior in the mid 1980s

small meeting place rather than a formal building at this time. The Abbot's Well is another link between the village and the Abbey, because water from the well in Christleton was channelled in pipes through Boughton to the site of the Abbey, now the Cathedral. The list of clergy is continuous from 1215 to the present day.

During the Civil War, the church did not escape the havoc and destruction suffered by the village. However because it was garrisoned by the Parliamentarian army under Sir William Brereton it was well protected, and any damage was comparatively light. As the Parliamentarians remained in control of the area after the Battle of Rowton Moor in September 1645, no revenge attack occurred to cause further harm to the building. Any damage was temporarily patched up until the nave and chancel were completely rebuilt in brick in the 1730s.

The Rector, Philip Smallridge, who was also a chaplain to Queen Caroline, rebuilt this part of the church in 1736. He managed to obtain money by the issue of a parliamentary Brief, a device used to make churches from a wide area contribute to the building of a new church. The sum of £1,250 was gathered for Christleton through this appeal, but £1,000 of this went in legal costs. The local people then contributed in kind by using their own transport and labour to enable the building to be completed. Recent research reveals that two important chapels were to be found within the precincts of the earlier church: the Brereton, or Cholmondeley, Chapel and the Cotton, or Venables, Chapel. Bennett's *Book of Inscription* (1910) states:

'In 1525 Eleanor daughter of a Sir William Brereton caused two windows to be made. One with shields with her arms, and those of her husband Thomas son of Thomas Bulkeley of Ayton. The second window, with Eleanor and her second husband Hugh Cholmondeley who possessed the manor of Rowton. This chapel was thought to be in ruins by 1619.

'The Cotton Chapel was to the south side of the church and had one window. In the 1737 plan it is styled the Chapel for Cotton Hall.'

Sir William Venables of Kinderton and second wife Katherine, daughter of Robert Grosvenor of Eaton, had a window adorned with two shields. The window may have been erected in celebration of Sir William being elected High

St James' Church, the 1737 Georgian building

Details from a Kempe stained glass window

Sheriff of Cheshire in 1526. The Arms of Cotton were borne by the Cottons of Cotton Hall.

The Cotton Chapel was present in the 1737 building, but there is evidence of a larger chapel belonging to the Townsend family. Robert Townsend, an Ironmonger of Chester, acquired substantial property in Christleton from his aunt Egerton. One record states that in 1712 his grandson Robert Townsend, then the Recorder for Chester, was given permission to build a chapel or oratory with burying place underneath in Christleton Church. The same record says that two of the Townsend pews had fireplaces.

One Sunday in January 1873 part of the roof of the brick building collapsed, and some of the congregation were covered with snow. The Rector Canon Garnett used the opportunity and his influence to ensure a substantial rebuild of the nave and chancel. He was determined to provide the best and spent more money than the church and village could afford to guarantee that the new structure would last for much longer than the previous buildings. The red sandstone blocks came from local quarries in Delamere and Waverton, and were used with creamy white sandstone from Stourton Hill, Wirral. This building, designed by William Butterfield, completed in 1876, and consecrated in July 1877 is the church as seen today.

The church has many interesting features, including the best craftsmanship that the Victorian era could provide. There are ten stained glass windows by Charles Kempe, designer of 4000 windows during the 19th century and recognised as one of the greatest influences in stained glass window design during the Victorian era. His trade mark was a sheaf of corn and the use of peacock feathers, however several of the Christleton windows also have a tower on top of the sheaf, reflecting the fact that his company had been taken over by the firm of Tower. The architect William Butterfield used the red and white sandstone to create his trademark chequered effect on the wall above the altar. He also had the font made in London of Derbyshire crinoidal limestone on a base of Sicilian marble. Edging in the sanctuary is also made of the crinoidal limestone.

St James' Church has been fortunate to receive many gifts. Among these are a Restoration board of 1665 painted by Randle Holme, a Mayor of Chester, to commemorate the Restoration of Charles II and a Constable Staff of the 19th century. More recent gifts include a processional cross given in memory of Canon Garnett and an oak font cover from 2000 given in memory of Canon Gordon Robinson. The organ was the gift of William Fleming of Rowton and was installed in 1878. Many items in the church were made locally. A metal labarum (a standard or banner) was made by a pupil from Christleton High School and a decorated iron screen, separating the Lady Chapel from the main body of the church, was made in the Kaleyards, Chester. Members of the church family have sewn vivid and beautiful tapestries, such as the altar cloth that depicts the Holy Land as seen from space and the tapestry illustrating the church year and its festivals that hangs in the Lady Chapel.

St James remains the place of worship for the people of Christleton, a place where worship has been continuous for well over a 1000 years. A complete history of St James' Christleton, together with a self-guided tour of the church and churchyard, can be purchased from the church.

Ceremonies And Festivals

St James' Day and the Flower Service

This ceremony has been held for many years to celebrate the Patronal Festival of St James. However, in recent times the date has been changed from 25th July because of the school summer holidays. This important annual event takes place on the Green in front of the church adjacent to the War and Garnett memorials, and is now held on the second Sunday in July. The village Rose Queen and her retinue traditionally lead the procession and arrive at the Green after parading through the village carrying their posies of flowers. In the early 1900s this procession was so popular that everyone in the village turned out, and the parade seemed to be at least 100 yards long. Everyone, young and old, would wear their Sunday best and it was a glorious celebration of what the village meant to people. The gentry in the big houses, such as Christleton Hall, The Old Hall, Christleton Lodge or The Grange, would also open their gardens to villagers on the afternoon of St James' Day. Even today, many former villagers make a special effort to return to celebrate this important parish occasion.

St James' Flower Service procession in 1911, led by Rev Hickey

St James' Flower Service, 1998

Local children in front of the altar during the Christingle Service at St James' Church, 1995

Confirmation candidates outside the South door of St James', 1998

The parade was usually led by the village band followed by the Rector, choir, and the children and teachers from both day and Sunday schools. Many photographs of these ceremonies were taken by village photographer, Reg Morgan, some dating back to before the First World War. For several years in the 1980s the service was expanded to include the blessing of pets and farm animals, and among these were cats, dogs, rabbits, guinea pigs, horses and snakes. However, the main focus of the ceremony today is the tradition of thanking God for the blessings of the land and the celebration of the village as a community. The service is led by the Rector, usually with the help of the Sunday School teachers, the choir and church musicians. At the conclusion of each service the Rose Queen and her retinue lead the congregation into the graveyard to place bunches of flowers on graves, particularly on those that are unattended, giving thanks to God for the life and example of the residents of the village that have gone before.

The Beating of the Bounds

Boundary stones traditionally mark out the divisions between the village, its townships and neighbouring parishes. In the past there would have probably been more than 20 stones marking the boundaries between Christleton Parish and its five townships: Little Christleton (Littleton), Row Christleton (Rowton), Cotton Abbots, Cotton Edmunds and Christleton itself. The majority of the stones surviving today are on the boundary with Boughton and can be seen in the vicinity of the old Glass House, the last house in Christleton before the Park and Ride site approaching the A41/A55 roundabout. This house dates from before 1500 and is recorded on all old maps of Cheshire, including John Ogilby's strip map from London to Chester. Christleton boundary stones are all rectangular in shape and probably all date from around 1848. They are either set into the walls of houses or placed adjacent to the main road. There is an unusual round boundary stone on the front of the old Glass House, which is possibly a Boughton Parish stone from an earlier date. A further damaged stone survives on the bank of the derelict branch of the Shropshire Union Canal just beyond Christleton Lock.

The best surviving example is a stone situated at the base of St James' Church Tower. This stone was rescued by St James' bellringers from the Christleton/Littleton Parish Boundary on Tarvin Road at Vicar's Cross when it was in danger of being damaged and lost during the road works in the 1970s. This stone is marked C.P.L.T. 1848 (Christleton Parish/Littleton Township).

Over the years most of the stones along the parish boundaries were lost, but they are now in the process of being replaced. The village of Waverton is also replacing its stones, many on the joint border. As a consequence, the traditional visiting of boundary stones during the Beating of the Bounds Ceremony is becoming possible once again. In Christleton the celebration takes place every 10 years although, to mark the Millennium, a special walk was organised in June 2000.

This ancient ceremony of walking round the outer edge of the parish boundary is usually combined with the custom of Rogation, the church festival of blessing the land, crops and animals of the parish. The Rector and walkers stop at boundary stones, or the site of former stones marked on the older Ordnance Survey maps, for prayers.

Another tradition that used to take place on a stone was the 'beating a boy with rushes or canes' or, more recently, the 'bumping' of a boy. Bumpers Lane in Chester gets its name from this ancient ceremony as there are many

Rev Alyn Arthur Guest-Williams during the Beating of the Bounds, May 1963

old stones along this boundary of the city. The term *Beating a Blue* is also referred to in this context, the *blue* being a boy from the Blue Coat School in Chester, an old educational establishment that existed just outside the Northgate. Today in Christleton girls and boys are allowed to be gently 'bumped' on a stone, and there is no longer a threat of anyone being 'beaten' on a stone.

After the 1993 walk when few stones were found to be surviving, Roger Croston and David Cummings, with the support of St James' Parochial Church Council and the Parish Council, and Ron Rimington, a local stone mason, raised funds and found a source of stone to replace three of the missing stones. The first two were erected in 1994 on the Cotton Edmunds boundary with Christleton near Stamford Mill, C.P.C.E.T, and at the eastern end of Councillor Walley's Crocky Trail at Cotton Abbots marked C.P.C.A.T. The third new stone, unveiled at Rowton in 1995, was carved from a piece of red sandstone rescued from the demolition site of the old convent near St John's Church in Chester. It is marked C.P.R.T 1645–1995, Christleton Parish/Rowton Township, and also commemorates the 350th anniversary of the Battle of Rowton Moor. Funds for the purchase of this stone were raised by selling accounts of the battle at a reconstruction of the event on Cotton Abbots Farm by the English Civil War Society. A donation from the proceeds of the booklet was also made to Rowton Parish Council towards their commemorative stone and plaque of the Battle of Rowton Moor, which can be seen on the Village Green near Rowton Hall Hotel.

The siting of the new stone along the Shropshire Union Canal replaced one that previously stood about 100 metres away in Foxes Lane, on land near the former chemical factory in Waverton. The site was not very satisfactory and the stone disappeared many years ago. It was felt that a new site on the canal towpath, which also marks the Rowton Township Boundary, would be more appropriate and would also indicate the spot where traditionally someone taking part in the Beating of the Bounds swims the canal. This was a very popular event in the past, with 20 or more village youngsters taking the plunge. However, only one brave soul, Roger Croston, has done this recently, with everyone else taking the longer but drier route along Foxes Lane, following the line of the old boundary (marked by oak trees) through what is now Capesthorne Road. Permission to place the new stone on the canal was given by British Waterways, and Rowton and Christleton Parish Councils.

After the completion of each Beating of the Bounds, a written record is compiled by village calligrapher Cliff Boddy. The latest of these from 1993, beautifully scribed on calfskin, can be seen in the Lady Chapel at St James' Church.

Christleton College Youths (The Bellringers)

Christleton has a long history of bellringing and in the 19th century the ringers, who styled themselves the *Christleton College Youths* (obviously a corruption of the Ancient Society of College Youths, the oldest, most prestigious ringing society in the country), were renowned nationally for their skill and dedication. The present bells are regarded as one of the finest rings in the Chester district for their ease of handling and their tone. At the time of writing, it is hoped that a date peal of 2000 changes will be rung during the Millennium year.

The Tower
The Parish Church of St James, Christleton stands on a sandstone outcrop, some three miles south-east of the city of Chester. There has been a church on the site since 1093 when the patronage (the right to present a priest for the living to the Bishop) was granted to the Benedictine Abbey of St Werburgh in Chester. However, recent archaeological evidence suggests that Christleton had been a Christian settlement for some considerable time before then.

There have been at least four churches on the present site. Of the previous buildings, only the tower of c1490 remains. The tower has been a victim of battle over the years. During the English Civil War Christleton was a Parliamentarian base, laying siege to royalist Chester a few miles away. Sir William Brereton, one of Oliver Cromwell's foremost generals, was based at The Old Hall and in 1645 the village was burnt to the ground by Royalist forces under the command of the King's nephew, Prince Rupert. Only The Old Hall and church tower remained. However, the tower obviously came under attack as small dents, the effect of cannon balls, can be seen on the north wall, some two metres off the ground.

The tower seems to have had no work done to it until after the Restoration of the Monarchy in 1660. On the south walk of the battlement is the following inscription: *R: PVL These battlements being ruined: wer rebuilded anno do 1678 G: Coo.* The clock, built by Thomas Moreton of Chester, was installed in 1868, but no further work was carried out until the late 1870s.

In 1869 Rev Lionel Garnett was appointed Rector of Christleton. Garnett was a man of vision and did not believe in doing things by halves. The Georgian rectory was deemed to be unsuitable and was replaced with a new, much larger building at the 'Top of the Wood'. (The house has since been divided and is now known as The Grange and Christleton Grange). Early in Garnett's rectorship, during the Sunday morning service, part of the church roof, straining under the weight of snow, collapsed, allowing Garnett the opportunity to have the church rebuilt.

It seems that the Rector, with the support of several leading parishioners, wished to build a much larger church somewhat to the north, which would have meant demolishing the tower. However, the leading ecclesiastical architect, Sir William Butterfield, persuaded the authorities that the Perpendicular tower should remain. The height of the tower was raised and the pyramid roof was added to give extra height. The architectural historian Sir Nikolaus Pevsner quotes the architect H S Goodhart-Rendle who described this as 'a sort of square, slated pigeon house with a spire roof, set inside the battlements.' Hugh Grosvenor, the first Duke of Westminster, gave the money for this particular piece of work.

During the rebuilding of the church 1875–77, Butterfield carried out additional work on the tower, including some minor masonry work and the setting up of the gargoyles on the four corners. Previously, the ringing chamber had been at ground level, with the ringing open to the view of the congregation. To accommodate the new font and baptistery at the bottom level of the tower, the ringing chamber was raised and a new exterior entrance to the staircase added to the south wall.

The Ring of Six 1743

Until the English Reformation in the 16th century, many parish churches would have had several bells and Christleton would have been no exception, especially for a church in the gift of Chester Abbey. It is quite probable that one or two of these would have survived the turmoil of religious and political upheaval

Christleton College Youths (Bellringers) circa 1900

in the 16th and 17th centuries, although there is no documentary evidence to support this theory.

By the early 1740s, the decision had been taken that St James' church ought to possess a ring of bells suitable for the art of change ringing, which had grown in England since the 17th century. So in 1743, Abel Rudhall cast a ring of six bells for Christleton at his bell foundry in Gloucester, including a tenor weighing approximately 6¼ hundredweight (cwt). The bells, as far as is known, were: Treble (inscription not known); 2 Peace and Good Neighbourhood, AR [Abel Rudhall] 1743; 3 Prosperity to the Parish, AR 1743; 4 Abel Rudhall of Gloucester cast us all, 1743; 5 John Bennett* Hugh Dean* Churchwardens* 1743; Tenor I to the Church the living call, and to the grave do summon all, AR 1743. The inscription placed on the shoulder of the tenor bell was a common variant of one used at that time, reminding those who saw it and heard the bell of the shortness of this life.

It seems that no full length peals were rung on these bells, but the churchwardens' terrier (register) and inventory of the times regularly record the ringing 'in a most superior manner' of extents of various Minor methods, such as Plain Bob and Kent Treble Bob. (An extent is the maximum number of changes that can be rung on a number of bells without repetition; on six bells, the extent would be 720. Methods rung on six bells are given the surname *Minor*.)

The Ring of Eight

Abel Rudhall's 1743 ring of six bells remained unchanged for 69 years until 1812 when they were augmented to seven; the new bell was a gift from John Hignett of Rowton. John Rudhall was commissioned to cast the new bell and it came from the Gloucester foundry in 1812 as the new tenor, weighing 8½ cwt. The fourth was lowered a semitone to compensate for the addition. However, a ring of seven bells is somewhat limiting as far as the art of change ringing is concerned, and 18 years later in 1830, an eighth bell, the new Treble, was added.

By now the Christleton ringers were becoming active and well-known locally and nationally. They rang the bells for services on Sundays and practice nights (for which they were paid £3 12s per year) as well as weddings and funerals; they were also paid 10s per year for ringing the curfew. Five new bell ropes were provided on an annual basis, which cost the churchwardens £2 15s.

The bells did not escape the rebuilding of the church and restoration of the tower, and in 1877 a representative of Warners Bell Foundry in London inspected the bells and found both bells and fittings were in need of a major overhaul. The bells were removed and taken to Warners Foundry where they were tuned and the second, being cracked, was recast. The bells were returned to Christleton and rung for the first time on the first Sunday in October 1877.

Because the bells were not good musically and there were design faults with the oak bell frame and fittings, it was decided that John Taylor and Co of Loughborough should redesign the interior of the tower and the bell chamber in particular. The old oak frame was replaced with a modern iron and steel one at a cost of £600. An appeal was launched and within a week more than enough had been raised to complete the work. The bells were removed to Loughborough in 1928 where they were broken up and recast. During their absence, work was carried out on the tower, including some minor masonry work to the mullions in the louvre openings. In addition, the floor was lowered by about one metre to create more space in a small bell

One of the Peal of Eight, St James' bell tower

chamber; this also ensured that the bells would be nearer the openings, thus allowing more sound to escape. The local firm, and bellringing family, John Mayers & Sons, carried out most of the building work under the direction of Taylor's bellhanger, Arthur Fidler. The new bells were returned to Christleton and were on display, initially on the church lawn by the Garnett Memorial and then inside the church, prior to being raised into the tower. They were hung in two tiers, with the second, third and sixth on top.

Since the recasting and rehanging in 1928, no major work has been carried out on the bells, with the exception of some minor repairs to some of the fittings.

Ringing yesterday and today

The Christleton ringers achieved national renown during the 19th century. On 26th January 1837 the ringers rang, 'in a most superior manner', a peal of Stedman Trebles, which was followed on 3rd February by another peal, also of Stedman, which is recorded on one of the many Peal Board records sited in the ringing chamber. These two peals were followed on 13th April by a third and, on 19th April 1838, the Christleton Society of Change Ringers rang the first peal of Stedman triples 'ever accomplished outside their own tower' at St John the Baptist in Chester. There is an interesting link between the ringers at Christleton and the ringers at St Peter's Liverpool (now demolished), and several of the peals rung at Christleton between 1830 and 1859 were by mixed local and Liverpool bands. The ringers have always played an important role in local events and festivities and many of the great national events of the 19th and early 20th centuries were marked by ringing peals. The deaths and accessions of William IV, Queen Victoria and Edward VII were all marked in this way, as were the coronation of King George V in 1910, the signing of the Treaty of Versailles in 1919 and the birth of HRH The Prince of Wales (the Earl of Chester) in 1948.

At a meeting in 1871, the ringers organised themselves with a Foreman (George Mayers), Treasurer (William Lunt) and a set of rules. This would have been done during the second phase of the Oxford Movement, when many clergy were almost at war with their ringers; it would be interesting to know whether these rules were imposed on the Christleton ringers and if they were voluntary. The rules were entered in the Vestry book of that year and a copy, beautifully reproduced by Cliff Boddy, now hangs in the ringing chamber.

In the 1980s and early 1990s, the ringers were active in the Chester Branch of the Diocesan Guild of Church Bellringers, twice winning the J W Griffiths Shield at the annual Branch Ringing Contest. As well as the juniors winning the George Weaver Cup in 1988 at All Saints', Hoole, the ringers represented the Branch at the Diocesan Contest and won, coming away with the 'ashes'. The 1980s and 1990s also saw an increase in the number of quarter peals being rung; these were rung to celebrate the births of Princes William and Harry, to welcome new clergy, to celebrate the release of Terry Waite from captivity in Beirut, and for confirmation services and, of course, the deaths of ringers and clergy.

A Christmas dinner was held just before Christmas 1986 and has become an annual event ever since for ringers, their families, the clergy and friends of the tower. Bellringing is an engaging activity and there is a great sense of camaraderie amongst ringers; and this is particularly true in Christleton. Yet it must be remembered that bells are rung primarily to call the faithful to worship, so for ringers the

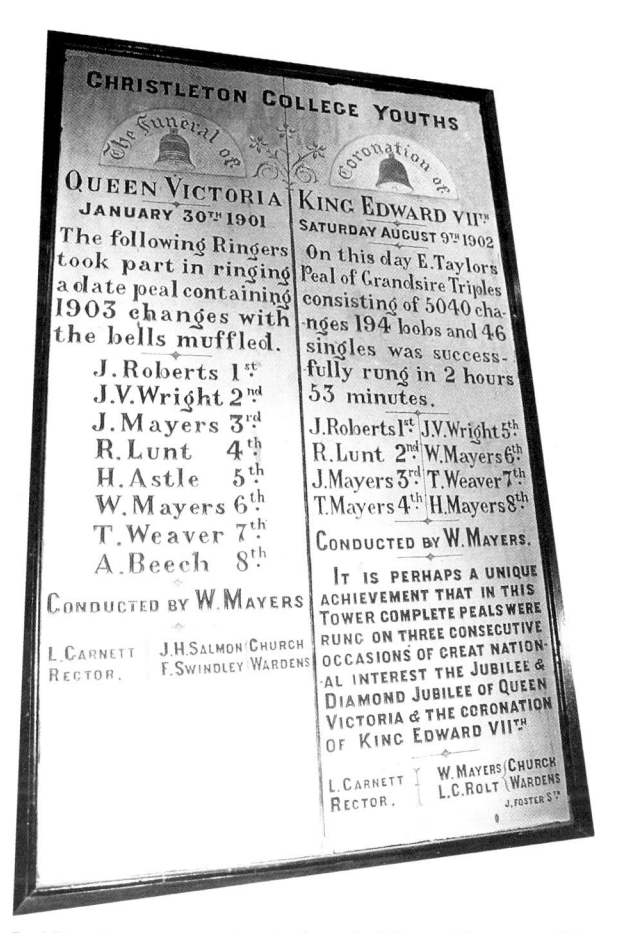

Peal Board commemorating the funeral of Queen Victoria in 1901 and the Coronation of King Edward VII in 1902

first duty is to ensure that the bells are rung on Sundays. There are not many churches that can boast of their bells being rung twice each Sunday, but Christleton is one of the few and the present ringers carry on the same ministry that their forebears, whose names and faces adorn the walls of the tower, were engaged in 250 years ago.

Tower Captains
George Mayers was elected at a meeting of the ringers in 1871, although the post was then known as Foreman. However, there are no records of any further elections until 1989. Indeed, all the Captains during the 20th century until this date were appointed by the rector, on the basis of long service in the tower.

1871 – 1878	George Mayers
1878 – 19—	William Mayers
19— – 1921	James Venables Wright
1921 – 1963	William Griffiths
1963 – 1975	William T Astle
1976 – 1988	Frank Poston
1989 – 1994	David S Fisher
1994 – 1995	Steven G Everett
1995 –	Roy Fisher

The Methodist Chapel And Methodism

Methodism in Christleton goes back well before 1888 when the present chapel was built. John Wesley visited Chester over 30 times during his ministry, frequently en route to Ireland. No record can be found of his having preached in Christleton, but it is very likely that he passed through the village on his way into Chester as the main road passed through Christleton. As he was an Anglican minister he would probably have at least paid his respects to the rector.

In 1765 a friend of John Wesley's and Methodist travelling preacher, Francis Gilbert, visited Christleton with Mary Gilbert his 14-year old niece. Francis, the younger son of the Speaker of the House of Assembly in Antigua, had left Antigua in 1761 on the death of his father and settled in England where he met John Wesley. During their visit to Christleton, Francis and Mary visited the Rectory and Mary is said to have been amazed at the model army that was laid out in the rector's garden. This suggests that the rector of the time was sympathetic to Methodism.

Many prominent families in the Parish of Christleton became sympathetic to the Methodist teachings. The prime mover in the building of the first Methodist church in Chester in 1765 was Thomas Bennett, a Chester ironmonger. It was sited near the Bars and called The Octagon Chapel. Thomas Bennett had been born in Christleton and after becoming a Methodist preacher he moved to Ireland. His mother, Mary Bennett, died in 1755 and was buried in the village cemetery. Thomas inherited his mother's property on her death and returned to live in Christleton. Another prominent local Methodist was John Dean. He was born in 1765 in Rowton. His family had a large farm in the township, and during his youth the Methodist Society in Rowton was formed. He subsequently became a Methodist minister. Richard Reece was born in 1765 and his mother Catherine (Hodson) was from a prominent Christleton family. Richard entered the Methodist ministry in 1791 and rose to the highest office in Methodism, President of the Methodist Conference in 1816 and again in 1835.

Although there was no Methodist meeting-house in the village of Christleton in the early 19th century, Methodism seemed to centre on the Rowton Society, which was within the Parish of Christleton. The rector's Return of 1811 states, '…a few Methodists whose number have not increased. Several of the latter have, of late, frequented the Church. They have no meeting-house.'

By 1817 there were sufficient Methodists in Christleton to justify entry onto the Chester Preaching Plan. Fortnightly services were arranged, but the location is unknown. In 1818 Thomas Floyd was the class leader and the society had 14 members including Thomas Peers, Maria Peers, John Kirkman, James Plevin, Mary Wood, Joseph Cross, Elizabeth Dean and Ann Plevin. Within four years the number of services had increased to two each Sunday, and this was linked to the amalgamation of the Christleton and Rowton Societies. By 1826 the Society had disappeared from Circuit records. It reappeared in 1828 until 1832 but never had more than eight members at any time.

Before permanent chapels were built, many societies fluctuated in size and changed their names as the meetings and services were moved to the most convenient house or farm building. However, for some reason the Christleton Society stopped meeting for over 50 years, until just before the present chapel was built. The next known record of Wesleyan

The Methodist Church interior, circa 1900

Methodism in Christleton is in the Preaching Plan for 1874 on which S Rowe from Birch Heath and W H Allwood of Christleton were listed as local preachers. A few years later Mr Rowe's address was Stamford Mill, which remained in the Rowe family until quite recently.

One of the principal movers in the development of the present church was Samuel Winward of Stamford Heath. The first meeting of this new Society was held around 1884 in a Mr Minshull's house in The Square, a small group of cottages built around a courtyard on what is still known as The Square. Samuel Winward and his daughter, then about 25 years old, were at that first meeting with five or six others, including Mrs Colley, Mrs Boswell and presumably Mr Minshull. In 1958 on the 70th anniversary of the Methodist Church, Mrs Darrock (nee Winward) - then an old lady of 98 - wrote a letter of reminiscence about the early years of the church and about the excitement and enthusiasm, which affected all involved and which enabled all the obstacles and difficulties to be overcome and a church to be built.

Following a meeting in October 1887 at Mr Minshull's house, it was resolved to go ahead with building a chapel. By February 1888 the design had been agreed and a tender from Mr J Youd of Christleton accepted to build a chapel at a cost of £277. The stone laying ceremony took place on 22nd March of the same year and the Christleton Chapel opened in early July. There were objections from the Rector Canon Garnett who had written to the Methodist Trustees declaring that 'the present Church accommodation was adequate for the population of the village.' After holding a special meeting, the Trustees replied to Canon Garnett, 'Assuring the Church people of [our] Christian feelings towards the Church, but that land having been secured and the deeds executed, the Trustees could not alter the decision.'

At a meeting of the Trustees on 19th December 1887 a further letter from the Rector concerning the 'advisability of building the Chapel' was considered. Judging from the Minute Book, the discussion became quite passionate with an entry stating, 'Evidence being given of the spiritual destitution of the village.'

After the building of the basic chapel in 1888, the Society developed rapidly. In 1892 the schoolroom and chapel extension were built, and it is thought that the kitchen and lavatories may also have been added at this time.

The vestry was added in 1899, thus completing premises that would suffice until almost a century after the original plans for a Methodist church were proposed. The church buildings remained largely in this form until 1983 when the kitchen and lavatories were rebuilt and 1989 when the entrance porch was rebuilt.

A church is defined not only by the building, but also by its Christian members and congregation. The Methodist Society in Christleton has fluctuated over the years but has been fairly steady during the last decade. The membership in September 1987 was 42; the membership in September 1999 was 42. The Methodist Church depends heavily on the efforts of its members to sustain and organise church services and events, and Christleton Methodist Church has been fortunate in always having had a good core of workers willing to respond to the current challenge. The minister of course has a significant role to play and the Methodist Society in Christleton has been fortunate in recent years in having had exceptional ministers with vision and dedication.

The Sunday School started the century with growing attendances and seems to have peaked in the 1930s when 60 or more children each week was the average. One year the Sunday School Anniversary claimed an attendance of 120. Sunday School Anniversaries required the dismantling of the wooden partitions between the chapel and vestry and the chapel and schoolroom (where the arches can now be seen each side of the pulpit). Staging was then erected behind the arches inside the schoolroom, and virtually the whole building was brought into use for these occasions. There are not many people left in Christleton who remember these early days but two who do, and are still active in the village, are Eric Beech, whose parents were amongst the earliest members, and Cliff Boddy, who was christened in the Methodist Church.

The Rev D Graham Evans is our present Minister, as well as being the Superintendent Minister of the Chester Methodist Circuit. Graham is the 28th Minister to have charge of Christleton Methodists and together with Rev Peter Lee and Rev Peter Sharrocks has spearheaded the ecumenical movement in Christleton with Churches Together In Christleton. There will be a new notice-board erected in 2000 which will celebrate the ecumenical movement in Christleton in the 21st century and a confident future by announcing that the building is not only *The Methodist Church* but also *Churches Together in Christleton*.

The Methodist Church

The Roman Catholics And The Salvatorian College

In 1934 the Salvatorians, a Catholic religious order, purchased Christleton Hall from the Hemelryk family, and it remained in their possession until the Law Society purchased it in 1972. During those 40 years, the property was extensively developed to enable the international religious order of priests and brothers to provide a training college for men preparing for the priesthood. In the 1950s the adjoining property, Stoneydale, was purchased to house a community of nuns, known as the Salvatorian Sisters.

As early as 1936 young priests were setting off from Christleton to work in the foreign missions in China. Others were being assigned to parishes or schools in England. By the outbreak of the war in 1939 there was a community of 50 or 60 men living and studying in Christleton Hall. A number of these left to join the forces but most remained. Priests are needed in times of war and peace.

The Cheshire Constabulary made a dramatic arrival in May 1940—it was the time of the evacuation of British and other Allied troops from Dunkirk. They came to round up a number of German students and lay brothers to take them to internment in the Isle of Man and from there to Canada. (When the war was over these same men went to work in China, the USA and Australia.) During this time life went on with its round of study, lectures, digging for victory in the kitchen garden or farmland, and serving in the Air Raid Precautions (ARP). Meanwhile young men were ordained and joined as chaplains in the Army, Navy and RAF, serving in North Africa, Burma and Europe. Great changes in seminary training began in 1962 with the result that Christleton ceased to be a major seminary. It became a junior seminary, a boarding school for boys aged 13–18 years.

From 1934 until 1972, many local Catholics attended their Sunday Mass and other religious services in the College Chapel. Most of these people became friends and supporters of the Salvatorian Community. The final Sunday Mass was a very moving occasion, but it was a 'grand and glorious' conclusion to a wonderful chapter of local history.

Memorial to the Salvatorian Fathers buried in the small cemetery at Christleton Hall

Churches Together In Christleton

For many years now, the different churches of Christleton have worked together on numerous occasions. However, the constitution of the group Churches Together in Christleton was only officially formalised in 1993. Since then members of the Anglican, Methodist and Roman Catholic churches have met together as a committee on a regular basis, either at the Methodist Church or the Rectory, to plan a number of events for the benefit of the community.

A Community Register was introduced which lists information about local groups and organisations and is of particular help to newcomers to the village. The Neighbourhood Link scheme was started in 1993 with an overall co-ordinator, five area secretaries and, to date, 40 representatives, whose aim is to serve as a link between their road and the churches. One of their tasks is to deliver information; for example each year Churches Together sends out a combined Christmas card, with details of all services, to every household in the parish. In December 1999 special Millennium packages were prepared and distributed by the group and their links. Each of these contained a Christmas card, a small white candle and candle holder, the Millennium Prayer and the Churches Together in Christleton Millennium Prayer, and a copy of the Millennium year *Programme for the Village*, to encourage the whole community to celebrate the birth of Jesus 2000 years ago.

Churches Together members setting off on a village pilgrimage in June 1996

The week of prayer for Christian Unity is planned in January, and a village coffee morning is traditionally held at the end of this. A scheme is decided on for Lent each year; this varies between study in house groups or in larger groups meeting at the churches or, as will be the case in the year 2000, a general gathering with a key note speaker for each week of Lent.

Various church services continue to take place on a joint footing: a Communion Service on the evening of Maundy Thursday and a post-Easter Service; a Sunday evening United Service during the Week of Prayer, sometimes with the clergy from the Roman Catholic, Anglican and Methodist Churches speaking on the same platform; and a United Communion Service at St James' on the first Wednesday of each month. Everyone comes together for a short service in the centre of the village at the War Memorial on Remembrance Sunday.

An outdoor service is also held, a village *Songs of Praise,* in May or June at Christleton Pit, where singing is accompanied by the Music Group as well as ducks, aeroplanes, wind and drizzle and sometimes sunshine. In 1997 this was preceded by a village pilgrimage to celebrate the arrival of St Augustine in Britain 1400 years ago and also the death of St Columba. There were exhibitions in both the Methodist Chapel and St James' Church.

In 1999 the group was honoured, if a little reluctant at first, to arrange the ecumenical Good Friday Service at Chester Cathedral. As many people as possible were involved from the different churches, and the result was an inspiring experience for many. Also in 1999, the churches came together for another new experience: a broadcast with Radio Merseyside for their popular programme *United in Song*. After several rehearsals, the recording was made one Monday evening in St James' Church and the broadcast went out on 25th July, St James' Day. It was an interesting and enjoyable experience.

The present committee in 2000 are Leo Carroll, Teresa Doak, Humphrey Broad-Davies, Anne Collier, Sheila Roberts, Jayne Roscoe, Marjorie Woods, Harold Whetnall, Tony Gardner, Jan Bowden, together with the clergy of all three denominations.

3 Times Past and Present

The Roman Bridges

The three bridges at Hockenhull Platts are known locally as *The Roman Bridges* and it is certain that bridges existed at the time of the Roman occupation of Chester. However these were probably constructed from timber and were in use until the late 15th century. When work was being done to underpin the present stone structures during the 1940s, some earlier timber-post construction (possibly Roman) was exposed. The three stone bridges seen today were probably constructed in the 15th century and are typical pack-horse bridges with a single arch construction. They are connected by a causeway or an embankment, more than 250 metres in length, built from earth and clay and topped with sets or cobbles. This enabled travellers along the old highway from Chester to London to cross the marshland surrounding the various courses of the river Gowy in comparative comfort.

The route was in active use in the 13th century, as the Black Prince's Register contains reference to the maintenance of the bridges at Hockenhull. In fact the Prince ruled the County of Chester until 1355, and it is recorded that he paid 'a grant of 20 shillings for the repair of the bridge of Hokenhull.'

The Black Prince, as Prince of Wales and Earl of Chester, had good reason to keep the road in good repair. He would travel along the highway from London to Chester, often in a great hurry, to obtain money and men from the rich landowners of Cheshire to enable him to fight battles overseas, for example the Battle of Crecy in 1346.

Nearly 200 years later a further reference to a bridge at Hockenhull appears in the will of one Ralph Rogers, a citizen of Chester, who in 1539 made testamentary provision of 10s for its repair. During his perambulations of Cheshire in 1620, William Webb wrote in his book, *The Vale Royal of England*, of a passage over the Gowy as part of 'our great London roadway to Chester, wanting nothing but a bridge for carts to pass that way when the river riseth, which were a very necessary and charitable work to be done.'

Whether the construction of such a bridge for carts was ever contemplated is unknown, but 55 years later the three stone bridges clearly shown on John Ogilby's map are only wide

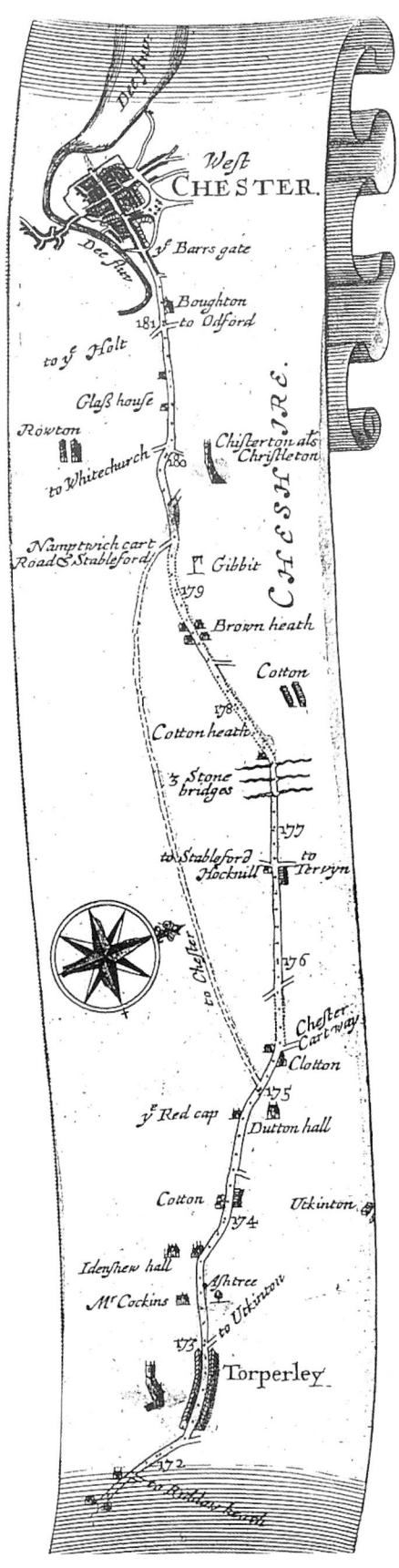

A section of John Ogilby's 1685 map, showing the Roman Bridges and Glass House

53

enough for use by the pack-horse trade or by travellers on horseback. Ogilby's *Britannia Road Book* was produced in 1675, and the section from Nantwich to Chester is of particular interest for local people as it also shows a gibbet at Brown Heath and the Glasshouse Inn at Christleton.

There are several references to the importance of the bridges as part of the route to Chester during the period when Edward I was building his castles in Wales, and between 1642 and 1645 during the Civil War. Tarvin Church, further to the east, was the main garrison of the Parliamentarian soldiers commanded by Sir William Brereton. He also had his forward headquarters at The Old Hall in Christleton. With his troops having an excellent lookout position over the city of Chester from the top of Christleton Church tower, he was well placed to attack Royalist troops leaving the city. It is certain that the bridges were the main communication route for Brereton's troops.

A local story reveals that a servant, called Grace Trigg, from the nearby Hockenhull Hall haunts the bridges after being beheaded for trying to save the family silver from being melted down into coin to pay the Parliamentarian soldiers. This act is commemorated in the name of the nearby public house in Duddon, *The Headless Woman*. The Hockenhull family was involved in shipping, and their wooden ships would tie up near their house at the Port of Shotwick on the inner estuary of the river Dee. The pack-horse route from the bridges through to Christleton and then the Port of Chester would have been their most direct route.

The area around the bridges is clearly described in 1685 by Celia Fiennes, the *fine Lady upon a white horse* from Banbury Cross, who was in effect one of the first travel writers to move around the British countryside. She writes in her journal, 'I went 3 miles on a caussey through much wood; its from Nantwich to Chester Town 14 long miles the wayes being deep; its much on enclosures and I passed by severall large pooles of waters but what I wondered at was that tho this shire is remarkable for a great deale of greate Cheeses and Dairys, I did not see more than 20 or 30 cowes in a troope feeding, but on enquiry find the custome of the country is to joyn their milking together of a whole village, and so make their greate cheeses, and so it goes round.' There is also some evidence to suggest that this early highway was once turnpiked. For example, a Cotton Gate is clearly printed on a number of early maps, situated on the bend to Cotton Hall, and it is suggested that it was part of a turnpike-road from Chester to Duddon Smithy in 1743. However, in 1769 the Chester Tarvin Turnpike Trust built a new turnpike-road from Tarvin to Chester along the line of the old Roman road (now Tarvin Road) through Vicar's Cross and then into Chester, so avoiding the pack-horse route through Hockenhull. The main reason for this may be that the Turnpike Trust could not persuade the Grosvenor family to part with their land at Hockenhull to widen both the bridges and the carriageway to take coaches and carts, and the decline of the route was inevitable. In 1780 Thomas Pennant, another famous traveller on horseback, writes 'about taking the horse road across Brownheath by Hockenhull.' P P Burdett's map of 1777 shows the new road structure with the Tarvin to Chester and Chester to Whitchurch turnpike-roads clearly shown, but the Hockenhull route is still usable. Although lines of oak trees mark many local parish boundaries in the area, the finest avenue is that from Hockenhull to Christleton.

The Roman Bridges

These fine oaks still dominate the skyline and are home to many bird and insect species, including little owls. Today, the former pack-horse route is most likely to be used by walkers, cyclists and horse-riders. Hockenhull Platts is a peaceful place, disturbed only by the sound of birds singing and the rush of the river Gowy as it passes through the middle bridge on its meandering course to the river Mersey and the Irish Sea.

Christleton In The Civil War

The Civil War between King Charles I and Parliament broke out in August 1642 and lasted until 1646. No doubt the people of Christleton, like most communities in the country, hoped that the dispute would be settled without their direct involvement. However, the location of the village on the outskirts of a city as significant to the struggle as Chester meant that this was not to be. Early in the war, in September 1642, the King visited Chester to confirm its allegiance to his cause whilst he was based at Shrewsbury recruiting for his army.

Meanwhile, Sir William Brereton, MP for Cheshire, had been appointed Parliamentary commander for Cheshire. During January 1643 he set up his headquarters at Nantwich. The main road between Chester and Nantwich passed at that time through Christleton (now Quarry Lane and Plough Lane). A few miles east of Christleton, the road passes through a gap in the Mid-Cheshire Ridge where it is overlooked by the old mediaeval castle of Beeston. The castle was seized and held in 1643 by Parliament.

In July Brereton made his first move against Chester, occupying Boughton for two days and firing at the outworks. Christleton was probably occupied by Parliamentary troops during this raid. The city's garrison was not caught off guard, however, and the Parliamentarians withdrew. Following this, the citizens pulled down the buildings in Boughton and cut down the trees and hedges to deny cover to subsequent attackers.

It was only towards the end of the year that the first serious moves were made against Chester. An attack was aimed south and west of the city, crossing the river Dee at Holt and seizing Harwarden Castle. This attack would, therefore, have bypassed Christleton. Its purpose was to blockade Chester by cutting it off from its supply lines to North Wales. At the same time, in November 1644, Brereton put a garrison into Tarvin, which had advance posts as far forward as Stamford Bridge. The Royalist forces in Chester mounted an attack against the Tarvin garrison on 12th November. They were held at Stamford Bridge where firing continued all afternoon. Eventually the Royalists fell back and were pursued as far as Gorse Stacks.

Brereton's advance into North Wales was short-lived, for at the same time several thousand soldiers from the King's army in Ireland were landed at Mostyn. Lord John Byron was sent to Chester by the King with his regiment of horse to be the new governor. With these reinforcements the Royalists went onto the offensive. The army marched out and must have passed through Christleton on its way to besiege Nantwich, seizing Beeston Castle on 13th December. The Royalist campaign did not prosper for Byron's army was defeated on 25th January 1644 at the Battle of Nantwich by a relieving force led by Sir Thomas Fairfax. The survivors of the Royalist army fell back to Chester, although a garrison was maintained in Beeston Castle. Throughout this time, the Parliamentarians maintained their garrison at Tarvin (or they quickly re-established it) for on 29th January there was another skirmish at Stamford Bridge.

Throughout the spring and summer of 1644, the war in Cheshire was dominated by the campaigns of the King's nephew, Prince Rupert. He had been sent north by the King to redress the balance following the defeat of Byron and also to counter the entry of a Scots army on the side of Parliament. Rupert was defeated by the combined armies of Parliament and Scots at Marston Moor near York on 2nd July 1644. Rupert, with the remains of his army, retired to Chester to recover before he returned to the King at Oxford. During this time, the Parliamentary forces were largely confined to Nantwich and it was only towards the end of the year that active operations were resumed against Chester.

In this phase, Christleton was to play a significant role. From November Beeston Castle was besieged. In December 1644 Brereton commenced the leaguer, or siege, of Chester by planting garrisons in surrounding villages, including Barrow, Tattenhall and Aldford as well as the one already established in Tarvin. This stimulated a vigorous response from the city horse with night-time raids on

A Roundhead Trooper

Tattenhall (9th January 1645), Aldford (11th January) and Barrow (12th January). Brereton reported to Parliament on 17th January that because of the activity of garrison (presumably the raids noted above) he had established Lieutenant Colonel Jones and Major Louthian at Christleton with his own regiments of horse and foot. In spite of its proximity to the city's defences, the village's strategic location obviously made it an important garrison from which to control the raids from Chester. A royalist source states that the garrison was secured by mud walls (earthen ramparts), so some form of defence was presumably thrown up around the village. In a report to Parliament, Brereton notes that 'we had entrenched our force at Christleton so that the enemy's horse shall not rush upon them and destroy them,' (Dore 1984, no. 7), although Nathaniel Lancaster (Brereton's chaplain) in his account describes them as 'slight mud-walls'.

This led to an attack on Christleton by the city's troops on 18th January 1645, no doubt hoping to repeat the success of their earlier raids. The resulting engagement became known in local sources as the Battle of Christleton. A force of 800 foot and 300 horse was drawn out of the city and laid an 'ambuscade' or ambush. However, Brereton's forces in the village had intelligence of their coming and observed them from the church tower. They saw how they placed ambushes of the foot on both sides of the lane from Boughton to the Glass House (now Christleton Road and Whitchurch Road). Their advance guard of cavalry came up presumably to entice the Parliamentarians into the ambush. Lt Col Jones led out Brereton's horse and attacked the Royalist advance guard with vigour. They fell back to the body of their army. Brereton's horse followed closely and charged through the main body routing the Royalist horse back to their own lines at Boughton, within range of their cannon. Meanwhile, Maj Louthian led out 700 foot and deployed them in the fields on both sides of the lane and routed the Royalist foot back to the city. Many were slain or wounded. The citizens had closed the gates of the city (presumably the one at the Boughton outworks) to prevent the cavalry routing through the defences and being followed by the Parliamentarians. This forced the Royalist horse to turn about and make a stand so the Parliamentarian force was drawn off. Lancaster reports that they took what prisoners they could and cut and slashed miserably those who couldn't be brought off. There were reports of 40 men drowning as they tried to escape across the river and 100 'sore wounded' in the city. More than 200 prisoners were taken including Col Werden, commander of city horse, and a great store of arms and equipment. Amongst the prisoners were two native Irish men. Parliament adjudged that any native Irish captured in arms were in rebellion against the government, so these unfortunate soldiers were hanged at Christleton on 24th January.

The city's position was becoming precarious so another relief attempt was mounted. Prince Maurice, with a force drawn from neighbouring garrisons, entered Chester on 19th February 1645, thus raising the siege. Brereton withdrew some of the garrisons from the villages around Chester, but he maintained his force at Christleton and the siege of Beeston Castle. However, Maurice had so weakened the garrison of Shrewsbury in order to relieve Chester that, on 22nd February, the Parliamentarians operating in Shropshire captured the town. Maurice himself was now in difficulties trapped in western Cheshire, so another force under Prince Rupert came north. Consequently, on 16th March, Brereton withdrew the garrison of Christleton to Tarporley. On 17th, as the combined forces of Rupert and Maurice reached Whitchurch, Brereton was obliged to raise the siege of Beeston and withdraw to Middlewich. On 18th March, the Royalists reached Tarporley. They burnt down Christleton and Great Boughton to punish their treachery. How effective this destruction was is uncertain. The village was certainly not used again as a garrison during the Civil War, which suggests that it was almost complete. On the other hand, the church certainly survived, and as The Old Hall also incorporates much early 17th century fabric that too must also have survived. It would seem likely, therefore, that other buildings might also have survived with varying amounts of damage. The Princes rendezvoused at Bunbury on 19th March and retired to Whitchurch. Brereton resumed the siege. Garrisons were placed at Rowton and Huntington though, as noted above, Christleton itself was not reoccupied.

On 9th June 1645 a large-scale raid was mounted by the city, comprising six companies of foot and three of horse. They set out from the city towards Stapleford, intending to raid the surrounding villages. They surprised and captured Captain Glegg and his company of horse. However, Lt Col Venables, the governor of Tarvin, marched a force towards Christleton, cutting off the Royalist line of retreat. During the skirmish that followed the Parliamentary prisoners were released and 200 Royalist prisoners and 30 horse were taken, along with numerous arms and much powder. The prisoners included Sir John Powell, formerly High Sheriff of Cheshire. The Royalist force was pursued towards Eaton, Rushton and Delamere. The next day 87 of the prisoners were sent from Tarvin to Nantwich where, on 11th June, three, being Irish, were hanged.

The next crisis in the siege occurred in May 1645 when the main Royalist army under the command of the King approached Cheshire. The King's cause was not prospering, and there had been considerable debate as to the campaign that the King's main field army, based in Oxford, should conduct during 1645. The relief of Chester was an obvious first step. By 17th May the King had reached Newport in Shropshire. The following day Brereton raised the siege of Chester and Beeston and withdrew his forces to Nantwich except for the garrison at Tarvin, which was maintained. The King's army, however, turned eastwards away from Chester and was eventually destroyed at the Battle of Naseby on 14th June 1645. Operations in Cheshire were not immediately resumed, apart from some minor raids. The Parliamentary soldiers and supplies of money and food were exhausted, and the Royalists in Chester were in no condition to take the offensive.

In August the siege of Beeston Castle was resumed. On the night of 19th September 1645, the Parliamentary forces made a secret march to Chester, presumably passing through Christleton, and during the early hours of 20th they stormed the outworks of the city. They managed to seize the suburbs but the city within the historic walls held out. Great siege guns were brought up from Tarvin and a breach was battered in the walls. Meanwhile the King, with the remnant of cavalry that had escaped from the Battle of Naseby, was at Chirk. He rode to the assistance of Chester, entering the city on 23rd September. The bulk of his cavalry, under Sir Marmaduke Langdale, was sent across the river Dee at Farndon and must have been quartered overnight in the area of Saighton and Waverton. Their plan was to trap and overwhelm the Parliamentary forces between the King's cavalry and the garrison in the city in the suburbs of Chester along Boughton.

However, a Parliamentary force of cavalry, under Major General Poyntz, was following the King and had reached Whitchurch where it received urgent pleas from the Parliamentarians in Chester suburbs. Poyntz marched his force northwards up the Whitchurch road overnight and, at first light on 24th September 1645, was approaching the position of Langdale's cavalry. The battle that resulted has come to be known as the Battle of Rowton Moor. It was, in fact, a scrappy, long drawn-out affair of three major engagements and is hard to follow from the contemporary accounts. The first engagement between the cavalry forces of Langdale and Poyntz took place early in the day on the heaths south-west of Waverton. Langdale had drawn up his troops on Millers, or Milners, Heath. Poyntz attacked but his approach was restricted to a narrow lane with thick hedges. The Parliamentarians were held and pushed back down the lane to more open heathland at its southern end. Here they were able to deploy properly and hold the Royalists. In this stalemate situation both sides sent messengers to Chester for reinforcements.

The Parliamentarians were able to organise themselves more quickly and had a shorter distance to march to join Poyntz. Col Jones with 350 horse and Col John Booth with 500 foot were dispatched from the suburbs at about midday, their march being marked by the firing of two cannon.

The Old Farm in Christleton dates from 1654

Meanwhile Langdale, followed by Poyntz, had moved nearer to Chester and taken up position on Rowton Heath. The traditional site of the battle is the triangular area of rough pasture to the west of the Whitchurch Road and bounded by Rowton Lane. One Parliamentary account says that the Royalists had the advantage of the wind and sun. As the time was now about three o'clock in the afternoon, this implies that the Royalists were facing eastwards. Presumably, Langdale had drawn his cavalry onto the heath to the west of the Whitchurch Road to prevent them being caught between Poyntz and the reinforcements from the suburbs. The latter must have met up on the outskirts of Christleton. The foot was stationed on the flanks of the cavalry and battle was rejoined. After fierce fighting the Parliamentarians gained the upper hand, the musketeers on the flanks causing casualties to the rear ranks of the Royalists. Langdale's force was broken. Some fled south towards Farndon Bridge and safety; most were swept through and around Christleton through fields, ditches and narrow lanes towards Chester.

The Royalists in the city had in the meantime collected together reinforcements from the forces that had accompanied the King. They were sent out under the command of Lord Gerrard. They had to march by way of the Northgate and around the eastern suburbs held by Parliament. Whilst passing the suburbs, they were attacked in the rear by yet more Parliamentarians coming out of the area. (Lord Lichfield, the King's cousin, was killed in this engagement.) The Royalists took up position on Hoole Heath where they were joined by Langdale's routed cavalry, which was being hotly pursued by the victorious Poyntz. Further confused fighting occurred. Langdale's force temporarily rallied but broke again under Poyntz's attack. Some fled towards Bridge Trafford and Delamere Forest, others into Chester by way of the Northgate. Gerrard's force seems to have held more firmly but was gradually forced back, pushing the Parliamentarians behind them right up against the earthwork defences. The Parliamentarians manning the defences fired on both without distinction. By now, dusk was falling and the fighting died down.

So ended the small but significant Battle of Rowton Moor. It was the last time the King commanded a field army in battle, although, in spite of Parliamentary reports to the contrary, he does not seem to have left the city and taken to the field in person. It also marked the end of the main Royalist field army. The foot had been destroyed at Naseby. The cavalry were lost at Rowton. It was also the last major attempt to relieve Chester. The lanes and fields between Christleton and Chester were filled with the wounded and dead, both men and horses, as well as great quantities of weapons and equipment. There is a tradition that the small, ruined sandstone building, which stands on the corner of Whitchurch Road and Rowton Lane, was used as a field hospital during the battle.

The King with the remnants of his force retired into Wales on the following day and the siege of Chester was intensified. Beeston Castle surrendered on 15th November 1645, and Chester yielded to Sir William Brereton's terms on 3rd February 1646.

The events that happened in and around Christleton can be reconstructed and their effect and importance measured, to some extent, from the historical records. What is much harder to gauge is the effect on the lives of the people who lived here at the time. There are only small clues about Christleton itself but a certain amount can be guessed from what happened elsewhere. No doubt men from the village joined the armies of one side or the other. Under the ancient arrangement (there being no standing army) the rectors of Christleton and Tarvin were jointly responsible

Andrew Gillit, General (retired), Sealed Knot outside the Ring o'Bells

for providing one musket furnished when required for the King's army (*Chesh Sheaf* 1961, 75). The musket comprised, in addition to the weapon itself, a rest, a bandoleer, headpiece (helmet), sword and dagger and, of course, a man to use them. One might expect that the proximity to Chester would mean that Royalist sympathies were strongest, but the burning of the village in March 1645 for treachery by the city's garrison might indicate the opposite. In this respect, an interesting document known as the *Cheshire Remonstrance* is preserved in the Randle Holme papers in the British Library. The Remonstrance was drawn up in July 1642, immediately before the start of the war. In Holme's words it was a 'remonstrance made under pretence of maintaining His majestie's royal and sacred Person and Prerogative: and the just Privileges of Parliament' (*Chesh Sheaf* 1956, 10). In other words, it was a petition largely Parliamentarian in sympathy. It was signed by 8000 names, including some who became significant Royalists, mainly arranged by parish. In Christleton 65 men signed, led by Minister Peter Ince. As none of the names is recorded by a mark, as happens in other parishes, it is likely that Ince himself wrote in the names. Peter Ince was not the rector at the time, William Mostyn was, so he was presumably a curate. He must have been a Puritan because he subsequently became a rector in Dorset and Wiltshire in 1646 but was ejected in 1662, after the Restoration, for nonconformity. He then became a dissenting preacher. His father, also named Peter, was a stationer in Chester and an associate of the leading Puritan, Calvin Bruen.

One of the units in Brereton's army, Maj Louthian's Company, was raised from Broxton Hundred (the western part of Cheshire) but numbered only 80 men in April 1645, perhaps illustrating the difficulty of recruiting for Parliament in this area. The armies were supported by levies of both food and money on the local populations. Those places where both sides had some control could be unfortunate enough to suffer levies from two armies. Christleton was such a place. When the village served as a Parliamentary garrison, several hundred soldiers were probably billeted on the families remaining. The construction of defences may well have involved the destruction of property. The burning of Christleton in March 1645 is a well-attested fact. In a catalogue of destruction drawn up by Randle Holme at the end of the war (Harl MSS 1944), there is the item 'All the houses, barns and buildings near to the Barrs [sic], with Great Boughton and Christleton'. In a terrier of 1663, listing the glebe-lands belonging to the Rectory of Christleton, there is the item 'Parsonage House with outhousings are totally burnt with fire' (*Chesh Sheaf* 1965, 24). However, as discussed above, some buildings must have survived. The soldiers from Chester and the armies of the Princes, who carried out the burning, were presumably only in the village for a few hours so the effect of the burning was probably mixed.

Brereton did not use the village again as a garrison; perhaps it was too close to the suburbs for safety while they were in Royalist hands, and once they were captured there would have been no need. During the siege the normal markets and distribution of produce must have been severely disrupted with concomitant bad effects for the local economy. At the end of March 1645, after the burning of Christleton and the retirement of the forces of the two Princes, Brereton, in a telling account, reported the difficulties of supplying his troops and maintaining the siege to Parliament. 'Our country is exhausted. Part, since our withdrawal from Christleton, Beeston and ffarne [Farndon], much impoverished by the enemy; the rest heavily charged with our own army and by supplying of victuals and accommodation for the armies. Our sequestrators can raise no money.' (Dore 1984, no 153).

The effects of the war did not cease when the city surrendered. Active Royalists were fined for 'delinquency' and their estates were confiscated. William Mostyn was the Rector of Christleton during the war. He was instituted in 1634 and died in 1669. However, Ormerod (1882, II, 782) records that he was ejected by one Samuel Slater in 1655. Slater was presumably of a more Puritan persuasion and more acceptable to the Commonwealth regime. Presumably William Mostyn was then restored to the living at the Restoration in 1660.

Life In Christleton In The Late 17th Century

Henry Prescott LLB, 1649–1719, was appointed Deputy Registrar of Chester Diocese in 1686. The following year, he was married for the second time on 11th August 1687 to Susanna Puleston, daughter of Sir John Puleston of Havod y Wern. She bore him 11 children but only Jack, Rector of Waverton, Harry, Ken and Margaret survived her. Henry was a keen traveller and often wrote about journeys made to the family property in Lancashire, to Buxton, Bakewell and Chatsworth in Derbyshire, and to Blenheim Palace and Oxford. Henry also collected Roman artefacts and coins and was an avid reader. Wherever he went he spent a great deal of time tasting wines and local ales and was something of a connoisseur. However, he always seemed to be searching for a cure for his over indulgence because he spent 'many turns on the Roodeye' each morning clearing his head.

At first glance the writings in this diary appear to have very little relevance to Christleton, but in fact they give wonderful first-hand descriptions of village life during the period 1686–1719. In his daily diary Henry records details of regular visits to Christleton when he came to see either Mr Gerard Townsend and his family at The Old Hall, or Mr John Witter, the proprietor of the old Glass House Inn on Whitchurch Road. His writings also give an insight into the life of the gentry during the reigns of James II, William and Mary, Queen Anne and George I. It also describes the build-up of tension in the country caused by the troubles in Ireland and the Battle of the Boyne in 1690, and the coming of the Jacobite rebels from Scotland in 1715. Henry's best friend was James Butler, 2nd Duke of Ormond and brother-in-law of the Earl of Derby. James was a loyal follower of William of Orange and must have influenced Henry's thinking. However, the accession of George I in 1714 disaffected many people. Henry was a sympathiser of the Old Pretender and after the 1715 Jacobite rising came out in support of him. After the failure of the rising, Lord Charles Murray and a large number of men were brought to Chester Prison. Many survivors of this uprising were shipped out to the plantations of America.

Henry is clearly an important figure in the social life of the city, and he often describes in great detail the food and drink available to him, as well as his favourite inns and eating-places. Among these are the old Glass House Inn in Christleton, the Ship Inn, the Yacht and the Coach & Horses in Chester, and the Coffee House in Bridge Street, now the Falcon Inn.

The key figure in his visits to Christleton is his friend Gerard Townsend, always known as Mr Townsend in his diary. From these visits come specific details about The Old Hall. 'He keeps an elegant dwelling house and garden, furnished and kept with extraordinary and fancy...I observe the greens and the order of his garden.' At a different time, Henry noted, 'I see the roof over the stable finished, and the brick in tolerable condition, not yet ready for the kiln.' (This could be a description of bricks being made out of local clay, and being prepared for firing near the Pit.)

Mr Townsend was a friend of Sir Richard and Lady Grosvenor and he kept a fine cellar, 'He receives us gently with 2 bottles of wine.' Going to church often appears to be preceded and followed by food. 'We have an elegant dinner at Mr Townsend's, and then move to church for a Christening. Later Mr Townsend treats us with a tankard of good ale and toast.' In addition, there are many details about the food provided for guests at The Old Hall. 'He keeps a good table and Mrs Townsend gives us a present of pork. We had pullets, pork and roasted surloyn of beef, and we drink a pot of coffee.' He often compliments his host's offerings, 'A pretty supper in which lobster is

The old Glass House

served,' and on another occasion he wrote, 'We had dinner of beans, bacon and pease, with cold beef and lamb which seems to please very well.' All kinds of fish and shellfish seemed to be plentiful at that time. 'We call at Mr Townsend's and dine handsomely on codfish and roast beef' and 'Upon appointment my Suzy, son and I set out in Mr Townsend's coach for Christleton. We drink a bottle of good claret and dine on oysters, pease soup, salted whiting and herrings.'

Henry also made frequent visits to the Glass House Inn at Christleton, where his friend John Witter was the proprietor and founder of a Gentleman's Club. The following entries describe some of the activities that went on there. There were many different topics of conversation, sport being prominent. 'Here we call at the Glasshouse where Mr Townsend, Hulton, Middlehurst and Witter have a Club. I sit an hour uneasily in their discourse on greyhounds' and 'There is a conference at the Glasshouse, about the running of horses at Farndon.' On another occasion Henry wrote, 'Near 12 I go to the Glasshouse, where the full company dine. They on pullets, bacon and surloyn. I on pikelet and pudding. The discourse is on the common subjects and hunting.' Amongst his descriptions of his friends and the food they ate, Henry wrote about items that went beyond the locality. His son Harry travelled to Virginia, then a colony, and Henry mentions this, 'I visit the Glasshouse where Mr Chancellor, Townsend, Hulton, Dodd, Middlehurst & Witter were met. We eat a meal of leg of mutton, & noble SirLoyn of Beef well and decently done to us epicures. The ale is tolerable so is the discourse. I write to my Harry now bound for Virginia.'

It appears that Sunday worship was sometimes followed by a hearty meal. 'After prayers at the Church we go to the Glasshouse. We had dinner there of spare ribs, roast beef, stewed hoggs puddings and mince pies well done, and eaten with a keen appetite.'

Henry provides some revealing insights into 18th century funerals. In 1706 the Bishop died whilst visiting a country parish, and Henry accompanied the hearse towards the city. They stopped at the Glass House, and all the funeral parade gathered there. 'Gloves are issued to all, and hat bands to particulars. Scarfs to a very few, myself of this number. We proceed to the Bars. Here the City Corporation and clergy served with gloves are ready.' Another reference to a funeral occurs on 23rd February 1719. 'Having received a funeral ticket, I go to attend the corpse of Sir Laurence Esmund at the Glasshouse, the house full with company and the road near it with company also. Horses and Coaches crowded. Gloves are distributed and I thought I saw Mr Bassona, Mr Holland and Mr Rymer. I escape that obligation and therefore retire about 6 to my chamber and cool posset. The corpse interred without prayers, he being a papist, in St Oswolds. Torches attending from the Glasshouse.'

There are references to Shakespeare's plays being performed in the area. On 20th September 1714 Henry and his son Jack (Rector of Waverton) met the High Sheriff Thomas Wilbraham near the Glass House. They also met with Thomas Brock, the Lord of the Manor of Christleton, and stay with him. 'They take a walk and over a pint of Dysons, and watch Shakespear's King Lear.' Four days later on 24th September 1714, 'The King [George I] comes to Chester and he goes to see Shakespeare's Anthony & Cleopatra, the following day Cymbeline, and later Spencer's Othello.'

Henry did not confine his writing to local affairs, and there are also several references to national events. For example, on 14th November 1715, 'The rebellion of the Old Pretender James, son of James II. We come to Warton [Waverton] about 3, drink two bottles of ale, and returning to Christleton (to our great surprise) we hear and see the great guns fire, and the bonfires raising a bright cloud over the city. We understand the rebels surrendered on mercy Sunday about noon. The number of captives 1500.' Just over a year later on 22nd January 1717, 'About 11 I ride out to Christleton. The weather is fair and frosty. I ride 3 turns around a field belonging to Mr Weston. I call and drink tea with Mr Townsend. The day upon the news of His Majesty's return is turned to a state one. The castle guns firing, filling the city with noise and smoke. Some bonfires and illumination with light.'

There are also very interesting entries relating to the weather and associated phenomena. 11th March 1716 was 'A sharp but kindly day. Accounts describe a phenomenon in the sky from 8 o'clock until 3 in the morning. Tis called the Aurora Borealis, a light or moisture sometimes dilated, sometimes embodied into column's sometimes broken and divided into figures and strands.'

Henry later described a period of very stormy weather with flooding. On 9th June 1718 he wrote, 'The weather continues disposed to rain. Here the clouds pregnant and dark are broke with long valleys of thunder, a most memorable clap which in the midst of common thunder distinguishes itself and makes all things tremble. The clouds again are ralleyed, and fill the horizon with gloomy terror, the lightning and thunder complete the scene above the shocks of human imitation. Seas break down on these parts and turn the roads into lakes and the streets to rivers.'

Nine months later on 29th March 1719, another celestial event is mentioned, 'A meteor appears in the sky.'

He also occasionally wrote about his travels out of the city. On 18th May 1704 Henry travelled with a regiment to Christleton. He rode in Lady Otway's coach with Dr Thane Chancellor. 'There were 500 in the procession. Sir Roger Mostyn, Mr Egerton, Mr Shackerley and Mr Bruen were among them.' It is interesting to note that from this list, Sir Roger Mostyn's family became Rectors of Christleton, Mr Egerton built The Old Hall, Mr Shackerley lived at Gwersylt Hall (later the home of John Williams great-great-grandfather of A A Guest-Williams) and John Bruen was a Puritan and magistrate. He destroyed the church crosses in Christleton, Vicar's Cross, Tarvin and Barrow but paid no penalty when facing prosecution at Chester Assizes. At other times, Henry's travels are more routine affairs. 'At 10 on a blustery day, I take horse and go by Hockenhull Platts to Tarvin. Call in and stay with the schoolmaster Mr Thompson.' He also went visiting with his family, 'My Suzy and three daughters and I go to the Wakes at Warton [Waverton].'

In November 1708 Henry made a visit to Gwersylt, the home of Sir Peter Shakerley. It was later the temporary home of Mr Townsend during the threatened rebellion of the Scots, and of John Williams, the head of the family who later took the name Guest-Williams. The other visitors on that occasion included Richard Middleton of Chirk Castle (whose sister Anne married Robert Townsend), Mr Hanmer, Richard Mostyn (Patron of St James' Christleton), Dr Thane Chancellor of Chester Cathedral, and the Bishop. 'Entertainment is generous and elegant. Upon the occasion of tobacco, my Lord banters Mr Chancellor the laying down of his pipe. Mr Shackerely equipped prevails me to go hunting. We meet a pack of beagles near the Vicarage, and the hare is found we persue the game. At the end of the hunt I am presented with the hare.'

Henry wrote a sequence of entries in June 1690 that describe a royal visit to Chester. On 6th June, the day before King William III arrived, the Bishop and citizens of Chester were expecting the Prince of Denmark. However, 'A misfortune of the carriage hindered his journey,' and the Prince was forced to spend the night at Christleton at Lady Bellot's. (Sir John Bellot was created Baronet in 1663 and was a descendant of Hugh Bellot, 1542–92, a former Bishop of Chester.) Consequently on 7th June, 'The Prince of Denmark passes through the city in a speeding carriage ungreeted. More Royal Horse Guards arrive. The King arrives in the city.' The excitement of the city at seeing the royal visitor the following day is well documented in the diary. '8th June: Spectators fly in every direction. The city is full. He arrives about 10 o'clock. The citizens receive him with solemn usage and eloquent speech. He travels through streets thronged with guards and packed with sightseers, strewn here with flowers, there with gravel, arrived at last at the Cathedral Church. The unrestrained crowd enclose, carry along and almost overwhelming the King. When the service is over the King goes on to Gayton for lunch. From there he inspects the fleet at Hylake [Hoylake].'

Henry's friend, James Butler, the Duke of Ormond, stayed with him in the city, and Henry travelled after him curious about seeing the then port. '10th June: The Duke of Ormond says farewell and returns to Gayton. I follow on a lame horse. The day grows warm, the way turns to sand. Curious of seeing Hylake, a most convivial harbour indeed, I press on. About 300 ships of every size are at anchor. the surrounding shore is inhospitable.

'11th June: About 10 o'clock The King boards ship, the sounds of cannon thunder on all sides. Prayed for good and favourable outcome. The wind slackens at about 3 o'clock. The King spends the night at anchor, having scarcely got out of the harbour.'

The most important entries in the diary relating to Christleton tell the story of the dispute between the Rector, Thomas Clopton, and Gerard Townsend. The dispute concerned the building of an oratory, or burial vault, for the Townsend family under the chancel of the church. Their relationship was extremely good in March 1709 but then deteriorated to the

The Old Hall

point, in July 1716, when the Bishop of Chester became involved. A heated argument took place, which eventually led to a reconciliation three days after the Bishop's intervention. However, the dispute resulted in the death of the Rector through stress and anxiety four months later. The following extract tells the story.

10th July 1716: I walk a good way and weather to Christleton to Mr Townsends where I drink tea. My Lord Bishop on his way to Whitchurch calls and sees the controversial chancel or oratory, finds no damage to the church or disorder. Mr Wishaw appears for Mr Clopton.

Mr Chancellor attacks him with too much passion and prejudice, and my Lord having heard the circumstances, upon his complaint of Mr Townsends leaving the church, and using Mr Clopton, a grave clergyman ill, uses sharp correspcious to him, telling him those faults were proper for his examination, and not to be so revenged by ejectment at law.

My Lord Bishop since, would not meet him there as he appointed, walks in displeasure towards the parsonage. Mr Clopton after several messages were sent, meets him. They go to the house and the company follows. Mr Clopton tells the story of their late differences about the Summer House as introductory to his reclaiming his right. He deny's that Mr Townsend ever had the Bishops, the Patrons or his concent, producing Roger Mostyn's and Mr Rowlands letters.

Mr Townsend gives another version of the facts, and deny's he pulled down one brick of the wall, or invaded another inch of ground. Because Mr Clopton had affirmed what Mr Townsend took to be an untruth, he proposed that the matter be decided by oath. This gave Mr Clopton occasion to reflect on him in his pulpit. This he did in terms so provoking and distinct and so frequently, that he (Mr Townsend) left the church before the sermon, that he might leave the subject which was directed against him. He also refused to take communion from the Reverend Clopton. He (Mr T) asserted that he had obtained the Bishops consent and that of Sir Roger Mostyn by his letter now mislayed, and that he had Mr Clopton expresses consent to build.

He produced a late letter from Sir Roger Mostyn as not expressing giving nor denying consent. Mr Chancellor attested positively the consent of the Bishop, the Patron and Mr Clopton, saying that without them he had not past his decree for the building of the chapel.

A personal reflection was made by Mr Clopton against Mr Townsend as guilty of prophane or common swearing, which was taken off by some present who had much more frequently used his conversation than Mr Clopton.

At last Mr Townsend's omission in not receiving the sacrament was peevishly objected to by Mr Wishaw. This seemed to shock the Bishop. He parts with the sentiment that Mr Clopton has quitted himself decently, and that Mr Townsend had shewed too much obstinacy in the controvercy, and had surprised him with a demonstration of a principle or at least an opinion contrary to the charitable doctrine of the C. of E. and parting with me he said, 'Mr Prescott, Mr Townsend is not the man you take him to be.' I pleaded his case and hope for a speedy reconciliation to the Holy Sacrament.

13th July 1716: Reconciliation and a lasting peace were celebrated by shaking hands, and drinking some of Mr Clopton's fine ale...

16th November 1716: After dinner my son and I go to Christleton. He calls to see Mr Clopton now weak, and then comes to me at the Old Hall. Later we call at the Glasshouse where Mr Townsend and friends meet at Mr Witters club.

22nd November 1716: Thomas Clopton died today.

Despite the dispute and the Bishop's warning about Mr Townsend's character, further diary entries reveal that Henry Prescott was still a very welcome visitor at the Old Hall, and their special relationship continued. He continued to visit the village and this entry is typical of his later writings. '27th December 1718: I rise about 8, and finding the frost wholly disolved, and a delicate air and glorious sun succeeding. I walk and come to Christleton before ten o'clock and am refreshed by the air and the exercise. I walk with Mr Townsend in his pleasant garden. After we drink tea and sit an hour with him and his lady. We go to Church and prayers. After, return to dinner at which Mr Davies the organist entertains in the parlour with the spinet, and his hopeful pupils Cotton and Carter.'

Henry died in 1719, but his diary remains to give some fascinating details of life in Christleton in the 17th century.

Note: the original spellings in these extracts have been kept to retain the authenticity of Henry's diary.

The Blacksmith's in Plough Lane, circa 1880

Christleton: The Self-Contained Village

A study of the 1851 census of Christleton reveals many details about village life. It seems that within the thriving village community there were many trades and talents and enough resources to feed and clothe the inhabitants, meeting almost their every need. There were 140 families at that time, making a total of 740 inhabitants. Almost half of these were young people under the age of 20, and surprisingly at a time when people didn't live so long, 27 people were aged between 70 and 90.

The Red Lion, St James' Church, and the old Cash and Carry Stores (on the right) in Village Road, circa 1920s

The majority of the inhabitants were born within the local area. A significant number also came from North Wales, many of whom were employed as servants in the houses of the wealthier families. These included The Old Hall, Christleton Hall, and the Rectory. Townsend Ince of Christleton Hall had five servants, although there were others employed at the Hall who lived in the village and therefore are not recorded as being at the Hall on census night. These included four members of the Poston family (housekeeper, maid, head gardener and gardener) who lived in Pepper Street. The Rector, Thomas Lloyd, is recorded as having three servants. Eighteen households employed 65 servants, a third of whom came from villages in North Wales. This is possibly the reason why there are a large number of families of Welsh origin still living in the village. The census also reveals that some of the wealthier families had already travelled to far off places, with children and adults having been born in Ireland, Portugal, Canada and the East and West Indies. Several of these families had interests in shipping, wine, wool, cloth and textiles, and some of the older gravestones in St James' churchyard show inscriptions recording 'Merchant of Liverpool', or 'Merchant of Manchester'.

The majority of servants were employed inside the houses, but there were also 20 employed on farms. There were 10 gardeners, and the map of 1895 on the inside front cover of this book shows the large number of formal gardens and parks within the village. Farming was by far the largest source of employment, with more than half the workforce working on the land. There were 17 farms in Christleton township alone, with the emphasis on dairy and mixed farming. Each farm produced milk, and some produced butter and cheese for sale locally. In fact one of the old dairies from 1730 still exists intact, adjoining a former farmhouse in the village.

With so many farms, there was work for two blacksmiths who employed 10 men. They dealt with the shoeing of the heavy horses, repaired tackle, and made and repaired machinery, including wheels and farm wagons. There were two slaughterhouses to provide meat for the two butchers' shops to sell, and the animal skins were taken from the slaughterhouse direct to the tanner, who worked from a yard at the back of the Trooper Inn. He too employed 10 men to produce leather, which in turn was used to produce shoes and other goods to be sold in the village, at least for the families who could afford them. Many children wore clogs, but there is no evidence of these being made in the village.

Local farms provided the shops with milk, cheese, butter, beef, lamb, pork, bacon, poultry and eggs. They also grew oats, wheat and barley, and supplied grain for animal food to be prepared at Christleton Mill, as well as flour for bread, which was baked at the two bakeries and either sold from there or delivered to homes by donkey cart or wagon. Vegetables such as potatoes, swedes, carrots, cabbage and

Joe Mosford local butcher, and staff, circa 1890s

other greens were also grown locally, and the parish has always had a good reputation for providing a range of food from local market gardens for the stalls at Chester Market. Fruit, too, was plentiful in season from local orchards, and fish from Mr Townsend's 'pond for fish' might have been available in the village. Salt was sold from the Salt Box, a house near the canal, and would have been used to help preserve meat products. Fresh produce was stored in the Ice House, near the Bottom of the Wood.

The village had nine dressmakers or seamstresses, and there were four tailors in 1851. It was possible to get clothes washed, as there were 11 ladies described as being washerwomen or laundresses.

If a house needed building or repairing, there were plenty of tradespeople who could help. The village census listed builders, masons, bricklayers, a brickmaker, a thatcher and several general labourers. As it was still the era of horse-drawn transport, if only for the wealthier families, the village provided grooms and coachmen. Three people were employed to collect the tolls at the Toll-gate near Christleton Bank, and nine men were employed on the canal as lock-keepers or boatmen.

The school provided work for the headteacher, three teachers and several pupil teachers, who looked after around 150 pupils. The village was served by a parish constable and a militiaman, and Mr Townsend Ince was the Colonel-in-Chief of the Royal Stockport Militia. There was also an attorney, a solicitor, four land-agents, and a surveyor. Eighteen people are described as 'Fund Holders' or 'Annuitants' (living off a pension), including Rector Thomas Lloyd. Eleven others are described as being in home employment, but the trade is not specified.

In 1851 St James' Church was the main place of worship, and there was a small congregational chapel above Thomas Johnson's Post Office in Pepper Street. The inns and beerhouses included the Trooper Inn, the Ring o'Bells (now the Parish Hall), the Red Lion (now the Ring o'Bells), the Bottom of the Wood, and the Plough Inn.

Christleton 1927–1953

The difficult decade

The 1930s, 1940s and 1950s were troubled times in the world, and Rector A A Guest-Williams did his best to guide his parishioners

Thomas Johnson's Post Office in Pepper Street, circa 1880

through the parish magazines during the Depression and the events leading up to and through the Second World War.

After attending two political meetings in April 1927 at the Boys' School, he wrote the following. 'It is perhaps as well for the clerical element to abstain from political discussion both in the pulpit and outside. Yet it is good to enlarge the mind by attending to one's duties as a citizen and the accompaniment of good fare affords food for thought. From this our thoughts travel on naturally to the supper at the Institute to celebrate the victory of the Billiard Team.'

He did not always refrain from expressing his political views, however, for the turmoils of the next decades over-rode his principle of clerical silence. In December 1931 he attacked the principle of free trade. 'The problem of the moment is wise spending for the sake of our country—it may mean considerable sacrifice. From the advertisements of various things it might appear that the only requisite was the spending of every shilling on cheap and shoddy goods that have obviously been imported into this country. To buy such is neither patriotic nor, in the long run, economical. As far as ever possible we must try to see that the money we spend benefits our own industries... Free trade would be an ideal thing if it worked fairly on both sides, therefore we must have strong protective tariffs ourselves... we must produce more and support home products and home markets. In a village we see the pity of a good man out of employment. It is our duty to try and help him by doing all we can to support local industries, the local dealers, the local traders and encouraging the latter to supply us with goods bearing the National mark.'

By January 1934, he gave a warning with the increasing hopes of improvement. 'There are prospects of better times and already there is a considerable decrease in the number of unemployed...We have most of us been passing through lean years and, if prosperity returns, let us remember the lessons of self-denial and thrift that we have been learning.'

However, there were some cheerful times in Britain during 1930s. In May 1935 the country celebrated the Silver Jubilee of King George V and Queen Mary. 'The May Jubilee Queen was crowned very fittingly by Mrs Garnett on the Grange Lawn, thus maintaining a link with the great celebrations that took place in the late Canon Garnett's days at the Diamond Jubilee

A Silver Jubilee programme, 1935

of Queen Victoria.' There were Jubilee mugs for all children in the parish, and Mr Peacock read out the telegram that had been despatched to Buckingham Palace from Christleton. The reply, received next day, was posted up in Morgans' shop window. On the death of King George the following February, Guest-Williams wrote, 'His very modesty proved one of his most regal assets. He was exemplary in his devotion to his subjects and that devotion was whole-heartedly reciprocated. Our new King Edward VII has gifts of his own that we have long appreciated.' There is no comment on the abdication, but a full account of the celebrations of the coronation of King George VI in May 1937 tells of the relay of the new King's speech, the evening bonfire and dancing in the Women's Institute Hall until 1 am.

The Second World War

A series of entries between May 1938 and September 1939 illustrate the unease and tension felt by Mr Guest-Williams and the village.

The Jubilee Fete – Rose Queen and attendants

May 1938: 'We are taking wise precautions in case of air raids. I trust they will be unnecessary, but the less care we take the more likely we are to attract attention.'

October 1938: 'Our hearts have been overcharged with apprehension at the crisis which threatens the peace of the world. We must hold fast by our faith and pray that the danger may be averted and that right counsels prevail. That is the first duty—then very calmly we must make ourselves ready to do the utmost that our King and Country may demand of us.'

May 1939: 'We all of us hope that there will be no war...Probably the best way of arresting the calamity of another war is to take a lesson from our own past mistakes; we were not prepared when the last war broke out...Individually we must do what we can. The young men from 20–21 are to have military training.'

On 3rd September 1939 a recording of the declaration of war by Neville Chamberlain was heard in the Boys' School after morning service. 'No-one was surprised, many were in a sense relieved that the period of tension was over. The younger folk, perhaps, with no recollection of the horror of the last war, seemed almost glad; but those of us who do remember the optimism of August 1914, and the hope we entertained of a speedy victory then, are grieved at the thought of the inevitable suffering that war brings...There are to be special services on October 1st throughout the kingdom. Then there is much to do, and the difficulties of lighting, transport and rationing are going to take up much of our time. May God give us strength...We have a splendid number of young men and women. It will be a great wrench to many a heart and home to let them go, but in sending them on their way we must first commit them to God's care.'

During the war years, the magazines chronicle village life in hard times and the activity of the parishioners in setting up and supporting many schemes that provided help for others as well as themselves. The winter of 1940 was very severe and an epidemic of influenza affected many homes. A Knitted Comforts Fund was set up in support of a scheme to provide parcels of knitwear for Christleton lads in the Forces and the local anti-aircraft and searchlight units. In March 1944, the letters arriving from the officers and men, who had received enclosures and who greatly appreciated their gifts, are referred to in the parish magazine.

Christleton's contribution to the War Weapons Week Collection in 1940 was an impressive £2365 6s 0d, of which £16 was raised by a gymkhana organised by Miss Smith and Miss Nevitt Bennett. 1941 saw the setting up of a collection centre for the Fruit Preservation Scheme, and the War Savings Campaign set its objective of £2,500 for an anti-aircraft gun. In 1942 a village highlight was a dance organised by girls from the Land Army for the Spitfire Appeal. The 'Wings for Victory' Campaign in 1944 achieved £13,452. Throughout the period there was continued fund-raising for the war effort. The Fete held at Christleton Grange raised £151 14s 1d for the Red Cross (Agriculture) Fund, and a further £1303 1s 0d was collected in October for Christleton's Victory Fund. All this money paid tribute to parishioners who gave, in many cases, more than they could afford and who were on a strict system of rationing. Ration books and cards were issued annually to residents of Christleton at the Girls' or Boys' Schools.

However, everyone was also encouraged to grow their own vegetables, and the Garden & Allotment Association was formed to extend food production. Its annual subscriptions of 1s 6d per head were used to purchase the right seeds and fertilisers and to establish a proper means of storing perishable vegetables. Some allotments still exist – behind the Glass House, for example – but others, such as those along the tops of the railway cutting behind Bridge Drive, have gone.

St James' Church also helped in the community effort. By November 1939 the blackout was in operation, which meant the 6.30 pm Evening Service had to be brought forward to 3.15 pm. A significant symbol of wartime and its precautions was the silence of all church bells. Their purpose at that time was to sound warning of an invasion of Britain. St James' Church gave some of its good iron railings in June 1942 to the Salvage Campaign, which recycled both metals and paper, and there were depots for clothing for those whose houses had been bombed. On Christmas Day 1943, with the threat of invasion over, the church bells were rung again. Guest-Williams wrote, 'thanks to the ARP [Air Raid Precautions] for lending us the lamps to guide our feet'; the blackout was still in place.

The first mention of evacuee children is found in September 1939. 'Christleton is to be a reception area for some of the evacuating districts in the event of any emergency. This means finding homes for perhaps 600 souls—mostly children attending school.' Later, the Rector wrote, 'We already have a quota of evacuees and in many places they have quickly settled down. But they will need supervision and must have discipline at home as well as at school.' In 1944 he reported on the departure of evacuees. 'St Patrick's RC Boys' School, Liverpool, is severing its connection with our school at Christleton. They give sincere thanks for hospitality during the past four years. Children and teachers have been very happy.'

Despite being a reception area for evacuees, Christleton was on the flight path of the German bombers en route to the docks at Liverpool and Birkenhead, and children on their way to and from school would stop to watch the dogfights overhead. Headmaster Tom Solloway would, at times, take his classes out into the playground to see the Battle of Britain of 1940–41 in the skies over the village. Air Raid Shelters were built in gardens and on village ground, notably beside the footpath between the present Primary School and Woodfields. Bombs, jettisoned by Luftwaffe planes fleeing from attacks by Spitfire and Hurricane fighters and local anti-aircraft fire, fell on some Christleton fields, and there were crashed aircraft at Littleton Hall and over the railway on the Huntington path. A Home Guard Unit was formed in Christleton and gave a display to parishioners in the fields on Windmill Hill, involving many smoke bombs. A Cadet Platoon was later organised in 1943 under Captain McKerrell Brown for lads aged 14–17 years.

The Rector gave the news in July 1941 of the first known wartime fatality: Charlie Rathbone died at sea from burns he received as a gunner. He was the great-grandson of Nurse Johnson and grandson of Mr and Mrs Partington of Little Heath. More bad news came of Eric Lockley, who had been missing for many months; in August it was confirmed that he had died of wounds 'some long time ago.'

The progress of the war took a turn for the better in July 1944. 'News of the success in its initial stages of the invasion of France for liberation from cruel oppressors.' In April 1945 Guest-Williams wrote, 'The long-expected advance of our forces across the Rhine into Germany has begun and great success has attended our efforts.' He also paid tribute to the departing American troops who had been based in Christleton. 'It has been a privilege to have had the opportunity of making friends among locally-based officers and men of the US Army. Colonel Brown has been with us for a considerable time.'

On 8th May 1945, the war in Europe ended and a nationwide Service of Thanksgiving was held in St James' on 13th, which brought together the Christleton representatives of the British Legion, ARP, Home Guard, British Red Cross, St John's Ambulance Association, National Fire Service, Police, Women's Volunteer Service, Cadets, Boy Scouts and members of the Land Army. In June the village held a Victory Tea and, after the Victory over Japan on 15th August, the celebrations were unbounded. Flags flew and the bellringers turned out two full teams to peal through much of the day. There was a service at 7 pm and an impromptu dance in the Boys' School with the Royal Corps of Signals Band, who were based at Vicar's Cross Camp.

The post-war years
Celebrations continued into 1946 and, on the Saturday before Whitsun – twice postponed by bad weather – victory programmes were held on the Grange field. A quarter peal by the ringers was followed by tea for all the children and a schedule of sports. In August the children went to Vicar's Cross to see the King and Queen pass by on their visit to Chester. Later that month, on 24th, a great Welcome Home Party for Christleton's service men and women was held in the Institutes. Sponsored by the Comforts Fund and the newly inaugurated Christleton Branch of the British Legion, it followed the ringing of bells and a church service of thanksgiving and was a great success. 'A happy event. It took hard work and thinking in days of rationing to provide every commodity in food, in drink and tobacco.' The final event paid for by the Victory Fund was a trip to the pantomime in Chester on New Year's Day for all the parish children aged 7–14 years.

The sacrifice of those who fell in both world wars was recognised during November 1947's Remembrance Day and the church service was well attended. A year later in November 1948 the Parish Council decided to have the names of those who fell in the Second World War engraved on a plaque inside the church. This was unveiled in February 1949 by the President of Christleton's British Legion, Lieutenant Commander Colin Campbell. The War Memorial on the Green was also inscribed with those names and it was re-dedicated by the Reverend J W J Steele, Service Chaplain to Western Command in Chester.

Despite the end of the war, rationing continued for a further five years, to the increasing criticism of the Rector. He wrote in January 1946, 'The past year has brought much relief from the anxieties of war, dangers and hardships. We still look forward to the end of separations and the irksome burdens of controls.' Food production in these years was badly affected by extremes of weather. The April 1946 edition of the parish magazine described 'a terrible winter of heavy snowfalls and rain, followed by a long, hot drought, has wrought havoc everywhere. Our crops are endangered. It will mean, therefore, that we have to be especially careful of our own produce of fruit and vegetables in our gardens and allotments.' This meant that two years later, in March 1950, there was still no end to rationing. 'New ration books from the Food Executive will be issued between 4 and 8 pm on Thursday 20th April in the Boys' School – a tiresome thing, no doubt, but apparently still necessary. The staff are always most helpful and obliging.' The last reference in the parish magazines to rationing was in April 1953. However, some events were not controlled by ration books. In the October 1950 edition, the Rector comments, 'This is an unusually large number of weddings to occur at this time of year. Happiness, we hope, is still un-rationed!'

The cover of the programme celebrating the coronation of Queen Elizabeth II

Village Trades And Industries

The canal industry

In 1935 the boating business was started on rented land next to Mr G F Wain's property Dinas, Rowton Bridge, Christleton by a small group of his friends. Their object was to build up a fleet of holiday hire cruisers to operate on Britain's canals. It was incorporated the following year under the name of The Inland Cruising Association Limited. The company began trading with five cruisers named *Stanford, Barbara, Beryl, Bobby* and *Jazz*. Six new cruisers were later added: *Freda, Betty, Audrey, Valerie, Pat*, and *Joyce*, all built by Taylor's of Chester. Docks and boat repair sheds were built in 1937–38, and a further large boat-building shed was added in 1938–39, bringing the total covered boat building and repair area to 4400 square feet.

This was the first hire fleet to be developed for operation on Britain's canals. The 11 cruisers and two camping punts were managed by Mr Gillmore.

The outbreak of the Second World War in 1939 brought with it petrol rationing, and boat hiring had to be abandoned. This was a major disaster for the company, which had now lost its principle source of income. It was not until 1946 that a limited amount of petrol was made available for leisure uses and the business was able to start trading properly again. During the war years some of the cruisers were hired out as holiday houseboats, on their moorings at Christleton, by people who had been bombed out of their homes or just wanted to get away to a quiet spot in the country.

At the end of hostilities the company had drifted into debt and two thirds of the fleet had to be sold to clear the debt and provide capital to restart operations. This only left four of the original fleet. However, the boating industry was growing fast and, by 1962, the Wain family had acquired all the remaining company shares from the original shareholders and set about rebuilding the fleet.

In 1956 the Chairman and Managing Director, Mr G F Wain, died suddenly and his son David Wain took his place. In the same year the company changed its name to Inland Hire Cruisers Limited. During the next 20 years the yard built 19 hire cruisers for its own fleet, as well as building, restoring and repairing many inland and coastal boats for private owners.

(1) A car on the frozen canal in 1963

(2) Boats on the canal, showing Rowton Bridge in the background in 1963

(3) Boat sheds at Christleton Marina, 1963

(4) Boat building at Christleton Marina in 1963

The company was dissolved in 1972, the fleet of boats was dispersed and the yard was sold with planning permission for three houses.

The mills

Christleton had two mills within the parish: the Windmill on the top of the sandstone ridge, belonging to the Sneyde Family of Keele, which produced flour for the village from around 1600 until the 1840s; and Butler's Mill, which was working until the 1970s producing mainly animal foodstuffs, but also produced flour for its own bakery in the early part of the 20th century. The latter depended on local farmers to provide the grain (wheat, oats, and flaked maize) to be mixed into suitable animal feed, which was distributed by their own wagons. The canal played an important part in the provision of grain, because the large canal barges, known locally as *Mersey Flats*, would bring supplies of grain to the mill from Ellesmere Port Docks. These double-width horse-drawn barges were regularly used on the Chester and Shropshire Union Canals between Ellesmere Port and Nantwich, and photographs at the turn of the 20th century show them being used in Christleton. The wooden section of the mill overhanging the canal contained a gas-driven hoist to lift the grain from the barges into the mill, although it is said that a pulley system using the horse was just as efficient for the task. The Butler family was involved in many aspects of village life. They had farms at Rowton, a mill, bakery and shop at Christleton, and Thomas Butler owned the shop in Village Road that is now the Post Office. He was also a guardian of the poor in Boughton and a very prominent Parish and City Councillor. He published postcards of village life around about 1910. The last members of the family living in the village, Mr and Mrs Tom Butler, died in the late 1980s; their daughter Irene (a member of the history group) and granddaughter Joanne died in a car crash just before that.

Farming and market gardening

Farming has always been one of the most important aspects of village life and cultivating the ground has long been a necessity, but now in the year 2000, the farming industry is rapidly declining. In the past all the village farms were dairy or mixed farms, but today there is only one dairy farm left within Christleton township, and many of the farm buildings have been converted into houses or flats. The dairy industry suffered greatly during the 1960s from foot-and-mouth

A Mersey Flat Boat on the Shropshire Union Canal, near Butler's Mill, early 20th century

disease, then soon afterwards from the changes introduced when Britain joined the Common Market. Milk quotas were established because of the national over-production, which saw a further reduction in the need for milk, and many farms went out of business. However, there was still a need for arable crops and much of the land surrounding the village was cultivated in this way. Maize, wheat, oil seed rape, linseed, potatoes, beans and other vegetable crops are now grown in rotation, and in recent years many acres of land around Christleton are used to grow turf for the gardens of new houses.

Christleton was always renowned for its market gardening produce that was sold at Chester Market or in the local farm shop. During the 1960s and 1970s land all around Christleton, but mainly between the village and the ring road, and in Littleton and Rowton was extremely productive and a great range of garden produce and flowers was available for sale. Arden's and Randal's farms were large egg producers. Kirk's Nurseries in Littleton was well-known for growing flowers and even had collections of orchids flourishing in their greenhouses. They also produced cauliflower, sprouts, lettuce and tomatoes.

Butcher

One of the most famous residents of Christleton was Joe Mosford, the local butcher. His family had come to the village in the early 1800s and had owned the Red Lion Inn. Joe had his slaughterhouse behind the present Ring O'Bells public house, then called the Red Lion. His two daughters, Mary Partington and Vi Mosford, were well-known in the village. Mary was known as Mrs Christleton from her active involvement in village life: she helped to found the Women's Institute, organised the village Fetes, was an energetic member of Christleton Players and the Badminton Club, and was Chairman of both the British Legion and the Parish Council. Vi, her sister, was a milliner and worked at Browns in Chester, and later had her own shop in Frodsham Street.

Joe bought Rock House from Mr Hullah, the schoolmaster, and had the front section added to create his shop. (This part of the building is now the dental surgery.) He had two stalls in Chester Market and supplied the meat for them, and for his shop in the village, from his own resources. He rented several fields locally and kept the cattle, sheep and pigs there until he needed them for slaughtering. He rented Badgerett, part of the present High School field, as well as a field near the Abbot's Well.

Kirk's Florist, Chester Market Hall, in the early 1960s

Joe later had a second slaughterhouse near the telephone exchange. He was a great character and at every Fete he offered a pig as a prize for anyone who could climb the 'greasy pole', situated outside his shop on the village green. He is also said to have travelled most Saturdays to Chester Market to sell his produce and, after a good day and early evening, was put onto his cart by other stall holders and taken home to Christleton by his horse!

Joe was followed by Bill Partington and then by Jim Partington, who took over in 1965. Jim is also one of the great characters of Christleton, although he was born near Eccleston Ferry. Many people will fondly remember his shop, which was one of the best places to buy meat and to find out all the local news. When the shop closed in the 1980s it seemed as though someone had switched off the lights and sounds from the centre of the village; everything seemed so quiet and still. Jim continues to work hard for the Parish Council, the Institute, the Cricket and Football Clubs; he could perhaps be known as Mr Christleton, following the family tradition.

Mr Crump shoeing Mr Greenway's horse in the 1970s

Blacksmith

During the 1880s, with so many farms in the locality all worked by heavy horse, there was enough employment for two blacksmiths' forges in the village. These were very active places, and there are several fine pictures in the photographic collection of the work being done: making horse shoes and shoeing shire-horses, making and repairing ploughs and even a penny farthing. The only forge remaining, at the corner of Plough Lane, closed in 1999 when Mr Crump retired. He was one of the last men skilled in both traditional work and in modern steel fabrication. Mr Crump could be seen working with horses on most days in the early 1970s, but this work gradually diminished as working horses disappeared from the farms. In the last 10 years he mainly worked in wrought iron. Among his finest pieces were gates constructed for the Duke of Westminster at Eaton Hall. This smithy, at the Bottom of the Wood, was originally owned by James Fleet. He was succeeded by his son Frank, the violinist, who was heard on an early radio broadcast and was also photographed in 1953 for a book about Britain published to celebrate the coronation of Queen Elizabeth II. In 1955 Frank retired and handed the business on to his friend Fred Williams, who was then succeeded by Mr Crump in 1968. The second smithy was on Little Heath Road, next to the present telephone exchange, and was last owned by Mr Cyril Rogers, who is also recorded on film with a shire-horse. This house is said to date from the early 17th century and was the earliest site used as a forge in the village; it was surrounded by a group of farms and situated next to the timber-yard and tithe-barn.

Tanner

With two slaughterhouses in Christleton, there was also a need for several tanyards to cure leather. There was one near the Smithy in Little Heath Road, another at Littleton where Dandy's Farm is now situated, and also one at the back of the Trooper Inn. The owner of the tanyard at the Trooper had cottages in Pepper Street built for several of his nine employees.

4 Personalities and Memories

The Mayers Family

The Mayers' family name dominates any account of the village for the last two hundred years. It appears that the family can trace their ancestry back to a Wilhelm Mayer, who reputedly came to Christleton from Bavaria in 1490 and married a Christleton girl. He was a journeyman carpenter by trade, and it is possible that he was employed in the building of St James' Church. The large family certainly seem to have had the building trade in their blood, as so many of them have been involved in it in some way ever since.

They have also been closely involved in bellringing in Christleton and Waverton. Thomas Mayers, the head of the Victorian family, was the father of two of the famous bellringing Mayers: George, headmaster and Parish Clerk, and Joseph, born in 1840. Samuel Mayers, Thomas' brother, was also a well-known ringer, and there were two sisters Julia and Margaret. Julia was a seamstress who lived at the Dixon's Almshouses in her later life and who made dresses for Lucy Anne Ince and Mrs Cullimore. John Mayers, another bellringer, moved to Waverton and had a house on the corner of Common Lane. William, his brother, made a set of handbells for Waverton Church Ringers and had his initials carved on the handles. Different family members carried out other trades. Stanley Mayers lived at 4 Canalside and had a motor repair yard, whilst Gilbert Mayers was a painter and signwriter. More recently George Mayers, from another branch of the family, had a transport business in Vicar's Cross. Today the family responsibility for bellringing is carried out by Rev David Fisher, great-great-grandson of Joseph, and another family member, Mrs Nancy Catherall (née Mayers), still worships at St James'.

However, John Mayers is probably the most famous member of the family. The Westminster Estate employed him as a building contractor on several major projects. He worked with the Duke's architect, John Douglas, who was responsible for designing most of the black and white timber framed shops and buildings in Chester between 1890–1910. These included the buildings in St Werburgh Street and, most famous of all, the black and white building forming the frontage

The Mayers family, circa 1890s, including blacksmiths, joiners and carpenters who worked for Thomas Mayers & Co (taken at the rear of The Nook, now Smithy Cottage)

of St Michael's Arcade. This building was originally built in 1906 in white marble and tiles, which can be seen today at the base of the steps in Bridge Street and inside St Michael's Arcade. However, the Duke did not like the overall effect on the street, and in 1909 William Lockwood, another of the Duke's architects, and John Mayers & Company gained the contract to rebuild it at a cost of £17,000. The working relationship with the Duke's architects might explain why the house, Two Gables in Pepper Street, Christleton, was designed by John Douglas in 1898 and then lived in by one of the Mayers family soon afterwards.

The Mayers' firm was responsible for Church View, the home of George Mayers the headmaster, the extension to the Girls' School, and the replacement Boys' School (now the Parish Hall). It is probable that they built several of the houses in Pepper Street and also refaced the Old Hall with red Ruabon brick. This was a new brick that they often used in their buildings during the 1890s. The firm also built the Campbell Memorial Hall in Boughton and the old Chester Library in St John Street using Ruabon brick. They assisted in the restoration of Chester Cathedral. It also seems likely that the Mayers helped to put the first sewerage system into the village, because several of the oldest iron grids on the pavements carry the mark *Thomas Mayers of Rowton*.

John Mayers & Sons was also responsible for other major building work, including the arcades, hotels and shops in Llandudno and

Joseph Mayers with grandchildren in the late 1800s

Colwyn Bay. They built a church in Ireland and a rather unusual Catholic Church at Amlwch, Anglesey. This church, called the Star of the Sea, is designed like an upturned boat with a number of concrete ribs giving it stability and strength. There are strips of stained glass windows running down the outside of the walls and a huge stained glass star over the front porch. The cross inside is made from cut glass placed in a wooden frame, which allows the sun and the moon to reflect through it when their light strikes it. This was one of the last projects carried out by the firm and is certainly the most unusual.

The Dixons Of Littleton

The first Thomas Dixon, a timber merchant of Chester, lived in a large house called Littleton Hill at Littleton, one of the five townships of Christleton parish. He had been a Captain in the Royal Navy and served under Admiral Rodney. Thomas was born in 1755 and died in 1811. He expanded his business by purchasing land around the old dock area of Chester to store his timber. The Port of Chester was a very active place at this time importing timber from Memel, Lithuania and Christiana (Oslo), as well as fine wines from Africa and Portugal. There were also 14 shipbuilding yards and Thomas might also have been involved in this trade. Clues can be found from records in the Chester Record Office: 'Thomas Dixon was granted lease of the old dock between the House of Industry and Mr Harrison's Iron Foundry.' It was in this area of Chester that some of the first iron ships were constructed: *The Royal Charter*, which later sank off Anglesey with its cargo of gold bullion, was the most famous.

Another record of a later date states that, 'Thomas Dixon Merchant. Granted lease of wasteland along the River Dee extending from the Dee Bridge for landing timber. 1812.' This refers to Thomas' eldest son. Thomas and his wife Anne had three sons, Thomas, William and James. It is probable that the other brothers were also involved in the trade, although James does seem to have been more involved in property dealing, as can be seen from the following extracts.

'James Dixon. Brother of Thomas Dixon Timber Merchant of Chester. Lease of a plot of land to be used as a shipyard, near the House of Industry.

'James Dixon Re Beaching estate at Coddington. Details of exchange of land in Christleton between James Dixon and Townsend Ince of Christleton. 1843.'

Thomas the younger clearly ran the family timber business and also became involved in land deals, many around the Port of Chester. He also became a banker founding the Dixon & Chilton Bank in Market Place, Chester in 1813. On the death of Mr Chilton, the bank moved to Eastgate Street and became the Dixon & Wardell Bank. Thomas then sold his Market Place property to Chester City Council for £2,800.

In 1859 a new bank building was erected in Eastgate Street, and the Dixon & Wardell Bank became the Chester Bank (Dixon & Co). It was a very imposing building designed in the classical style and had fluted columns capped by Corinthian capitals. It later became Parrs Bank, then the Westminster Bank, and is now a branch of the National Westminster Bank. Thomas gave a very grand supper for all the workers on his new bank project on 30th November 1859, which was much appreciated and enjoyed. He was held in the highest regard both in the city and in Christleton where he worshipped. A white marble tablet was erected in St James' Church to celebrate his work.

Thomas is also mentioned in a number of Christleton Parish Highways Committee

> *The Parishioners of Christleton being most desirous to record their feelings of high regard and esteem for*
> *Thomas Dixon of Littleton Esq, in the said parish*
> *for the great interest uniformly taken by him in all matters relating to the church*
> *and the keeping of its paved precincts, in due order and decency [when in office or otherwise] as well as more*
> *especially for his zeal and liberality in co operating with the recent repairs of the Church and Chancel*
> *being unanimously agreed*
> *that this tablet and inscription*
> *dedicated to him*
> *shall be placed therein as a lasting testimonial*
> *of their obligation and respect.*
> *April MDCCC.XLVII. Rev. T Lloyd Rector.*

Text on the white marble tablet in St James'

Accounts and also in records concerning the use and enclosing of the commons at Littleton. He seems to have been involved in the administration of almshouses in Chester, 'Thomas Dixon Esq of Chester Conveyance of property in Bridge Street to create new trustees for William Jones Almshouses.'

The artist, W W Ouless, was commissioned to paint a portrait of Thomas, which was presented to him at the Town Hall, Chester on 3rd June 1875. The Mayor, Alderman Roberts, said, 'that it was his pleasant duty to say a few words on this very pleasing occasion.' He did not recollect that it had fallen into the hands of any mayor of this city to offer congratulations to so valued a citizen, or one who had served the town so well as their friend Mr Dixon. If he attempted to say anything regarding Mr Dixon it would be indeed very poor praise in comparison with his life itself, a life and history which were well known to them all. He had therefore to call upon his grace the Duke of Westminster to make the presentation, which he had gladly consented to do.

The Duke of Westminster said, 'Mr Mayor, ladies and gentlemen. If it is an honour to take the chair, as my friend, the Mayor has said on this occasion, I certainly think it a far greater honour, allow me to say, to have the pleasure of coming forward to present the picture to our friend Mr Dixon. All of you may not be aware that Mr Dixon was born in Chester in the year 1790, and I think it was in the year 1800 he went to the King's School, in this city, and in 1813 founded his present bank. As we all know, to manage and maintain a bank, and one of the character which Mr Dixon's has always held in this city, requires not only very active management, but also very constant attendance, and is in itself a position of very great delicacy and very great anxiety to all connected with it. In all the events that have happened in the eventful years that have passed since then I believe his bank has always stood its ground, notwithstanding the shocks that have occurred to every commercial enterprise in this country. It would be almost dreadful to think of the number of secrets that have been known to our friend, as well as all that he has known of the private affairs of so many citizens of Chester. But we must all feel that in his hands they have been perfectly safe. In the year 1814, Mr Dixon was appointed to the honourable office of Sheriff of Chester. Later on, I believe in the year 1836, Mr Dixon was made Mayor of the City of Chester, and in the year 1847 he became a county magistrate, and has since then given his attention, diligent attention, to the affairs of both the city and county.'

After further complimentary remarks the Duke proceeded to make the presentation. Thomas Dixon replied, 'In the first instance I have to thank the Duke of Westminster for the kind manner in which he has alluded to my services. It has always been my wish to do everything I could to promote the welfare and happiness and good fortune of the people of this city. I have to thank my friends for the kindness which they have done me, and the manner in which they have chosen to express their feelings towards me. The portrait will be in existence long, long after I am gone, it will be handed down to my descendants as an heirloom, and preserved by them as a mark of your kindness towards me.'

Thomas died in 1878 aged 88 having played a prominent role in the life of the city. In addition to the positions mentioned by the Duke of Westminster, Thomas Dixon was elected Councillor in 1835 and Alderman 1835. He was became a Justice of the Peace in 1856 and is listed as a magistrate in 1862. A very gruesome part of his duties was to commit both men and women to the lunatic asylum. There are many records of such actions in his

Littleton Hall in the early 1800s

name at the Record Office. There is also a painting of him as Mayor in the City Records. He married his first wife Phillis in 1812, and at the same time, his house was renamed Littleton Hall. Thomas and Phillis had seven children born between 1815 and 1830: Phillis Anne, Thomas, William James, Ellen, Ambrose, Henry, and Edward. Of these Edward and Ambrose were the two most prominent. Edward was a noted property owner and Ambrose was known as a banker.

However Thomas' younger brother James, who lived at Littleton Old Hall and later at 14 Stanley Place, Chester, is responsible for the Dixon name remaining in the public eye in Christleton throughout the years. He married Mary Anne and they had a son James. After their son's tragic death at age 30 and James' death a year later, Mary Anne, together with her brother–in–law, William Griffies Dixon of Nant Hall Flintshire and also of Wrexham, set up four almshouses at Little Heath in Christleton overlooking the village pond in memory of James.

The Dixon's Almshouses were intended for the use of poor residents of Littleton, and separate trusts were established not only to build the houses, but also to provide income for future repairs, insurance, and a weekly pension for the incumbents, as the following extracts show. '5/1. 2nd March 1868. An agreement between The Rector & Churchwardens of the Parish of Christleton and Mrs Dixon. Declaration of Trust concerning the sum of £2800 @ 3% Consolidated Bank Annuities for providing the dividend or interest thereof for the payment of a weekly stipend of 8 shillings to each of the inmates of the Dixons' Almshouses. '5/2. An agreement between Thomas Griffies Dixon and Mrs James Dixon to the Rector and Churchwardens of the Parish of Christleton. Conveyance of land for almshouses at Littleton and declaration of trusts concerning the same, and £200 @ 3% consolidated Bank Annuities for providing for repairs and maintenance of the buildings and for establishing a charity to be called Dixon's Almshouses.'

Apart from the £200 for minor repairs, £2,800 was set aside for weekly pensions, £500 to provide some medical attendance and fire insurance on the buildings.

J O Scott, son of the famous Victorian architect Gilbert Scott, designed the almshouses. (His father had been responsible for the repair and rebuilding of Chester Cathedral at about the same time.) They were built in timber and brick and fitted into the style of buildings being built in the area under the influence of the Grosvenor family and their architects, John Douglas and William Lockwood. No doubt the family obtained the timber for the almshouses from their timber-yards down on the river Dee. The almshouses have been in continuous occupation since that time and are highly favoured by the older members of the community.

The Dixon's Almshouses

The Dixons were also benefactors to the village in other ways. In 1860 James Dixon had given £100 of India Stock to the care of the rector, the income from which was used to benefit the poor of the parish. Edward and Anne Dixon, who lived in Stanley Place in Chester, gave £150 and £50 towards the new boys' school, and Ambrose Dixon offered £1,000 as a gift to the church when a new building was contemplated in 1876. The latter sum was eventually turned down as it had been stipulated that the money was to be used to provide a new site for the church building, but the Rev Garnett and churchwardens decided to keep the tower and rebuild the body of the church on the same site. The third Thomas married Anne Mary and had four children: Thomas Henry who lived at Gresford, and Phillis Annie*, who married Dr F M Granger of Bodfari; the other two daughters married Rev C H Hylton Stewart and Col Simpson. The following extract from the Gresford Church Magazine of July 1881 provides a glimpse into Thomas Henry's life. 'On the Queen's Birthday the members of the Gresford Volunteers were invited by Mr and Mrs Thomas Henry Dixon to their residence [The Clappers] to celebrate the Day by giving a royal salute of 21 guns. At eight o'clock the first gun was fired and at intervals of a quarter of a minute the salute was concluded. After three cheers for Her Majesty, the men were invited to partake of an excellent supper.'

There is a large box tomb in the churchyard at Christleton containing the remains of many members of the family, with separate graves for James Dixon and family, Dr and Mrs F M Granger (Phillis Annie), their son Sir Rupert Granger and his wife, Lady Judith and their family.

*Named as Phillis Anne in church records, Phillis Annie on grave.

Canon Garnett

After 37 years as Rector, Lionel Garnett was offered the status of Honorary Canon in August 1906. A proud parish presented him with an illuminated address, fees and a hood for his MA degree. To Mrs Garnett it gave a silver tea service and bracelet.

In November 1910 the departure of Canon Garnett 'within the next few months for reasons that can't be given' was announced. He wrote in January 1911, 'I have seen 42 New Year Days as Rector of Christleton. I have grown old here and my ways are old. My successor, Reverend G M V Hickey, comes as a young man and will no doubt bring new ways.'

The photographs of all the Garnett family appear in the February and March editions of the parish magazine collection at the Cheshire Record Office, and the Canon looks very much

Rev Lionel Garnett

the patriarch. He was the first married rector for more than a hundred years and seemed to regard his parishioners as extended family.

Advice was always forthcoming: whether it was on how to make a good, home-made drink at 3d a gallon for harvesters or how to create cheap blankets for the winter. 'Paste a few newspapers together to the required size and spread them beneath the quilt. Paper is a very powerful non-conductor of heat and acts as a very warm blanket. The only objection to the plan is the crackling sound of the paper, but then you must not expect to get everything for a penny or so!'

Always having to raise money for many village schemes, he was frugal with expenses (except in the building of the church) and in 1891 decided to change the evening service in winter to Thursdays at 7 pm to preserve fuel. 'The fire lighted for Thursday evening will warm the church for Friday morning's service.' He paid for the excess costs of the parish magazines himself, and the bound volumes of the first six years, which are currently in the Cheshire Record Office, are impressive. They contain a great range of religious tracts, articles about everything from equal rights to British birds, poetry and long, serial stories with beautiful etchings. In 1881 he had to cut down to free sheets of local news only, which were also hand-written for a while in 1883, until circulation improved again.

He never failed to bring the needs of individuals before the parish in the belief that help would be forthcoming. In March 1904 he wrote, 'Problem: a labouring man with a wife and family, himself ill – nigh unto death for five months – a child ill almost as long. Doctor's bill £8 17s 6d – how is he to pay it? The best solution—a little help. It is a deserving case and I shall be glad to receive contributions.'

His stewardship of the village was immense, and he was responsible, together with his great supporter Lucy Anne Ince, for the rebuilding of much of the village, including the Church, both Girls' and Boys' Schools, Christleton Institute, and Christleton Grange. He started the Fete and Flower Show to raise funds for the building and running costs of both schools and

The Christleton Band, circa 1890

A Little Owl with its catch at Birch Heath Common

A Comma butterfly on buddleia in Rowton

An Early Purple Orchid

A Common Spotted Orchid

Pen 2SL (known as Salad), with her cygnets at Christleton Pit

1. The Dixon's Almshouses beside Christleton Pit, 1997

2. The plaque at Christleton Pit commemorating the North of England Heritage Pond Award

3. The Pit Group restoring the edge of the Pit in 1997

4.

5.

4. The Dedication Service following the refurbishment of the Dixon's Almshouses in 1998

5. Swans on the canal by The Mill, Christmas 1997

6. Best Kept Village Award on the Village Green in 1999

6.

1. The Methodist Church in spring

3. Christleton Hall (now The College of Law)

5. The English Civil War Society re-enacting the Battle of Rowton Moor

2. The Old Farm in Village Road

4. The Old Hall in winter

6. Romany Caravans on Birch Heath Common in 1964

7. St James' bellringers outside the tower

8. The interior of the Methodist Church

9. St James' choir

10. The Restoration Board in St James' Church

11. Frank Poston, former Captain of the bellringers, 1989 (the original lychgate cross and Parish Hall prior to alterations are shown in the background)

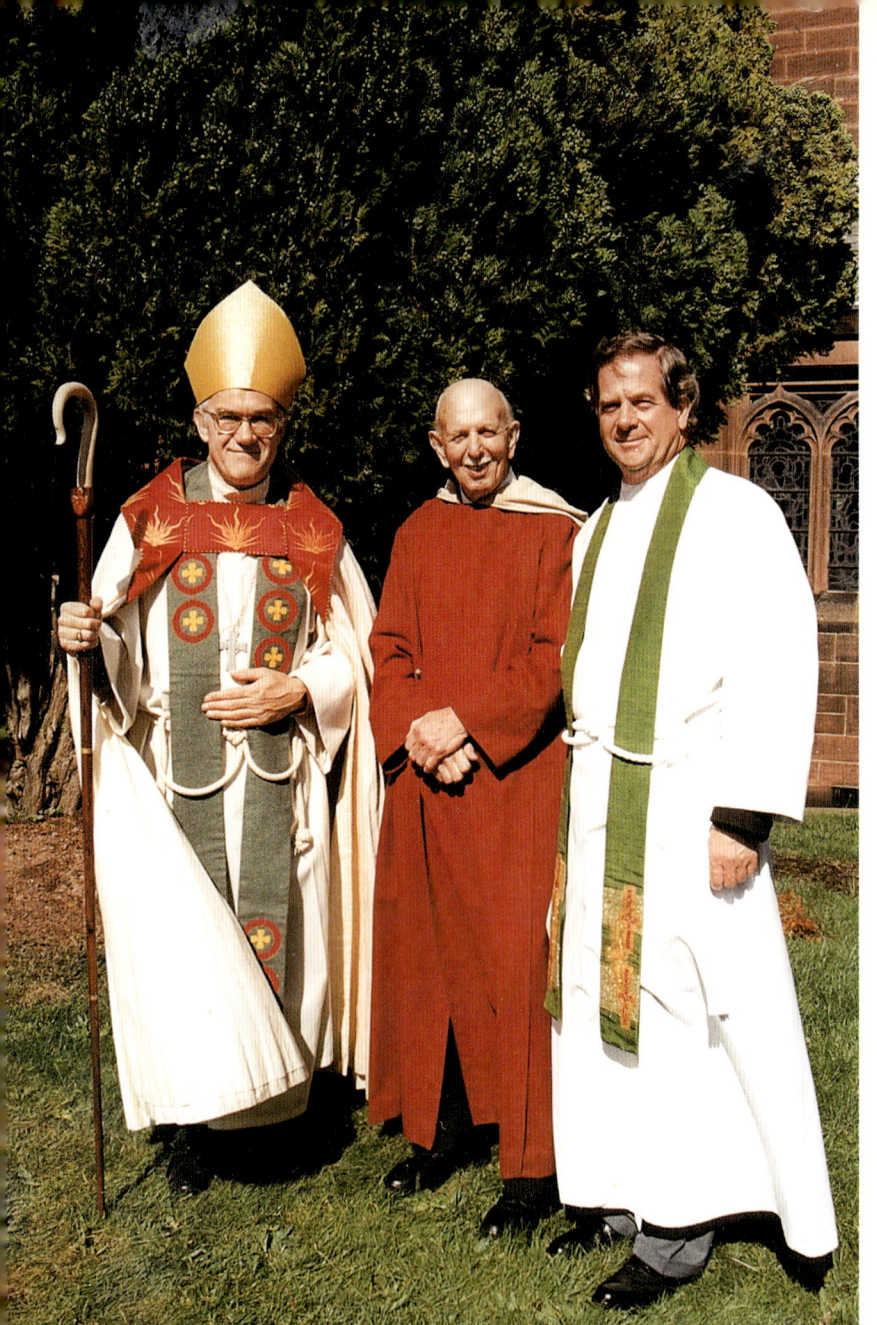

1. L – R: Bishop of Chester, Rt Rev Dr Peter Forster; Cliff Boddy, Verger Emeritus; Rev Peter Lee, Rector of St James' Church

2. L – R: Geoff Lawson, present Headteacher; Les George, first Headteacher; Phil Hodges, second Headteacher of Christleton High School

3. Eric Beech, retired farmer of Brown Heath Farm

4. Portrait of Alyn Arthur Guest-Williams, Rector of Christleton 1926–1965

5. Jim Poston on his 100th Birthday in 1978

6. Christleton Toddler Group at the Parish Hall, March 2000

7. Christleton Under-5s Community Playgroup, February 2000

8. Christleton High School training orchestra and brass group performing in the Spring Concert, March 2000

9. The 1997 Primary School production of Joseph and His Amazing Technicolor Dreamcoat

10. Primary School children fundraising for Comic Relief

11. Primary School in the Junior Playground, March 2000

1. Christleton Players performing a scene from the Wakefield cycle of Mystery Plays at Eaton Hall in 1965

2. Bilma, Bilques, Ruth, Ruth Mary and Anju from Ladakh with Gertrude Wright

3. Members of Christleton Wednesday Group presenting a cheque to Dorin Park School, one of the organisations benefitting from the Group's fundraising activities for the year

4. A flower-arranging demonstration held in the Parish Hall for Chester Flower Club

5. Floral exhibits at the 1999 Village Show

6. Children from Christleton Primary School performing the traditional maypole dance at the Village Fete

7. Christleton Guides and Brownies walking in the procession on Village Fete Day 1999

8. The 1999 Christleton Rose Queen, Anna Nilssen, with her retinue – Lawrence Jones, Louise Sloan, Lara Nilssen, Sophie McCahey, Dawn Capper, Holly McCann, Charlotte Seddon, Rebecca Newmarch, Katie Heritage and Eleanor Sowden

Rock House, home of William Huggins and later the Mosford family

the rebuilding of the church. He formed two bands to give young men in the village something to do; he encouraged the bellringers; and started both the Cricket and Football Clubs. He and his family were involved in all aspects of village life. He gave the Lych Gate in memory of his mother and was responsible for persuading Lucy Anne Ince to erect the Pump House on the village green.

His personal interests were in sport. He was a keen skater and loved cricket, which he described as 'one of the oldest and best English games, calculated to do nothing but good.' He was a good batsman, but whether he played in the return match with Waverton in August 1878 when the scores were Waverton 102, Christleton 14, he did not say. He commended the new Bishop Jayne in 1888 to his parishioners thus, 'He was at Oxford with me, a scholar of Wadham College and a good oar.' He had been a housemaster at Eton before coming to Christleton and had been in charge of rowing. In the history of Christleton he was a giant: dictatorial and Victorian in every sense, but he was also a devout Christian who gave himself honestly and entirely to the service of his parish in changing and difficult times. There is no record of his death in the parish magazines, but it is said he died of smallpox in 1911, contracted whilst working in the village.

William Huggins

William Huggins, the painter, moved to Rock House, Christleton in 1878 after the death of his wife. He had been born in Liverpool in 1820 and had lived there and in North Wales. By the time he moved to Christleton, he had achieved a considerable reputation as a painter of portraits, landscapes of the Cheshire countryside, and animals, particularly of big cats. It is even said that he kept a menagerie of wild animals at his house, Rock House, to enable him to paint from life. He died at his home, now the dental surgery, in 1884 and is buried in the churchyard. Many of his paintings can be seen at the Walker Art Gallery, Liverpool.

The Memories Of Frank Poston

Frank was a long time resident of the village and a respected captain of St James' Bellringers. These memories were written down in a long letter to David Cummings in 1989.

'The purpose of this letter is to try to describe just what our village and its people were like 70 years ago, and perhaps even earlier. Please forgive me if I use an odd old Cheshire slang word or two, remember such words were commonplace when I was at school. Words such as "canna, binna, but you munna wearit." Had you gone a little further than Egg Bridge [Waverton], you would not have understood what people were saying. A few of my notes have been handed down hearsay, so may have gathered a little moss, but most are from my own experience, or stories passed on by my father, who, as you know, died in 1983, in his 106th year.

'We were very good friends, particularly in my younger days, and during the last years of Father's life. He was an upright Christian, like Washington he never told a lie. I have even been told that he could curse like a trooper, but I only heard him swear once in my life, and that was at me. He was one of 15 children, all brought up in the cottage in which I live [the Old Surgery in Village Road]—where they put them all I do not know. Dad used to say that when they went to bed, they slept head to tail. He lived all his long life in and around the village, and was born in a thatched cottage in Pepper Street next to the old Post Office [Two Gables]. Mum, a Lincoln Imp, and he were married in 1906. I was born in 1911 and like Father have hardly ever been outside the village, except for that stupid period of war from 1939–45.

'Let's talk about some of the Rectors in my lifetime. Canon Lionel Garnett (1869–1911). We met once, when I was two months old, when Geoff Smith and I were the last two babies he christened. He was a good sportsman, all sports including rowing, running and boxing. He was Chairman and Treasurer of the Cricket Club and was a regular player. Matches and individual scores were reported in the parish magazine, and one [magazine] I have seen shows five Garnetts playing in the village team. Another has a report of eleven Garnetts playing and winning against a village XI.

'The Park [the grounds of the Rectory] was a massive field, and it contained a cricket wicket. All the outdoor events were held on it. Things like the Village Show, which was a very big one in days gone by. The Park was flanked on one side by Birch Heath Lane and the Wood on the other as far as Smithy Cottages. The Park ran alongside Plough Lane as far as the Finish Field Farm. At the beginning of that [far] drive, in the Park hedge was a wicket gate. The Rector used to ride on horseback through the Park to the gate and out onto the road, when visiting Brown Heath, Plough Lane and Cotton.

'The Wood started at the Rectory and finished at Smithy Cottages. It was beautiful; all the tall trees were beeches, growing so close together that inside it was almost dark. At the Smithy end, in the centre, was an underground icehouse, round in shape and the size of a living room. The whole of the wood floor was covered with bluebells, and at the tops of the beech trees [there was] a rookery of some fifty nests.

'[The next Rector], Godfrey Hickey (1911–1926) had been curate of Handbridge but came to us from Duckinfield so I was told. A tall big boned man, he wore rimless glasses, a straw boater, and had a large framed green bike with a big red ribbon on the rear carrier. His wife was no bigger than sixpennyworth of copper, and they had three children. The younger son Mark and I started ringing together 64 years ago. They lived at Lyndhurst, Village Road until the new Rectory was completed in Plough Lane. The Rector was very fond of music. He formed a glee club of some 50 voices, [which won] up and down the area. I didn't much care for him and knew the feeling was mutual. While being prepared for confirmation, he told me that he wasn't sure about putting my name forward before the Bishop, but at 15 years old I was an impudent monkey and soon told him what he and his Bishop could do with their confirmation. However, I was confirmed with the others at Plemstall Church by dear old Bishop Padgett.

'Mr Hickey was continually having, what he called, debates with people, even in the local press. I called them arguments or even rows. One day he had one of his arguments with the newly formed branch of the W I. He later changed livings with the Rector of Trowell [near Nottingham], Alyn Arthur Guest-Williams, and he was a wonderful man.

'Mr Guest-Williams (1926–1965) had been

Precentor at Norwich Cathedral. A lovely dream of a man. The trouble was his dreams got longer as the years passed. His wife was a charming lady, tall and very slim, and she was a very good musician. They had no children. He was a specialist in antiques and he also played the stock market and was a connoisseur on port. Mr Guest-Williams was very gentle, and our ladies fell in love with him. It wasn't long before our ladies were conjuring up false stories about him. At some time he had an operation, which left a large scar on the side of his neck. Rumour soon had it that the scar was caused by a German bayonet during the war and that the brave Rector just continued praying for the German soldier who did the deed. He knew what the ladies were saying and loved every minute of it; I am sure he wore narrow dog collars to exhibit the scar a little more.

'The Rector and his good lady purchased and came to live in Major and Mrs Currie's empty home, the Old Hall. Richard, his brother, was a scream. He wore khaki shorts and an old felt hat, no socks, and smoked a small pipe. Looking much like a gardener, he was mowing in the front of the Hall, when a chap addressed him, 'I've come in reply to an advert in the local paper, for a sexton. What is the old so-and-so like to work for?' Richard answered, 'I don't know what he's like to work for, but if you knock at the front door my brother will tell you.' The chap got the job. His name was Jackson. The Rector told me one day that, 'Richard came for a two–week holiday, but alas that was seven years ago.' Alyn Arthur retired in 1965, but stayed on at the Old Hall until his death. Mrs Guest-Williams died before him, and they are both buried at Gresford Church.

'Charles Mack (1972–1986) came to us from Bredbury, near Manchester, with his wife Betty. They had a son Charles Anthony and daughter Angela and they were a grand family. Many of our church elders abdicated when they first arrived, but that didn't worry Charles. The rank and file stuck and that was all he cared about. He was very hard working, and if you were with him, you had to be the same. He said to me one day, 'The ringing chamber needs painting.' Fourteen days later he said, 'I've put the paint and brushes behind the tower door, get on with it, there are enough of you.' The lads wouldn't tackle it, so I had to pay a professional to do it. If I hadn't, Mr Mack would have done the job himself. Charles Anthony joined us ringers whilst at school. He was a charming person. Sadly he died of cancer at 24. His dad never recovered from

Jim Partington in his butcher's shop in the 1980s

that. In 1986 he helped us pull down the ringers' stall on the evening of the Christmas Fair and he died later that night. Father and son lie side by side in the churchyard. It left many of us very sad at heart.

'Now David Garnett (1987–1992) is our Rector. He came from Heald Green, near Manchester, and has a charming wife and two young sons. It will be good if they outstay their namesake, Canon Garnett, who stayed for 42 years. But it will not be easy. My mum told me that when she first arrived in Christleton and was out scrubbing the steps, an old lady stepped across the road and shouted, ' Our done you like it?' Mum replied, 'I do not know.' Again the old lady shouted, 'You wonna, cause they donna won't to know ya round 'ere. I've lived 'ere 56 years an am still a stranger!'

'We older people say the weather and the climate are changing. When I was young, in winter on a cloud-filled moonless night, gosh was it dark. It was as black as a bag. Should you be outside, and that wasn't often, the darkness was awe-inspiring. Of course, remember there was not one street lamp. No light from the cottages as the oil lamps used indoors were very poor. No cars with headlamps, not even a horse and trap. The stillness was amazing. Should another person be afoot, you could hear the sound of his hobnailed boots on the cobblestones from the other end of the village. There were no kerbstones or footpaths, but the stones were smaller on the side of the roads. The odd cow or calf may have given out a cry, and a dog or fox would bark. The church clock striking the hour and that was it, except for the owls. They would hoot all night, and we had a lot of them. I must not forget the railway, for that is another sound we no longer hear. On a dark, silent night you would think the line ran straight past your door. On the down line, you could hear them as far away as Waverton, and each blew its whistle before entering the tunnel, which runs under the canal. On the up line, there seemed to be a lot of goods' trains starting from the city. They would huff and puff and their buffers and chains would clink and clink, and if the firebox was open, the whole sky appeared to light up. At full moon the exact reverse happened. You could read a paper it was so clear, and the reflection of the houses and trees was grand. You could watch the owls hunting by moonlight, and you were no longer afraid by night.

'At daybreak, you would hear the 'Boaties' cracking their whips along the towpath, and the rooks in the wood, some 50 nests, would be cawing their heads off. You could hear dear old Joe Mosford, the butcher, chopping the meat on the block and the ring, ring of his brass scales when weighing it, often at 5 am. Cows would be bellowing, and pigs squealing for their breakfast. The handle of the village pump hitting the sandstone trough when operated by the early birds. Later in the day, Charlie Booth with his handcart would come from Chester, with a voice like a foghorn, shouting, "Rags and bones, bottles and jars, rabbit and skins." Then the cockle and mussel man would arrive all the way from Parkgate with his pony and flat topped cart, crying "Shrimps, cockles and mussels, Dee fluke and samphion" (an edible seaweed). Mrs Hewson with her Hurdy Gurdy [would arrive] all the way from Chester just for a few coppers.

'You were born at home whether you liked it or not. No ambulances dashing mum to hospital in those days. Nurse Ball, who lived in Quarry Cottages, would arrive on her old rusty bike dressed in her white starched apron and carrying her little black bag. In no time at all, you had a little brother or sister. Almost all we Christletonians were born with [the help of] that little black bag.

The old Post Office cart, circa 1890

Digger Swindley outside The Old Farm, circa 1910

Our village butchers were quite successful, having two shops in Chester Market. They had two or three fields and would purchase a number of cattle and sheep together and would turn them out to grass until required. Mr Joe Mosford was renowned as a judge of the weight of cattle on the hoof. Then, sales of meat were conducted from the Slaughter House. The Slaughter House was situated about the middle of our Ring o' Bells' car park. [The] killing and dressing of the meat went on from Monday to Thursday afternoon. It was then scrubbed down and converted into a shop for weekend sales.

'The iron gate and sandstone posts at the side of the church, leading to the footpath to Littleton, are the originals used as the entrance to the old school, which was situated on the green at the front of the church. Later the Parish Hall became the Boys' School, but before that it was a pub by the name of The Ring o' Bells. [The present Ring o' Bells used to be called The Red Lion.] The gateposts to Birch Heath Lodge and High Walls have acorns on top of them. Canon Garnett's widow told me that all four came from the old church building. She lived at The Green (now the nursing home) for several years, later at High Walls, and the last I remember of her was at the old Glass House just before the Second World War. She was a very interesting person who used to ramble round the village sketching. She once designed the front cover of the church magazine, I think.

'The new [primary] school stands on Hospital Field, Faulkner's Farm, which we called The Croft. The gardens on either side of the stile path were also part of the field. The farmhouse and buildings were in front of the present school building on Quarry Lane. Faulkner was sitting on the shaft of a heavy cart, which had enormous wheels, when, only 600 yards from the farm, the carthorse slipped, and Faulkner was thrown under the wheels and killed. On the opposite side of Quarry Lane stood Bush Farm, one of the Lunts worked it. The house called Greystones is the original stable for Bush Farm. The land on the other side of the school, now Woodfields, was the house field of Digger Swindley's old farm, the 1653 one. Digger's house field was quite large, its border joined Village Road on one side and Quarry Lane on the other and went on right up to the edge of the old Girls' School front playground. Digger had an old black mare called Bellwell Rino. Gosh, she was almost as old as the farm. She dropped dead one day in the house field, and the vet was allowed to hold a post mortem. He found eight tennis balls in her tummy! The girls had lost the balls over the hedge, and the mare, whose teeth were worn out, swallowed long grass and the tennis balls without chewing. They buried Bellwell Rino in the field one dark night, and now Woodfields stands on top of her grave.

'A cannon ball from the Civil War period was also found in that field and that went to the museum. There were no houses in Quarry Lane, except for two thatched cottages against the Girls' School, and the lane was only half its present width. The Girls' School was paid for by Mrs Ince. We all started school down there in the Infants. Mrs Fleet was our motherly teacher and she was the blacksmith's wife. Miss Huss was the strait-laced spinster headmistress. At eight years of age we boys went up to the big lads' school [the Boys' School]. Some sort of 11+ exam took place in those days. Fred Aspinall was headmaster then, and Sammy Earlam had preceded him. Morris Hullah came after Mr Aspinall, and Tom Solloway finished me off.

I keep harping on about the village being self-contained. Most of the natives worked and stayed in the area, and the city seemed a long way away. Seventy years ago there were only five cars in the village, all chauffeur driven (so you dina get a lift from that lot), and, of course, one could walk faster than a horse and cart. Up to 1905 the only way to get to the city was on Shanks's pony. In 1903 the Corporation began using trams with a terminus at Stocks Lane; this shortened the walk. Then in about 1920 Charlie Woodfine from Tarvin ran a small bus named Dinky each Tuesday and Thursday. He would pick up the ladies for shopping at 10.30am, park at the Queen's Hotel in Seller Street, and bring them home two and a half hours later, often stopping at one's door, and the conductor, young Charlie, would carry your purchases into the house. In 1930 the City Corporation replaced the trams with buses, which terminated at the top of the village. I remember the first Sunday they arrived, half the village queued just to ride on a bus into the city centre. Buses to the Trooper Inn began three months later. The buses and trams were in an apple-green and cream livery, and the fare from Christleton to the city centre was 3d.

'Mrs Ince of Christleton Hall was an autocrat who, with Canon Garnett, reigned supreme with Sam Earlam as their lap dog. Mrs Ince owned almost all the village houses. There were a few exceptions, but otherwise the lot was hers: every house, cottage, shop, workshop, farm, blade of grass, everything within a mile of the top of the village. If not directly working for her, the roof over your head was hers so you could look out. I think that at one time she thought the church belonged to her too. She employed about 20 in the hall grounds: horseman, cowman, pigman, coachman, head gardener and all his team. The walled kitchen garden itself was about three acres. About the same number were employed indoors, from the head butler down to the scullery maid. They all started work at 6.30 am, had about half an hour off for breakfast, a similar time for dinner, and then finished the day at 5.30 pm. Some worked in the evening too, especially if there were guests for dinner. On Saturdays they worked until 3 pm, and on Sundays about half were always on duty looking after security. They all dressed in their Sunday best, which was provided by My Lady. On some Sundays, as the bells started for Matins, they would parade in the coachyard, about 40 servants, and Mrs Ince would inspect them. They would then walk her to her front pew in the church and listen to the Canon's sermon telling the whole congregation what a heaven-sent benefactor they all had got. Then the servants would accompany her back to the Hall.

'She often used to ride in her carriage and pair around the village, and should a cottage gate or door be left open, the carriage was stopped and the footie would be sent to close them. That didn't happen very often or you were out on your ear. Mrs Ince was the last person to be put in the large family vault which runs parallel with the path leading to Pepper Street. Tom Johnson, the local coal merchant, told me a story about her funeral. "You know kid, I was standing at the church porch door after the service. (The woman had been a customer, but like us all, I was one of her tenants and had to attend.) Then Jack Roberts came down from the tower having been ringing with the team, with bells muffled of course, and he said, 'I owe you a bob or two, for that coal you delivered. Come in 'ere.' So we both went inside the vault, 'cos we couldn't exchange money in the churchyard with everybody looking, could we? Jack put the money on Mrs Ince's coffin. Eh kid, I was upset. I didna like taking money off Mrs Ince, but money is money, so I took it in the end, but it worrited me for a long time."

'I fell in love with Miss Olive Garnett twice before I was five years old. The first time was when she took me around the village on her donkey. When I come to think of it, I'm not so sure if I fell in love with Miss Olive or her donkey. She was a lovely person, unmarried at the time and living with her mother at The Green. By the way have you heard that The Green, like many other local houses, is haunted? Several of my friends have seen the apparition there, at some time or other. In fact, it was only a few years ago, that a service of exorcism was held there by our church people. More to follow...'

In fact that was the end of the letters from Frank as he died quite soon after sending this letter. He had not been well for many years and suffered particularly from asthma in later life. Despite his breathing difficulties, he took a very active interest in the Bellringers and the Tower until just before he died. David Cummings remembers accompanying him to the Tower one day in the middle of summer, and Frank was wearing a wonderful Cossack type hat to keep his head warm. He was quite a character and he gives some wonderful descriptions of the Christleton of his youth. Some of his letters have been censored, especially his stories about Sam Earlam, but there is a great deal of accuracy in the detail of life at the Hall, because his grandfather and grandmother were Head Gardener and Housekeeper respectively. His father was also a gardener there at the turn of the century.

The Memories Of Cliff Boddy

I was born in a house in Fir Tree Lane, Littleton. My mother was an orphan who had been adopted by a Mrs Boswell from Fir Tree Lane. My father came from Spital Walk, Boughton, near St Paul's church. I had two brothers, Stanley and Austin, but I was the eldest in the family. We all wore wooden clogs, and they made a great noise as we walked to school mainly over cobbles. Everyone had clogs, and you could always hear them clip clopping along the lane. We got them from a shop in Watergate Street called Cowleys. In fact I think it's still there. We started school in the Girls' & Infants' School at the bottom of the village near the blacksmith's. You could start at three years of age in those days if you wanted to. My teacher was Mrs Fleet, the blacksmith's wife. When I was five I went up to the Boys' School opposite the church, and the teacher I remember was a man called Hullah. He was there before Tom Solloway.

Sunday School visit to Rhyl travelling to Chester Station by wagonette

I always used to walk to school, even when I went to Love Street School in Chester. It was about three miles walk each way every day, and then Woodfines of Tarvin started a bus service. The bus ran from Tarvin and Tattenhall through Christleton to Chester. We paid him 9d return per week on a Monday morning and used to start school at 8.30 am. The teachers could be all right, but they were very strict and often kept order by using a stick, but I never had it. I stayed at Love Street until I'd taken my school certificate, and I left in 1928 when I was 15. There was a slump then and no jobs, none at all. I wanted to be an architect, but there was no chance at all of anything like that. I had to take the first job that came along. I went to an electroplating company in City Road, where the Bank of Scotland is now, and I started as an apprentice silversmith; I stayed for 45 years.

One of my proudest jobs was doing work for the Mayor of Denbigh. He brought in a pair of Elizabethan maces from about 1580. They had been knocked about and had been repaired before with pieces of any old metal, brass and tin. It was terrible—a sacrilege. I had the job of restoring them as best I could.

It took two or three weeks, and when they were ready, the Mayor himself came to collect them. He had a shock and said that they weren't theirs, but I showed him the hallmarks and he knew they were. He then had some proper cases made for them, all plush lined. I was very proud of that job, and it was one of the most interesting I did. I developed an interest in heraldry after that and copperplate handwriting.

The track between Christleton and Littleton was mainly a dirt track, and it was called the Quoit alley. I suppose because they used to play quoits there. I can remember a brickfield near the stile in Fir Tree Lane going across to the Manchester road. It was a big field. I remember all the kilns looked like beehives. I remember those kilns quite well, but by the time I'm talking about the bricks weren't made there any more, and the kilns were falling to pieces.

We knew that the Pit was a marl pit and there were always lots of fish in it. As boys we would sometimes spend afternoons there, and you could catch as many as 80 small fish in one afternoon. You could also walk across it in places. We knew where the ford was so we could go across when we wanted.

It wasn't Dandy's farm in Littleton then, it belonged to a Mr Bentley and it was a mixed farm. They grew hay, oats and wheat, and they had cattle of course. There would be about half a dozen men working on the farm. He had horses, of course, in those days to do most of the heavy work, and cowmen too. I remember they started work at Bentleys at 6 am, but they used to stop for breakfast about 8 am, having washed first in stone cold water outside by the pump. I sometimes used to help collect hay in the holidays, but I preferred playing about in it. Sometimes children would work on the farm, doing jobs like picking stones up from the fields, and the schools used to close for this time.

There was only one farm in the village making cheese: that was Lunt's. He farmed where the Ardens had their farm in the village until recently. There were two or three brothers. William Lunt, I think, rang the bells and Frank, the cheesemaker, had a short leg and used to limp. They also used to make black puddings in the village and sold them in Millwards shop. I don't think Digger Swindley from the Old Farm ever did so. Millwards was a great village shop: they sold everything, including the sweets that I liked and all kinds of things like mops, buckets and brushes. Anything you wanted, Millwards would have it. There used to be an advert over the door of the shop for their coach building works, which was in Bold Square, Chester. Today the shop is Drakes, the hairdressers.

There were two blacksmiths in the village. There was Fleet, of course, near the Bottom of the Wood. Joe Fleet was the father and Frankie the son, and when Frank died, a chap from Saighton came along and took it over—Fred Williams, I think it was. The other smithy was near Arden's Farm; it's the one called Smithy Cottage. Rogers was the man there, a chap with a big flying moustache. I knew him quite well, and he could swear for half an hour and not repeat himself. He could honestly. On our way home from school, we used to sit down and watch him doing his work and we used to pinch the nails from his box. Of course, he would chase us off and his language... That's where we learned our bad language. There was also a shoemaker near the corner and a Mr Woodcock worked there. He had a club-foot and he mainly repaired shoes rather than made them. There was a saddler too up an alley near the ladies' hairdresser shop today.

Digger Swindley used to live at the Old Farm and he used to chase us many a time. He had a walnut tree in his field, and of course, we lads liked to pinch his walnuts when they were ready. He wasn't a very tidy farmer and there were always a lot of cowpats about his yard. He and his wife came to church every Sunday morning. I remember that he always wore a long frock-coat. Digger wasn't the only one as Mr Heap from Rowton also wore a frock-coat together with a top hat. The Ince family came to church on Sunday mornings, and they and their guests always sat in the front pew, the Townsend Ince pew. I remember Major and Mrs Currie. She was a nice lady, very flamboyant. I think she was an actress before she married the Major, but they had no children. Other important families included the Sidebottoms, Macfies, Singes, Porrits, and the Flemings. They were nearly all merchants in cotton, wool and that sort of thing in Manchester or Liverpool.

I joined the church choir when I was 11 when the Rector was Mr Hickey. Later I remember Mr Guest-Williams coming, after exchanging parishes with Mr Hickey. I also remember Freddie Finch, the choirmaster and organist. He was only a small man, effeminate in a way, but I mustn't call him that because he was a most kind man. I always was a big lad and found it difficult to sit on the front row in the boys' pew. So one Sunday he said to me, 'You are getting too big to sit there. Go and sit with the men in the back row.' So I did. I started as a boy soprano, but then developed into an alto and sang this until I was 60. In those days a male alto singer was looked at in a funny way. I still sing alto occasionally, but it is not the same as it used to be. I then began to sing tenor, and I sometimes sang bass when they were short.

I wonder what Freddie would say if he knew that one of his 'laddies' was still singing in 2000. Not so well as before, perhaps, but still trying and remembering. I recall one boy all those years ago who was always sent home for not behaving at choir practice, but he always managed to be in his place on Sunday. Sometimes it was a case of, 'Come and sit by me laddie, where I can keep an eye on you.'

My memory goes back and remembers the boys who sat in the choir stalls 70 years ago: Bill Payne, Alan Mathews, Dennis Morgan, Sonny Dutton, and the Needhams, Mac and Possy. It was a privilege to wear your Eton collar all day on Sunday. These are the boys who made the gardeners' lives a misery on Flower Service Sunday when the Big House gardens were thrown open and the fruit trees were very vulnerable.

The dedication of the Garnett Memorial in 1912

The senior members in the choir then – their names come back to me – were George Dean, Mr Mellor, Bob Gregory, Bill and Sam Pickervance, Mr Wynn, Baden Brammall, George Ashton, Bill Johnson and many others whose names escape me. In those days *Messiah* and the *Crucifixion* held no terrors for our choir, neither did an anthem every month and settings for canticles and communion. If a psalm had 70 verses, we sang them all. If there were three psalms for the day, we also sang them.

After the demise of Freddie Finch, several organists took over the choir. I remember Mr George Guest senior, George Guest, Mr Sutton, Sam Barker, Norman Rimmer, John Reed, Ron Smith, Bob Owens, Ken Stark, Carina Moffat and, of course, our present organist Steve Roberts. All worthy musicians to whom our choir, past and present, owes a great deal.

In the old days, our pipe organ had to be blown by hand, and I remember one Sunday when Freddie put his hands on the keys after the sermon expecting sound, no sound came out. He dashed around the back and found the organ blower fast asleep on the seat.

Mr Guest-Williams was a very interesting man. He was a real scholar. He was a member of the Royal Society of Antiquarians. His sermons weren't everyone's cup of tea but they were very clever and very deep. He used to preach over the people's heads to tell you the truth, but he was a real gentleman. He was also most generous. He helped us in putting on our Sunday School and Choir trips. We went to Rhyl mostly, and in the old days we used to go to Chester Station by horse and cart before going by steam train to Rhyl. Once or twice we went to Beeston Castle by canal barge and spent all our time rolling down the hill. We would catch the barge, a Mersey flat boat usually used for carrying grain, by Butler's Mill. There was a bread shop at the mill and we also got bread from Morgan's Post Office in Pepper Street.

I also liked working for Charles Mack. He was straightforward and called a spade a spade. He helped us out in our choir work, but we were a little disappointed when he first came. As he was an organist and a Choral Scholar from Cambridge, we had expected him to give us settings and real church music, but he wasn't that bothered. He really wanted the congregation to sing.

Another person I remember well was George Guest; I actually called him young George. After Freddie Finch died we had several organists, and the first one to stay for a long period was George Guest's father from Helsby. By then his son was 18 and was assistant organist at Chester Cathedral. He came to join us and he was the best organist we ever had. All the boys loved him because he would join in and would swing the tunes. He became the eminent Dr George Guest of St John's College, Cambridge and was a great friend of mine.

I had many friends in the village. Fred Watkins was one, but he came from Wem, so he was a foreigner. Frank Poston, Bill Astle and Frank Mitchell were others. They were in the Scouts with me in 1927 with Mr Tarbuck, who had been a policeman in Liverpool. His wife ran the Wolf Cubs and Mr G F Wain ran the Rover Scouts. We had a long army hut to meet in, where the present Scout headquarters are. We did all the things that Scouts do, tying knots and physical training, and we danced every Wednesday night—a proper dance with ladies. This dance in the Scout hut was always well attended, even in the holidays. We also used to go away for camps. We went to Heswall several times and to Arrowe Park, Birkenhead for a big Jamboree. We used to go to Riley Bank at Mouldsworth quite often. Once we went to Criccieth in North Wales; we went there in a big lorry owned by Les Astle. He later married Mrs Tarbuck's niece, I think.

I remember the Fetes. They were sometimes held in Hunters Field opposite the pond, sometimes down in Birch Heath Lane, and sometimes in a field at the side of Faulkners Lane on Mr Cullimore's land behind the quarry. I can remember the big marquee they used to have. It was a proper show in those days with vegetables, cheese, flowers, sheep, cattle, and horses. They were very popular events, with people coming from Hoole, Waverton, Tattenhall and all around.

During the war I served in the Grenadier Guards at Windsor Castle. Bill Jones from the village was also there, but he joined before me and was killed in Africa. It was a war of nerves at Windsor. There were soldiers and policeman at every post around the castle. If you were on guard, you always had a policeman with you. You used to see the Royal family now and then, but those corgis always used to warn you first. The policeman always gave the order 'Up Sentry', and you then presented arms.

Lord Montague of Beaulieu was our Captain, and our Adjutant was Lord Hamilton from Scotland.

I was a caterer to start with at the training depot. It had a huge wall with a big gate that had a sign over it saying, 'Abandon hope all you who enter here'. I was there about three months. Everything had to be done at the double. Oh dear, dear, it hurts me just to talk about it, but it hasn't harmed me has it?

These are the memories of an old chorister who would like to be a boy again and sing through the past years. *Tempus edax rerum* (time, the devourer of all things).

The Memories Of Eric Beech, Farmer

This farm (Brown Heath Farm) belonged to Major Currie, who had inherited it from Townsend and Mrs Ince. It was one of eight on the estate, all small dairy farms. Water was not laid on and cattle had to be driven to the local pits in winter. There were wells on all the farms, and at Brown Heath water can be found about 17 feet below the surface. We later fitted a petrol-driven pump on our own well and it's still in use. In 1996 it almost dried up for the first time in living memory. I can remember Frank Evans, who farmed the land where Ethel Witter now lives, having to pump water by hand from the village pump to get water to his animals because it was too severe to drive them to a pit.

The land around the farm has always been well drained, being of a very sandy nature. In fact there are sand-holes on nearby Plough Lane that used to be worked by hand. Things have always grown well here. Swindley's Farm in Village Road was very neglected, and my father was given the tenancy of his two fields in Plough Lane in September 1936, with no rent due for three years because of the poor state of the land. There were even potato drills from 1914–1918 still in one field. This had been a time of compulsory ploughing up. Two other fields in Plough Lane still belong to the John Sellers' Trust.

During the war the landlord built us extra stalls for 20 more milkers, and I fitted drinking bowls in each stall to save turning the cows out for water. We had two horses, a shire and another, an old army horse called Bob, a real favourite of mine. He died after slipping into a ditch one extra cold winter. The former died through accidentally eating wheat. All the ploughing, reaping, mowing and carting was done with these two horses. When 1939 came farmers had to plough up a proportion of their farms and were given a grant of £2 an acre. In those days you'd expect to get a ton of wheat or barley an acre without fertiliser and herbicides, but now four tons is the norm. Likewise, potato crops were eight tons per acre and now the figure is thirty tons. No wonder there is overproduction. In my early days on the farm, we had a single furrow plough and drag harrows, and I learned to work the fields with the horse. One acre a day was really good going. Now you can do one acre in half an hour. We purchased some cattle food from Butler's Mill on Whitchurch Road. We bought flaked maize and bran from them and mixed it together with oats grown on the farm, but it wasn't really balanced food; it was much later that

Horse and plough at Littleton

concentrates were produced giving the cattle a much better diet. The produce from Butler's Mill was delivered by horse and cart, and we also used to have a rag and bone man coming around the village in his horse and cart.

Every year the pattern of the year would be the same. We ploughed in autumn and let the soil become broken up by the winter frosts. It would then be ready to plough over much more easily in spring. We planted swedes, mangols and kale, and seed merchants from Manchester used to come to the farm to buy our best specimens. Some of our swedes, when grown with mangols, used to weigh over 26 lbs in weight. We also kept shorthorn cattle, which, when we needed to take them to market, had to walk through the village and on to Chester, going along Foregate Street before entering Sellers Street and then to the market on Gorse Stacks, on the other side of Cow Lane Bridge. Our milk was collected twice a day by a man called Morgan from Chester, and he also distributed milk twice a day from his churns, using the old tin measuring jugs. We didn't always have the horse fully shod at the blacksmith's because my dad thought it was too expensive, and in those days the horses didn't go on the roads a lot. So he sometimes had only the front two done, as the full set would have cost 4s 6d.

I was given the tenancy of this farm in spring 1940 when Phyllis and I were married. She was a farmer's daughter from Staffordshire and the mainstay of her father's farm. Shortly after she left, they found they couldn't manage without her, so they retired and had a farm sale. In 1941 we bought the tractor from them, and because we didn't have sufficient work to justify a tractor, we started the first contracting business in the area. There was plenty of work – too much at harvest-time – and you couldn't please everyone at the right time. Now there are seven tractors on the farm.

Christleton Mill

We had a prisoner of war (POW) to help in busy times, and in 1943 two lived with us for three months. One was used to farm work, and the other, a bricklayer, came in very useful at times. In 1944 we rented 14 acres of land at Guilden Sutton and we still have it. I had a pupil come to live in, but we didn't hit it off too well, as he thought he knew more than I did. He stayed six months. In 1945 David Kedward came as a pupil. He was everything you could ask for on the farm and also with the contracting. Eventually in about 1956 he married a local girl and we let him have the contracting business. We were also able to help him to get the tenancy of a small dairy farm at Blacon. After about ten years, he bought a farm at St Clears in South Wales and is now one of the leading farmers in the area.

We grew much of our own food for the farm stock and took many prizes at the Cheshire, Tattenhall and Christleton Shows for our produce. Artificial insemination started in 1967, which was a great change, and we were able to use the best bulls from the centre at Tarporley. Now farmers have their own refrigerated supply of semen and do the job themselves.

In 1948 we bought a threshing machine and went for miles around using it—a very dirty job. By 1950 we had our first combine harvester, which cost £900. Now they cost up to £250,000. We also saw the introduction of tuberculin testing of cattle and we were able to benefit, helped by a government grant. This year also saw the start of pick-up bales, a wonderful invention, and we had several machines to help us do this. In 1953 we fitted a coal-fired grass dryer, but it was very hard work. We ground the dried grass and cubed it and we also produced lucerne, which was very high in protein. In 1955 I took on another pupil, David Dodd, and later helped him get the tenancy of Barrowmore Farm. He has just retired.

Milk was now being pumped into bulk tanks. In my father's day he could produce about 35 gallons a day. When I retired we were producing 500 gallons a day. We milked by hand twice a day until 1944, then by machine into buckets, and eventually we constructed our own milking parlour. We had our own electric welder and made most of our own steel fabrications, including gates and trailers. Sparks from the welder caused a fire, and our youngest son Ian set a shed full of haybales on fire. What a mess that was! There was little concrete on the original farm and over the years we have done quite a lot, including the farm drive.

In 1967 a very bad outbreak of foot-and-mouth disease hit the area and we lost 90 cattle. They were shot and buried on the farm. Having just started with contagious abortion in the herd, we were able to make a fresh start. The government helped us restock with compensation, but we had also recently doubled our farm insurance. However, we were without cows for several months. (The outbreak of 1927 was also very bad in this area, but strange to say the Methodists did not get it.) Cattle were now loose housed and were able to lie down in home-made cubicles, 175 in all.

We acquired a self-unloading trailer for silage and the grass from far-off fields in 1970, but the more machinery you had the more breakdowns there were. I remember John Arden starting here in 1971 and then farming where his father farmed in Plough Lane. Flail hedgecutters became popular in 1976. Hand-cutting had been such a tedious job. In those days potatoes were £4 for 56lbs, but today (1999) we are selling at £2 for 56lbs. During the early 1980s we fitted automatic concentrate feeders to the parlour and the cows had collars on to activate them.

On 7th June 1982 hailstones one inch across knocked holes in our plastic roof and we had to replace it with galvanised sheets instead. However, in 1985 we gave up the milking herd and went over to keeping beef cattle. We had a visit from a former Italian POW in 1986 and we celebrated his working on the farm 40 years before. He was willing to do any job. Sad to say, he's been in a wheelchair for nine years due to a stroke.

Since giving up milk, we've tried pedigree Charolais cattle and our bull took second prize at Crewe Market and sold for £1280, much more than the first prize winner. We also started wintering sheep for hill farmers in 1988. About 200 animals are brought here in the winter from Dolgellau, and they seem to thrive on the grass we have on the fields. In fact, they need twice the number of trucks to take them back than they came in because they put on so much weight. We also let some of our fields for growing turf, which is happening a lot these days because of the great demand.

My son Brian farms here now and he has two sons, Simon and Michael, who've been to Reaseheath Agricultural College. It would be good to keep the farm in the family for the years ahead.

In 1987 a ringed swallow had three broods in one of our barns but didn't come back in 1988, having been caught up in the gales of that year. I've occasionally seen a kingfisher on one of our ponds, and we sometimes have a tawny owl sitting in the open barn. At times, a sparrowhawk screams over the fields and frightens off all the other birds. Of course, the swans also feed on our grass when they come down to the canal. I have always loved nature

A fallen tree at the High School

but in my early days I used to shoot geese. Thousands of wild geese would come in skeins off the Mersey marshes and the Rogers family would have the first shots at them as they came over Plough Lane. Although they would rise up into the sky when someone shot at them, I managed to shoot one down once. I wouldn't do it now, of course, and prefer playing snooker. I didn't start that until in my 60s, but I used to be a good tennis player in my youth. We had a tennis court on the farm and played regularly.

I first attended school at the Christleton Girls' & Infants' School, and then for a time I went to Tom Solloway at the Boys' School. However I left Christleton School aged 12 and for a short time I went to a private school, but I left school at 14 and began working with my father on the farm. I was paid £5 a year and my keep. Not much, was it?

One of my friends was Frank Poston, and he used to deliver meat for Joe Mosford. I can remember us going up to the Pit to skate in winter, and one day we saw an Austin 7 towing skaters around the ice. I also used to swim in the river Gowy in a pool on the bend near the Roman Bridges. During the last war I was needed on the farm but I became a captain in the local Home Guard and helped to look after the village, making sure that the men in the platoon were in good order and able to put out fires, amongst other things.

There were lots of characters in the village: Joe Mosford, Digger Swindley, Thomas Johnson of the old Post Office, who retired to live at Elmfield in Plough Lane, and another Thomas Johnson, who was a coal merchant and lived near the Red Lion. He had three teams of horse and carts and kept his animals in stables near South View. He used to work from Waverton Station where the coal was delivered by rail. I also remember the Mayers family: William, who owned the Smithy in Little Heath Road, and Stanley, who ran the garage opposite the Trooper. There were old-fashioned pumps there then and he was so slow in selling the petrol that it used to run back into the pump instead of into the car.

I also remember Frank Fleet, the blacksmith, who took over from his father Jim, who had been there since the 1930s. He appeared on a radio programme once, singing *Under the Spreading Chestnut Tree*, which to him meant the tree at the entrance to the Secondary School that came down in a gale about 10 years ago. Mrs Fleet used to teach at the Infants' School.

I've always attended the Methodist Chapel, in fact I was christened there. I used to go three times on a Sunday with my father and mother. We children would sometimes sit at the front and be talked to by the minister. Other times we stayed out at the Sunday School. There used to be so many children that there were seven or eight teachers. Sadly we don't even have a Sunday School now. One of the first superintendents I remember was Joseph Ryder, a gardener at the big house in Vicar's Cross where the Rugby Club is now, and another was a really nice chap called Willis, who had been a local farmer.

Wing Commander Jas Storrar, Vet And Fighter Pilot

Wing Commander James Storrar, who died in April 1995, was a resident of Christleton for many years, living at The Grange in Village Road. He was a giant of a man, well over six feet tall, and a flamboyant character who was very much the picture of a successful Battle of Britain pilot. His jackets were lined with red silk and his Jaguar XJS 12 had the registration JAS. James Storrar was born at Ormskirk, Lancashire in 1920 but attended school in Chester where his family had run a veterinary practice since the early 18th century.

In October 1938 he joined the RAF on a short-term commission. The following year he was

Jas Storrar and his dog

posted to 145 Squadron, which was then flying Blenheim bombers from Croydon. He was still a teenager when the war broke out, but he flew missions to protect troops of the British Expeditionary Force as they were being evacuated from the beaches at Dunkirk. In March 1940 the Squadron converted to Hurricane fighters and James, or Jas as he was known, came into his own. Flying in the Battle of Britain brought him great fame and he notched up 15 confirmed kills as a Hurricane pilot.

By mid-August 1940 he had already been credited with nine kills and was a relative veteran when Germany launched its massive bombing raids on Britain. 'At first, seeing so many German aircraft filling the sky, I thought we must lose the war,' he once recalled. However as the battle escalated, James was often compelled to scramble three times before tea. On his third sortie one summer's day, he found himself flying alongside a Ju-87 Stuka. 'I could quite clearly see the pilot looking at me, and could see his hand on the stick,' he said later, but he soon sent the plane blazing into the sea. That day 145 Squadron was credited with 25 kills but also lost six of their own planes. 'I looked no further than breakfast the next day, of having a cup of tea and offering up a silent prayer,' he remembered. 'When we lost six pilots I didn't think of them, I thought of me. As long as it wasn't me, it didn't matter.'

After that terrible time during the Battle of Britain, the depleted squadron was sent to Scotland to rest and reform, and James served briefly with 421 Flight before moving to 73 Hurricane Squadron. In November 1940 they sailed for Takoradi, West Africa, aboard the aircraft carrier *Furious* and then flew across Africa to Egypt. On 4th April 1941 James spotted a Lockheed Lodestar that had made a forced landing in the desert. He landed and discovered that the Lodestar was General Wavell's personal aircraft. After he had helped the Lodestar's pilot to get the engine going, he found his own aircraft would not start. He was obliged to walk across the desert to Tobruk. A few days later, whilst enjoying a rest at Takoradi, he was asked to take a Hurricane to Freetown, Sierra Leone. However, bad weather forced him down in the jungle and it took him two days and three nights to walk more than 70 miles to the Firestone rubber plantation near Monrovia.

In 1943 he returned to Britain and, aged 22, he was given the command of 65 Spitfire Squadron, flying bomber escorts and fighter sweeps over France, Belgium and Holland. In the course of a screaming dive on a Me 109, James overstressed his aircraft and it had to be written off after landing. The next year he moved to a Transport Command Unit flying an air delivery service but returned to operations in the autumn of 1944 as commander of 64 Squadron. He later commanded 165 and 234 Squadrons and in 1946 was posted to Italy as commander of 239 Wing, which was equipped with Mustang fighters.

Whilst in Italy he met his wife Winifrede (Freddie), who was a WAAF (Women's Auxiliary Air Force) driver, and they were married in Venice. Although after the war he was offered an extended commission, he opted to study veterinary science at the University of Edinburgh and later joined the family practice. In 1949 he joined 603, a Royal Auxiliary Air Force Squadron, and resumed flying. He went on to command 610, the County Of Chester Auxiliary Squadron. He was awarded the Distinguished Flying Cross in 1940 and Bar in 1943.

Just a week before he died, he had attended a reunion in Copenhagen of the pilots he had led in a wartime air raid against the Gestapo headquarters in that city.

One of his most audacious exploits was to fly a Hurricane under the Grosvenor Bridge in Chester.

Although he is perhaps best known for his exploits in the war, he really was at his best as a veterinary surgeon. He loved animals and his work: he didn't consider it a job but a great pleasure to work with them. He also gained enormous respect from the local farming community and made many friends in the city, including the Grosvenor family, especially Anne, Duchess of Westminster. He and his wife lived most of their married life in Christleton and are buried in the churchyard.

5 Education

Education has always played an important part in the life of the village, from the days of John Sellers' Charity School, founded in 1779, through to the Primary and High Schools of today. The dame schools, the private schools at Holly Bank (now Birch Heath Lodge) and High Walls, the Catholic seminary, and, more recently, the College of Law at Christleton Hall have also had a major influence upon the life of the village. In fact, the population of Christleton doubles each day with the influx of pupils and students to its educational establishments.

John Sellers' Charity School

The first recorded school was the Charity School provided by John Sellers of Littleton. This was set up in the corner of the present churchyard between Christleton House, the church tower and Pepper Street, and there is evidence to suggest that the first school was a two-storey building and that the gateway to the footpath to Littleton was the original school entrance.

The Trust Deed states that the proceeds from the rent of lands in Christleton were to be used towards instructing 'the poor children of Christleton & Littleton in reading, writing and arithmetic, including mensuration, gauging and navigation, in spinning, sewing, knitting and other manual work.' The Trustees had to supply 'books, wheels, or other implements required, and, if the money was available, to apprentice the poor children.' Later in 1805, the Trust was expanded with a bequest of £100 from John Hignett of Rowton, which was to be used 'to educate the poor children of Rowton and Christleton.'

The Minute Book, which cost 5s 6d, is still in use today, and one of the first entries on 24th June 1787 states that John Williams of Christleton, School Master, should be paid quarterly the sum of 2s 6d for instructing the boys. Elizabeth Johnson was to instruct the girls, also for 2s 6d a quarter. She died in 1844 aged 69 years and was reported to have been 'a faithful and respected mistress of the girls for over forty years'. At that time John Edgar was the head. He was followed by George Mayers who, although initially untrained as a teacher, served for many years as headmaster. He lived

John Sellers' Charity School in present churchyard in the 1870s

The former Dame School at Hen Davarn and the village Smithy (right) in the 1900s

with his wife Mary in the School House, now Church View, which was built for him by the Trustees.

The Charity School took its role seriously, and on 8th July 1789, the record states, 'The children shall constantly attend divine service at the Parish Church of Christleton twice in every Sunday. Boys...shall come to school from 1st April to 29th September at seven o'clock in the morning and that they do stay at school until five in the evening being allowed two hours from 11 to 1 o'clock for dinner time and from Michaelmass to the 1st April school hours from eight o'clock until four o'clock with same allowance for dinner time.' Despite the lengthy hours and restrictions, the school expanded rapidly. In its early days, there were no more than 10 boys and 10 girls, but by 1840 those numbers had risen to 70 boys and 60 girls.

The finance for the day-to-day running of the Charity School came partly from the parents, who contributed 1d a week, and partly from the contributions of local gentry and collections in church. (One entry in the Minute Book refers to a payment of one shilling for Mary Wilding of Littleton for seven or eight weeks; at this point she seems to have run away.) The church played a vital role in the life of the school, and the rectors and their wives were actively involved in the day-to-day running and administration.

Dame Schools

The church also supported the dame schools, one at Rowton and the other in Little Heath Road. There is evidence of yet another built at a later date to the rear of the house called Hen Davarn, near the old Smithy. Catherine Mayers, George Mayers' sister, ran one of these schools. The dames who ran the schools did little to educate the children and were in effect childminders. The reminiscences of Catherine Faulkner of Rowton give an insight into life at this type of school. 'As an infant I went to Mrs Weaver's Dame School in Perch Cottage, Rowton. Our playground was Sycamore Bank near the canal, and when playtime was over Mrs Weaver would come out and call "Books, Children" and any who lagged in the least behind got the rod. While lessons were on, the old lady would sit by the fire, the children having their backs to her, and she would get out a long churchwarden's pipe and have a smoke. It was woe betide any child who turned round to have a look at her.'

Christleton Academy

At about the same time, Christleton Academy, a boarding school, was being run in the building now known as Birch Heath Lodge. Ephraim and Benjamin Parkin were the proprietors, and Thomas Lakeland and his wife Mary ran the school. They catered for 15 boys aged 9–15 years of age and were helped by two servants. The boys were often seen about the village in their formal clothing. Thomas Welsby, a 12-year-old pupil there, wrote to his father John Welsby, a wine merchant in Chester, to tell him about life at the school in 1823.

Dear Father,
Considering the season of the year undoubtedly you'll be surprised at receiving this letter from me, not so much to learn when we break up, for that I daresay you know already, as to see the improvement in my writing. I am at present reading in Latin, Caesar's Commentaries in Gaul, and have advanced in Miscellaneous Questions and in the use of arithmetic. I have likewise paid great attention to my other studies, and I daresay you will be pleased with my improvements generally. We break up on the 16th June and the school will reopen on 16th July. Messrs Parkin and Tosh desire their best respects. Mary Jane is very well and in good spirits as myself. She desires to join me to you, and my dear mother.
Sincerely dear father
Your affectionate son
Thomas Welsby

(Tosh is clearly Thomas Lakeland and Mary Jane, his wife, who also acted as matron.)

It is not known how long the school survived, but Thomas Lakeland died aged 39 years and was buried in the churchyard. The school building became a private house called Holly Bank, which later became the home of Canon Garnett's eldest sister, Annie Rolt.

Christleton Academy Private School in the early 1800s

Girls' School

In 1850 it was decided to enlarge the John Sellers' School as it was becoming too small for the number of pupils, and consideration was given to creating a separate school for girls. The Trust therefore acquired land at the Bottom of the Wood and opposite the Woodfield from John Brockwood, Lord of the Manor, and Benjamin Parkin. The Trustees, led by Rector Thomas Mostyn, also tried to persuade the government to help them establish a 'Church of England Girls' School'. A yearly grant for upkeep was awarded and Joseph Mayers, the local builder, completed the new school building in 1856 for £400, which was paid by Lucy Anne Ince. It was decided that the annual income from the Sellers' Charity should be equally divided between the two schools. The girls' school became known as the New Church of England Girls' School and, soon after this, the Charity School became known as Christleton Boys' School.

The new school opened in 1856 and Catherine Faulkner records her time there. 'After leaving Mrs Weaver's school, my sister and I went to Christleton New Girls' School. The teacher was Miss Bennett and the school was held in a room over Betty Dutton's house, the nearest to the Bottom of the Wood, and it had a separate entrance...I was one of the first pupils to go to the New Girls' School.' She also remembers meeting Mrs Currie. 'I remember a widow lady named Mrs Currie and reflect how generous she was to the poor people of the parish. As a child I broke a leg and remember Mrs Currie bringing me a squeaking doll to amuse me. Later I went to Miss Lovatt's Private School in Boughton, and later to Miss Douglas' School which was held in the Salt Box House adjoining the Brown Cow in Waverton.'

Control of the school became the government's responsibility, and an annual inspection was held to ensure high standards and that the pupils were worthy of the annual grant. One report for the school dated 1865 says, 'The discipline in all respects is excellent. The Religious Knowledge and Needle Work deserve high praise. The Girls show much more quickness of understanding, in what they read than last year. The weak points are the reading of the class, and the writing of the older scholars. The practice of learning to repeat poetry has had a very good effect on the reading of the higher classes.'

The old Girls' and Infants' School and Sadler's Stores, Quarry Lane, 1972

Finance became a vital issue because the grant depended on a high attendance figure. Regular pleas were made to parents to ensure that their children attended school and were not kept from school to work on the land. An entry in the parish magazine for 1877 is typical of many. 'We are sorry to say that owing to irregular attendance during the past year, many scholars have failed to qualify for the examination. This entails a loss of grant which the funds can ill afford. We do beg that parents send their children to school more regularly.'

Total expenditure for the year in 1877 was £208 2s 10d and the government grant only £109 6s 0d. The balance had to be found locally, and funds were raised at a parish tea, from a church collection, and the endowment of income from the Sellers' Trust of £11. The Duke of Westminster gave £15, Townsend Ince £10, Thomas Dixon £10, and the Rector Lionel Garnett also £10. It was to help solve this annual state of affairs that Mr Garnett started the village Fetes and, for many years, the proceeds from the Fetes went towards the running costs of the schools.

In 1873 the Girls' School was extended to provide additional accommodation for infant children and became known as Christleton Girls' and Infants' School. Later it became the Christleton Elementary Girls' and Infants' School, and finally in 1902 the National Girls' and Infants' Voluntary Aided School. The Charity School seems to have lost its status in 1904 and to have come under government control. However, the John Sellers' Charity continues to play a part in village life by issuing each autumn small grants to schools and individuals for educational purposes.

Boys' School

The establishment of the separate Girls' School in 1856 meant that there was more space for the boys in the building in the churchyard. However, although the Sellers' building had been extended in 1846 and again in 1873, it still was not big enough to cater for the needs of the village or for the new developments in education. It was in his comments on the Inspector's Report in 1878 that Canon Garnett first raised the issue of a new school for the boys. 'Numbers at both Boys' and Girls' Schools have greatly increased—at the former inconveniently so, frequently exceeding 100, and the building is too small to accommodate them properly. (It is allowable, I suppose, to wish for a better school, but we must not talk about more building until we have paid our debt on the Church).'

This new Boys' School was eventually built opposite the church in Pepper Street on the site of the former Ring o'Bells public house. The publican and coachbuilder, James Parry, sold the land to the Parochial Church Council for £600. The total cost of the new school was £1200.

Lionel Garnett was on the Board of Managers of the two schools and used the parish magazines to publish the school accounts, Inspectors' Reports and regular appeals to raise funds. The accounts for April 1873 to March 1874 appeared in his first edition. 'Received Government Grant: £97. Endowment: £11 10s 0d. School Pence: £68 6s 7d contributing to a total of £290 4s 7d. Expended were Salaries of £198 6s 8d. Pupil Teachers and Monitor: £40 6s 8d. Books etc: £10 11s 11d. Land Tax: £0 2s 0d.'

There were, however, unavoidable absences and closures of the schools, sometimes for weeks, through outbreaks of diseases such as

Mr Cummings' class in the Infant Playground, 1972

measles and scarlet fever. A series of extracts from the 1906 school log-book shows the hazards of disease in the early years of the 20th century.

'Nov 1906. The school was closed by order of Dr Kenyon, because of an outbreak of diphtheria.

Nov 14th. School closed again for three weeks because a child has caught diphtheria. She has a malignant throat.

Dec 3rd. School resumed work. 80 children present. While the school has been closed, the building has been fumigated very thoroughly, sulphur having been burned for three successive days, walls having been brushed and desks scrubbed with carbolic soap.'

In 1887 a new Education Act dealt with the national problem of attendance by making school Guardians appoint Attendance Committees, which were to be made up of six to 12 members of the Board. Their duties were to publish and enforce the Act's provisions relating to the employment of children and their attendance at school, and 'to take proceedings in the case of children under 10 years being at work; of children over 10 being at work without a School Certificate and of children over 5 not sent to school but left to run about the streets.'

The Guardians, one of whom was Lionel Garnett, also had to pay the school fees (not more than 3d) for the children aged 5–14 of parents who, 'though not paupers, are too poor to pay for them.' Published responses to the frequent appeals for special subscriptions for the schools brought up the same supportive names: the Curries, the Dixons, William Fleming, the Lace family, and they usually paid £5 each time. In April 1875, only four months after his last appeal for money, Canon Garnett tried to reach a wider conscience. 'Parishioners are bound to keep up their schools in an efficient state; if we don't we must have a School Board with powers to levy rates, and people say that is an expensive luxury. We had better on the whole try to do without it!'

Extracts from the Inspectors' Reports in general education reveal little of the teaching methods and what was actually taught. Reading ('want of fluency in Boys 1st and 2nd Standards'), arithmetic and spelling ('weak in all Girls' standards except perhaps the 5th'), and writing ('much improvement in the style of paperwork') are referred to in most reports. 'Needlework is carefully taught' and 'Some of the Geography papers of the 4th Standard are

Christleton Boys' School, 1900 (now Christleton Parish Hall)

meagre and not very accurate' provide scant reference to other curricular areas. The religious knowledge report of 1879 gives greater details of the work covered in a subject that undoubtedly filled a major portion of each day. 'RI has been given in this [Boys'] school as usual with exceeding care. Not only was a good and sound knowledge of prepared portions of Holy Scripture shewn, but the Catechism was capitally known and intelligently understood. Group 1 also gave some very good answering on the order of Morning and Evening Prayer. The slate work was neat and accurate and the paperwork creditable.' Learning by rote was obviously a prime teaching method, 'The little ones of Group III (Girls) answered brightly and with intelligence and repeated the catechisms, texts and hymns well.' Inspectors commended the behaviour at both schools and commented, 'discipline is excellent and teaching thorough...quietness and good order were pleasing accompaniments to the knowledge of the children.'

In the classroom, teachers relied upon young, untrained personnel to instruct in the basic curriculum, some of whom progressed via a Queen's Scholarship to teacher training colleges. One such pupil teacher, Robert Smith, embarked upon 'a 2-year training to qualify him as a schoolmaster at Chester College' in January 1875; however, he died suddenly from typhoid fever in January 1876. There were lighter moments for the pupils of both schools. A description of the School Treat in August 1881 offered thanks to Mrs Ambrose Dixon for entertaining the children at Christleton Bank, when 250 'had a real good time of it' with bran pies, balloons, nuts, sweets and buns. At the 1884 Treat, the Christleton Brass Band made its first appearance and 'acquitted themselves wonderfully well.' In November 1887, Mrs Townsend Ince sent the school children to see 'a very good panorama in Chester.'

It was Mrs Dixon who introduced the annual School Outings. Such outings provided opportunities to explore areas outside the village in times when few travelled far from home. A report by Canon Garnett describes the first one in August 1889.

We left Christleton at 9.30 (in horse-drawn carts), called in at Christleton Bank to give cheers to Mrs Dixon and got a special train at Chester Station for Rhyl arriving at 11.15. We marched at once to a Cocoa House where Mr Mason served out a bun and cup of milk all round. Then we proceeded to the seashore where we scattered in every direction in search of amusement. Some bathed, some waded, some dug in the sand and picked shells. Some rode on horses, some on donkeys, some listened to Christy Minstrels, others looked at Punch and Judy. All spent four happy hours or so, then we gathered again for an excellent tea, got into our train and reached Chester at 6 o'clock without accident or loss. Mrs Dixon met us on the road and we gave her a round of cheers by way of thanking her for a day's pleasure.

The school log-books give many interesting anecdotes of life in the schools, some sad, others amusing.

'May 1863. The teacher washed some of the children this morning who were too dirty to sit down to lessons. Sent home two girls on Thursday afternoon, to have their hair cleaned as they were in a filthy state.

'Sept 1863. School closed as children were away gleaning in the fields.

'April 1874. Julia Rowe aged 9 died of Rheumatic fever. The children attended the funeral.

'1922. The children could not be sent home from morning school, because of the depth of water around the school building. The sewage pit opposite has overflowed into the playground. Afternoon school cancelled as the children's shoes and socks were wet through, and it was impossible for them to walk through the water.'

There were also some happier moments.

'1883. Holiday on Wednesday & Thursday on account of the marriage of the Rector to Miss Thompson of Boughton Hall.

'1900. Miss Rolt visited school to show the children Indian Curiosities, and left some for the museum.

'1902. School closed for four days for the Coronation Celebrations.

'1925. Special holiday for the King's visit to Chester.'

Many of the old log-books from the 1900s are missing, so little detail is known of the schools at this time. However figures like Sam Earlam, Tom Solloway, Mr Hullah, Mrs Gooyer and Marion Kershaw left their mark on the education of village children. They were all popular and long-serving headteachers who were respected pillars of the community. The church choir, Sunday School, St James' Lodge, British Legion, village parties, Fetes and entertainments owed much in these early days to the energies of such teachers.

In 1955 the Girls' and Boys' Schools became the Christleton Church of England Aided School; it changed again in 1963 to become Christleton Church of England Infant and Primary School. The two schools were closed in 1974 and were replaced by a new County Primary School in Quarry Lane. The Boys' School became the Parish Hall and the Girls' and Infants' building was converted into five small flats.

Christleton Primary School

When Marion Kershaw retired in July 1972, the new headteacher David Cummings and his staff had to take the pupils from the two old buildings into the modern era. The style of the new school building was completely different. There were open classroom spaces with carpeted floors, indoor toilets and even a hall for assemblies. There was a playing field on site, so the days of walking to Little Heath to play football were over. However, for a time conditions were not that much better as, due to the three-day week and industrial unrest, much of the new furniture, lighting units and equipment could not be delivered.

The school finally opened its doors on 22nd April 1974 and the children walked in classes with their teachers from their old schools to the new building. Amongst the first visitors were Mr and Mrs Wilf Mitchell, the Mayor and Mayoress of Chester. The new building brought with it a new era of education and a new status as a County Primary School. The aim of the headteacher and staff was to make the school a living part of the community. Continuity was provided by long-serving members of the support staff, such as Jean Carline, Joan Walley and Ethel Morris, who all served the schools for more than thirty years. Parents were encouraged to play an active role and a School Association was formed and still has a very prominent part in school life. The governors have also played a vital part and continue to support the school.

The school succeeded in improving academic standards by treating children as individuals or as members of a small group. The children also worked with teams of teachers, who shared both expertise and resources. The school expanded the curriculum with the introduction of art, pottery, needlecraft, dance, drama, and music. The children also tried a variety of sports, including swimming, table tennis, orienteering, football, netball, athletics, cricket, and gymnastics. Educational visits were an important part of the learning process, and children visited museums in Chester, York and Liverpool. They were taken on day and residential visits to Delamere Forest Outdoor Centre, Burwardsley Outdoor Centre, Tattenhall Arts Centre, Bangor in North Wales and Keswick in the Lake District.

Learning about the local heritage and environment was also encouraged through work in geography and history (the research for this history book began at that time).

After completing a natural history survey of the village for the Cheshire Wildlife Trust in 1972, the school became involved in a long-term project study at Hockenhull Platts Reserve, which has now been carried out for 28 years. The children researched and wrote a school project about the Pit (the village pond). This won second prize in the National Save the Village Pond Campaign in 1974–5, and two pupils, Christine Evans and Liam Carlen, appeared on the BBC programme *Animal Magic* with Johnny Morris and Tony Soper. This later resulted in the children becoming involved in the Pit rescue project, and several conservation awards were made to the school for this work.

Sport has been an important part of school life. The school has won Dolphin Trophy Swimming Awards and reached the National Table Tennis finals. The table tennis teams also won the Cheshire, North-West, and Northern Championships during the 1990s. The school is also noted for its maypole dancing and has given displays at Christleton Fetes and Shows, as well as at Chester Town Hall and at the May Fair at Tatton Park.

Music has played a significant role. The choir performed twice with the Gateway Theatre Company in two productions of *Joseph and the Amazing Technicolor Dreamcoat*. This production was later staged at the school in 1997 to mark the retirement of David Cummings that year.

The choir has also given many performances at Christleton High School in the joint Charles Mack Memorial (now Spring) Charity Concerts. These have raised over £12,000 for a variety of causes since their inception in 1987. Both the infants and juniors still produce their separate Christmas productions, and the juniors show their talents at the annual Strawberry and Wine evening.

The school regularly holds services at St James' Church. Although not a church school, it has always had strong links with the church

Christleton Primary School, summer 1989

community in Christleton. The present Rector, Peter Lee, takes assembly in the school each week and is also a school governor. It was through the church and Mrs Gertrude Wright that the Primary School formed links with St James' School, Leh, Ladakh, in northern India. One of the highlights of school life during the 1980s came when five girls from Ladakh spent a winter in Christleton. It gave everyone a chance to live and work with children from a different culture and faith. The visit of Bimla, Bilques, Ruth, Ruth Mary and Anju was a good lesson on how people, in communities with so little, can work together for the common good. After their visit, the Primary School raised the money for three classrooms for the new school at Shey and provided uniforms and clothing, books and materials.

Links between the High and Primary Schools were started in 1974 through regular liaison meetings. These have been a vital part in the smooth progress of children between the schools. Joint induction courses for all new Year Seven children to the High School were started at St Mary's Centre in Chester during the 1970s, and now take place at the High School each July. David Cummings retired in 1997 after 25 years and David Harker took over as headteacher for another era of educational change.

Secondary Education

Until the 1950s, fee-paying private schools and grammar schools provided the only secondary education available to children who lived in the rural districts of Cheshire and some of the Chester suburbs. The grammar schools only catered for the one in three children who had passed the 11+ examination. The rest of the children spent their school life in all-age village schools which had no specialist teachers or accommodation. During the 1950s and 1960s there was a large school building programme throughout Cheshire, as a result of which, all children were given access to secondary education in appropriate buildings. On 1st September 1958, Christleton Secondary School opened with 490 pupils from 75 square miles of Cheshire. The school was officially opened on 3rd October by Sir Edward Boyle, Parliamentary Secretary to the Ministry of Education. A young art teacher, Philip Hodges, designed the school's crest for the opening, and pupils in the school workshop made a large metal version of this for the entrance of the school. The names of the school Houses were suggested by the school's first metalwork teacher, Mr G W Jones. The names have historical associations with Christleton and the land on which the school was built: Badgerett was the name of a small copse; Bythom and Ketlan were family and field names of local landowners; and Lawns had been the name of the land where the school now stands. (The site of the school, including the playing fields, had previously been the grounds of The Grange, the old Rectory.) Mr Jones died in 1960 and a silver bowl, made and designed by silversmith Keith Smith, was commissioned in his memory. It is awarded annually as the Inter-House Trophy.

Two factors have been a feature of Christleton School since it opened: first, it has been a successful school and consequently popular with pupils, parents and teachers; secondly, the school has always had a perpetual shortage of accommodation. Two national events proved significant in increasing the shortage of space at the school. The raising of the school-leaving age from 15 to 16 in 1973 and the introduction of the comprehensive system in 1974 increased the number of pupils at the school and the length of their school life.

From the school's beginning in 1958 an increasing number of pupils stayed on voluntarily to the age of 16 in order to take examinations. This was further encouraged by the introduction of the CSE examination in the mid-1960s. After 10 years, the first pupils asked if they could stay on beyond 16 to take 'A' Levels, and by the early 1970s Christleton School had a thriving sixth form and was regularly sending pupils to colleges and universities.

The raising of the school-leaving age from 15 to 16 transformed the structure of the curriculum. Previously, pupils in the first two years followed a basic general course of study, and in the third and fourth years pupils were placed on one of four vocational countywide courses: technical, commercial, rural and practical. The raising of the school-leaving age led to those courses being abandoned. During the first three years pupils now followed a basic course of general education. In the fourth and fifth years all pupils studied nine subjects, six of which were compulsory: English, mathematics, science, a humanity, physical education and a creative subject. The three other subjects were the pupil's own choice.

The change to comprehensive education in 1974 was countywide. Christleton Secondary School became Christleton High School. Whereas Christleton Secondary School had taken children from 75 square miles of rural Cheshire after the grammar schools had removed the top third, it now took all the children from the villages of Christleton, Littleton, Waverton, Vicar's Cross and Barrow. More teaching areas and additional playing fields were added to the school in 1972–73 in readiness for the anticipated 1020 pupils for the comprehensive school (although at the time there were already more than 1000 pupils in the school). It was assumed that there would be 180 pupils in each of the first, second, third, fourth, and fifth years, and that 30% of each year group would stay on in the sixth form. There was, however, an unforeseen development. The new Dee High School (now Bishops Church of England High School) was scheduled to open in 1974 and was due to take children from what had previously been a part of Christleton High School's catchment area. Construction delays meant that the new school would not be ready until 1977. The education authority decided that the children, who were to have gone to Dee High School, should go to Christleton, and that the first two of these three groups of children should stay at Christleton for the whole of their schooling.

Consequently in 1974, 311 children entered the first year at Christleton School, followed by 306 in 1975 and 300 in 1976. The school faced tremendous challenges in terms of organisation and accommodation. In 1980 and 1981 the first comprehensive years progressed into the sixth form, and nearer 50% of the fifth year stayed on instead of the projected 30%. In 1981 the school's population reached 1400. In spite of all this, the school flourished and achieved success with children at all levels.

By 1983 the bulge had passed through, and the school had settled to its normal size of around 1100 pupils. At that time, predictions indicated that pupil numbers in all secondary schools would plummet by the late 1980s as a result of the falling birth rate. Cheshire anticipated a fall of 30% overall, with the biggest fall in the Chester district. Within the Chester district, Christleton High School was expected to experience the greatest fall of all, approaching 40%. However, the acceptance of parental choice has meant that Christleton has remained an oversubscribed school.

Many people have worked hard to make the school a success. Mr Les George was the first headteacher of Christleton Secondary School and he remained until his retirement in 1980. Mr Phil Hodges, who was one of the original 17 teachers appointed to the school, succeeded him, and on his retirement, Mr Geoff Lawson took over in 1990. Deputy headteachers, teachers, registrars, secretaries, caretakers, cleaning staff, technicians, catering staff, sports hall and swimming pool staff have all made an invaluable contribution to the life and success of the school.

The school has also been fortunate in the quality of its governors, who have always given considerable support and service to the school. The school's first chairman of governors was Alderman William Dutton, who continued in this capacity for many years.

One of the strengths of Christleton High School is the team spirit that exists between the pupils, their families and the staff, which was fostered from the start by Mr George. Many parents, some grandparents and several members of the teaching and support staff are former pupils of the school. This spirit has led to achievements in all aspects of the school's work: academic performance, the arts, sport and community involvement. In October 1998 the school celebrated its 40th anniversary, and many former pupils and teachers gathered to join in the festivities. Former teacher, Mrs Whalley, then in her 90s, was present as were Gerry Fair and Dick Tucker, two of the original governors. There have been many teachers who have spent a significant part, in some cases all, of their teaching career at the school. David Crook, who supervised the creation of the wrought iron jardinière inside the main entrance, taught at the school for 40 years from May 1960 to April 2000. Every subject in the school has achieved success over the years; the eight acceptances at the universities of Oxford and Cambridge in this Millennium year are an indication of this. (Six of these eight pupils also attended Christleton Primary School.)

Significant success has also been achieved in national competitions in mathematics and science, as well as in the Young Enterprise and Duke of Edinburgh Award schemes.

The High School Association has worked hard during the years to raise tens of thousands of pounds to help the school develop. It became clear in the 1980s that the existing buildings were, in many respects, inadequate. A major building programme was undertaken to equip the school more appropriately. For example, the school now has well-developed facilities for music, drama, technology, science and sport.

Drama has been one of the school's most high profile activities. The combination of the talents of staff, pupils and parents has created many professional productions. All aspects of staging plays and musicals, including acting, direction, the sets, costumes, make up and props and sound and lighting, have been developed; high standards have been expected and achieved. The 1960s saw productions of Mozart's *The Magic Flute* and a sequence of Shakespeare plays, *The Merchant of Venice*, *A Midsummer Night's Dream* and *Twelfth Night*. Two of the most successful productions were performances of the musicals *Oliver* and *My Fair Lady*, as good as any West End production at that time. During the 1970s musicals such as *The Boy Friend* and *West Side Story* were performed, as well as three productions written by members of the staff: *Alice in Wonderland*, *Love in Idleness* and *Jason and the Argonauts*. Among the shows in the 1980s were *Jesus Christ Superstar*, *Larkrise*, and *Godspell*. More recent productions have included

Christleton High School, April 2000

George Farquhar's *The Recruiting Officer*. Many former pupils have gone into the professional theatre and broadcasting after having their interests stimulated at the school.

The swimming pool was built as a result of the efforts of Mr George, teachers, pupils and parents. During the first four years after the school opened, more than £4,000 was raised to build the pool. (The land, the building and equipping of the original school cost £160,000.) It was initially an open-air pool but was later covered and heated by the County Council on condition that other schools could have access to it. The Inter-House Swimming Trophy, the Prescott Cup, was presented by the current Deputy Prime Minister, John Prescott, in appreciation of the help and advice he had received during his studies at the Grange School, Ellesmere Port and Ruskin College, Oxford from Les George. The sports hall was added in 1974. The sports hall and swimming pool have added tremendously to the life and development of the school and the local community, which runs the hall in a joint venture with the school.

Sport has also provided many successes. In the first year of the school's life, the 1st Soccer XI won the Chester District Cup. After the school became a comprehensive, the 1st Soccer XI went on to win the Cheshire Championship. Although boys' and girls' teams in the more mainstream sports, such as rugby, cricket, hockey, netball, swimming, and gymnastics, have had their successes, specialist activities have also produced individual achievers, including the National Schoolboy Cycling Champion, Lee Minshull, and angling champion, Wendy Locker.

Good humour has always been a part of life at the school. Teachers' marriages always seemed to inspire good-natured practical jokes. One young teacher, on receiving good wishes for his marriage, was deluged in confetti from above. It was later discovered that one of the confetti makers had accidentally left a pair of scissors in the pile of confetti. Fortunately they only stuck into the floor.

The thousands of pupils who have attended Christleton School since 1958 have spent their school days in a beautiful environment. There is no doubt that this environment has contributed to the success of the school. The school is conscious of its responsibilities to the village community, and the reputation of the school has enhanced the name of the village.

Under-Fives Community Playgroup

Founded as a private playgroup in 1968 by Beryl Hood and Chris Charlesworth, the group started operating from the Scout Hut. Following the retirement of both women in 1983, the continuing need for a playgroup for the under-fives was recognised. In 1983 the community playgroup was set up with Eunice Fish as the supervisor, Carole Penney and Margot Kirch as the two deputies, and a committee of mothers dealing with the business and financial aspects. The playgroup is now a member of the Pre-School Learning Alliance and has had two good Ofsted reports since 1997.

The aim of the playgroup is to provide a safe, caring and happy environment where children are able to learn and develop at their own pace. For many children it is their first experience of play away from their parents or carers and, as such, it is a useful introduction to pre-school learning. There is a wide range of individual and group activities through the morning, and the curriculum works towards approved learning outcomes.

The playgroup meets every Monday to Friday during school term-time from 9.00–11.45 am. Carole Penny is now the supervisor and her deputies are Brenda Rogers and Lyn Burns. The cost in 2000 is £3 a session and there are more than 50 children on the register.

Children are admitted at the age of two and a half. During the late 1990s it was felt that extra provision should be made for those children who would be starting school the following September, so the Rising Fives Club was set up. This group meets on Thursday afternoons and during the summer term a member of Christleton Primary School staff visits the children and talks to those who will be going to the school the following term.

The playgroup takes an active part in the village Fete: the children, dressed in their costumes, walk in the procession and their parents and carers run a stall. In 1999 the stall won the Junior Best Dressed Stall cup. In addition, there is a summer outing, a visit to see the Christmas play performed by the infants at the Primary School, and a Christmas party with entertainer and Father Christmas. As the playgroup is dependent upon fundraising, there are numerous other events held for the parents and carers throughout the year.

Christleton Toddler Group

The Toddler Group was formed in 1980 by some local mothers who recognised the benefits that they and their children would gain from organised meetings. These mothers included Helen Clifton, Christine Robinson, Sheila Murphy and Penny Danzak. Originally the group was called the Mother and Toddler Group and met at the WI Hall. It then transferred to the Methodist Church Hall for a short period, before moving to the Primary School. The name was changed to Christleton Toddler Group to encourage more carers, fathers and grandparents to attend. The number of children attending grew and a new venue was found at the Parish Hall in 1987, where the group still meets today.

The Group meets every Tuesday between 10.00–11.30 am and costs £1.50 per session per family. Approximately 40 children attend each week, with ages ranging from one week to three and a half years. There are lots of toys, a book area and an activity, such as painting or sticking. The session closes with all the children singing one or two nursery rhymes.

The Toddler Group organise and participate in many events. Activities for 1999 included a Barnardo's Sponsored Toddle at Chester Zoo when children had to toddle half a mile to raise funds for Barnardo's and the Group. The children took part in the village Fete procession dressed as stars and the mothers and carers organised a ball pond at the Fete. Nearly New Sales of clothes and toys were held to raise funds. The toddlers enjoyed a musical workshop during October. In December some of the toddlers sang carols at Birch Heath Lodge, the residential nursing home, and a Christmas Party was held for all the children.

The College of Law

The College of Law in Christleton was formally opened on 29th March 1974 by the

Christleton Parish Hall

The front entrance to Christleton Hall, now the College of Law

Lord Chief Justice of England, the Right Honourable Lord Widgery. The Hall, originally built in the 18th century for the Ince family, had changed from a large family house to a seminary in 1934. The Salvatorian Brothers had added a north wing in 1935 and a classroom block in 1963.

The College renovated the interior of the building, enlarging rooms to create classrooms and more teaching space. In 1974 there were eight classrooms, two reading rooms and a library, as well as lecturers' rooms and administrative offices, all set in extensive grounds. At the time of opening there were 15 full-time professionally qualified lecturers.

Two of the primary objectives of the Law Society were to promote the study of law and to establish colleges at which students could receive instruction in all branches of law, in order to sit professional legal examinations. The Christleton college was set up to provide a branch in the north of England. Control of the College is vested in a Board of Governors appointed by the Law Society and administered by a Board of Management.

In recent years the Christleton branch has expanded rapidly and now teaches a variety of courses to over 1500 students a year. These include the Post-Graduate Diploma in Law, the Open University Qualifying Law Degree, and the Legal Practice, Professional Skills, and Bar Vocational courses. All of these aim to equip students: 'with the skills and knowledge needed to analyse legal problems and provide solutions to them; how to transfer and apply knowledge and expertise from one legal context to another; the essential skills involved in thinking like a lawyer, such as researching and using legal materials, and constructing and articulating legal arguments; how to take advantage and realise the potential of IT in the context of legal study and practice.'

More recent facilities at Christleton Hall include a library with 300 study places, a student common room and a refectory, which opens onto the walled garden. There is a European group with language classes, and there has been investment in information technology. The current Director of the College of Law is Janet Lea.

6 Social and Sporting Life

Christleton Village Players

Christleton Village Players was one of the most influential societies in village history. For more than 50 years they entertained the village and the surrounding area. The Players often dominated the headlines in the local papers and were a recognised force within Cheshire theatre circles, especially during their later years when they were led by Mr Peter Dornford May, the County Drama Advisor. The group was formed at a meeting on 9th March 1928 at Christleton Scout Hut. Colonel Shaw proposed that a dramatic society, to be called the Christleton Village Players, should be started. Membership was restricted to residents of the parish and those who had some local connection, and the subscription was 1s a year. It was also decided that no person under the age of 18 could join.

Their first production in December 1928 was *Babes in the Wood*, written and produced by Colonel Shaw. In 1929 the Players became members of the Village Drama Society, which was affiliated to the British Drama League.

The next production was *Make Believe* by A A Milne and took place in the Boys' School. The Rector, A A Guest-Williams, was asked if electric current could be permanently fixed for the use of stage lighting. However, the new Women's Institute Hall became available in January 1930 and was placed at the disposal of the Players, if they agreed to assign the profits to the building fund. This offer was accepted and the Players moved their productions to the W I Hall. It was also agreed that the scenery could be hired out to the Christleton W I for their productions. It was further resolved at a committee meeting in March 1930 that if the Players disbanded, their stage properties would revert to Mr Guest-Williams as Rector.

Three short plays were chosen later that year: *The Twelve Pound Lock, The Monkey's Paw,* and *Have you anything to declare?* They were performed on 29–30th September. The play *Baa Baa Black Sheep* was chosen for the 1931 performance, but the Players had to do a great deal of fundraising to buy curtains for the

The Christleton Players in a scene from *Double Doors*, 1954

stage. Whist drives and dances were the favoured events, and Mrs Mary Partington, 'Mrs Christleton', was chosen to head the fundraising committee. After purchasing the curtains, they were left with a bank overdraft of £2 9s 5d, so more fundraising efforts were needed.

In 1934 there were many discussions about the choice of play, seating arrangements, improvements in the quality of programmes, and where to place advertisements. Finally *The Distaff Side* was chosen as a play. One of the suggestions acted upon was that they should advertise on the local buses. The start of the Second World War caused the productions to stop, and there were no meetings between 24th July 1939 and February 26th 1947.

At the first meeting after the war, committee members all agreed that new blood was needed and that young people (still over the age of 18) should be encouraged. However, later in 1947 Mr Wain proposed that 'they form a junior section to get young people interested, and to give them training.' They did lower the age limit to 17 years in 1948 but ruled that new members must have resided in Christleton for six months. *Fresh Fields* was chosen for the next production and the admission prices were 5s and 3s 6d for reserved seats and 2s unreserved. The other minutes for that meeting invited Mr Douglas Williams to give a price for playing incidental music on all three nights of the production. It was agreed that giving flowers and presents should be strictly kept until the last night of the performance. Mary Partington suggested, 'that it would be nice if we had refreshments on the last night after the performance.' It was decided that everyone should bring his or her own food and Mr Hunter would provide the alcoholic refreshment. Mr West suggested that they should have a lucky number programme at each performance and that the prize would be one dozen eggs. The Chairman also recommended that they should provide a special bus to Chester after the performance. A footnote states that it was agreed that no alcohol should be given to the players during the show!

The Players began to organise theatre visits from 1948; the first play they went to see was Terrence Rattigan's *The Winslow Boy* in Liverpool. Miss Kershaw, the Girls' School headmistress, is mentioned as a member in early 1948 and was given a part in the play *When Fools Rush In*. In 1949 it was finally proposed to lower the age limit for membership to 15 years of age to enable junior members to join. The proceeds from the plays that year were given to the new Village Playing Field Fund. One member, Mrs Taylor, asked for permission to use the services of some of the members to put on a play in Chester. It was agreed as long as all the cast were from the Christleton Players and that the production was approved before the play was advertised in the city.

Mr Cracknell, one of the leading members, resigned from the committee in 1953 over the part he had been given. He said it was obvious that some members were critical of the selection committee's casting, and it was not showing the right spirit when members refused to undertake a part that the selection committee had offered to them. Mrs Kay Davey said she also wished to resign from the society, as she no longer found pleasure in the activities. When the committee asked her to reconsider she agreed, but would not serve on the selection committee. It was agreed that future policy would be decided at the next Annual General Meeting. At this AGM membership applications from outside the village did not meet with approval. However, in May 1956 it was agreed that members from outside Christleton could join, as long as they did not form more than 10% of the membership.

It was the appointment of Mr Peter Dornford May as County Drama Advisor that really increased the profile of the Players. He and his family came to live in the parish. His arrival, together with the new stage and facilities at Christleton Secondary School, meant that the Players reached new standards of performance. Mrs Kay Davey, now President, was reported in a Chester newspaper in 1964 as saying, 'that she was convinced that the Christleton Village Players' progress was due, in no small measure, to the facilities at the Secondary School, and the enthusiastic support given to them by Mr Leslie George, the Headteacher and prominent member of the Society.'

It was Mr Dornford May's staging of the series of outdoor performances at Eaton Hall 1964–1968 that raised the Players' profile. Large numbers of villagers were needed to perform and stage these large productions. The need for even more actors, for example in the Wakefield Cycle of Mystery Plays, ensured that the Players had to be drawn from an even

The Christleton Players, featuring Beryl Hood, Joan Pollitt and Stan Jones, performing in a pantomime at the High School in 1958

wider area. The peak of the Christleton Players' achievements was reached in Mr Dornford May's staging of these plays under the patronage of Anne, Duchess of Westminster. The proceeds were given to the National Society for the Prevention of Cruelty to Children. There were enormous costs for the Players and there were doubts at the beginning as to whether they could succeed in such major productions. However their success is now history and they gave pleasure to thousands of people.

In June 1964, they performed *A Midsummer Night's Dream*, followed in 1965 by a production of the Wakefield Cycle of Mystery Plays. *As You Like It* was performed in 1966, and June 1968 saw a production of *Twelfth Night* in the Courtyard. Mr Dornford May also became involved in the Chester Mystery Plays, and many members of the Players were drafted into these productions. In June 1974 the expanded Christleton Village Players presented *The Cheshire Saga* at Chester Castle produced by Hilary Egan. The society celebrated their Golden Jubilee in March 1979 and, later that year, presented *Chester Tales* in Chester Cathedral.

For many years at Christmas time, the Players presented the nativity scene from the Mystery Plays on the Village Green and, as part of the 1975 Festival of British Villages, they performed a traditional mummer's play led by Mark Dornford May. They also performed in St James' Church. However, it was the large-scale, successful productions at Eaton Hall and Chester that brought the Village Players to the peak of their achievements and to the notice of a much wider audience. After the death of Peter Dornford May, the activities of the Village Players came to an end, but they had been a great influence in village life for more than 50 years and had provided live theatre for generations of local people.

Wednesday Group

The Wednesday Group came into being in 1960 when a small group of ladies, who were collectors for Barnardo's Children's Homes, met together to extend their activities and raise more money for Barnardo's. More events were planned and more meetings were needed and, as Wednesday seemed to be the most convenient day for everyone to meet, the expanding group decided to call itself the Wednesday Group and to appoint a Chairman together with a small committee.

It was decided from the beginning that, in order to minimise expenses, meetings should be held in members' houses on the first Wednesday of each month, and this formula has remained constant for the past 40 years.

Over the years support has been extended from Barnardo's to include many other charities, mostly child-centred and almost all local. The group has tried, where possible, to provide specific equipment, as it was felt that the donation would meet the charities' or individuals' direct needs and would not disappear into administration. Examples include metal rods for a child with brittle bone disease; a special hearing aid for a profoundly deaf child; household goods in a newly-opened home for young adults with learning difficulties; baby monitors for the neonatal unit at the Countess of Chester hospital; and equipment for the new community physiotherapy service in the early 1980s. More general funds have been given towards a spina bifida unit, Riding for the Disabled in the Wirral, hospices in the area, and the local myalgic encephalitis (ME) branch to name but a few. This gives an idea of the range of recipients helped by the Wednesday Group.

Forty years ago the original fundraising event was a Handicraft Fair, featuring work produced by the group members. However, ideas expanded and several events have become part of the village calendar, notably the lunches provided by the members themselves. These events include the 5K run round a village circuit, a stall at the village Fete, and an autumn charity Christmas cards sale.

Other activities have included musical evenings, jumble sales, fashion shows, antiques' roadshows, quiz evenings, bridge drives, railway teas, and safari suppers. Many thousands of pounds have been raised over the years. Originally, the annual total was £100; this slowly increased until, for several years now, the totals have been around, or even in excess of, £3,000.

In all these efforts, the Wednesday Group has been generously and faithfully supported by village inhabitants and friends.

Football Club

Christleton Football Club was formed in 1897 and the games were played on the Park with the support of Rector Lionel Garnett. There were two teams. The Christleton Wednesdays, nicknamed the *Pals*, played in a Wednesday afternoon league, which was formed to accommodate shopkeepers and staff who worked on Saturdays. The other Christleton team at that time was called the *Bible Class* and played friendly matches on Saturdays. Although early achievements are sketchy, the Christleton team was highly regarded by 1910 under the chairmanship of Mr J V Wright, a founder member of the club. The full team of 1910 was C Walley, E E Shaw, C Allan, A Gregory, C Harding, H Waring, Cooper, J Bramhall, Griffiths, R Carr, F Pierce, W Amer, Thomas, H Ankers, N Wright and J Edwards. Their team photograph also includes Thomas Mayers, the local builder, J Wright, Major Townsend-Currie and Canon Garnett.

When competitive football restarted after 1918, the Christleton team continued to make their mark in the Chester & District Football League, where they played until being admitted to the present West Cheshire League in 1966–7.

After 1945, Ron and Grace Mayers collected clothing coupons to try to purchase a new kit for the team. Both took pride in the turn-out of the team and, for many years, the kit was handwashed by Grace. All the committee members currently share these duties. In 1947 the club meetings were held under the chairmanship of Reg Steventon. Reg's son, John, played in the 1947 team as did Harold Carman who went on to become chairman in 1956. Harold's brother, Arthur, became secretary 1954–1959 and 1965–1978. Another well-known village personality butcher Jim Partington was an excellent footballer and Jim was cutting and rolling the grass in 2000.

Peter Davies joined the club in the early 1950s. He later became treasurer, but it was his alliance with Ron Mayers that led the way to many Chester & District League championships and trophies during the following 50 years. Under the managership of Ron Mayers, the team won the Chester FA Challenge Cup in 1955–56, 1959–60, 1963–64, 1967–68, 1968–69, and 1970–71.

During the 1965–66 season members of the club enticed Sid Dandy, a farmer from Littleton, to join them. He had been running the Guilden Sutton football team but had, for many years, been influential in the affairs of Christleton Cricket Club. He became an enthusiastic manager, gaining notoriety for his caustic comments directed at his own players,

Christleton Wednesday Football Club, 1907–8

and he became one of the most liked characters in the league. When Christleton FC joined the West Cheshire League in the 1966–67 season, the team won the Division 2 title at the first attempt, scoring 154 goals on the way. Bobby Lewis scored a club record of 60 league and cup goals during this season. Three years later, in the 1969–70 season, Christleton won the 1st Division Championship and the Chester Amateur Cup.

The teams in the post-war years contained many members of well-known Christleton families: names such as Mayers, Steventon, Challinor, Partington, Carline, Dentith, Lloyd, Boddy, Fleet and Carman are included in the teams. In recent years the teams have been made up of players from outside the village community.

The club merged with the Cricket Club in 1975 to form Christleton Sports Club with new grounds and facilities at Little Heath.

Successes during the 1980s include winning the Pike Cup and the Chester Senior Cup in 1981–82; the Chester Senior Cup again in 1982–83; and in 1987–88 the prestigious Tetley Walker Top Club/Team Award for excellent grounds and facilities and for being the most sporting team. During the 1990s the club again achieved regular success, winning four consecutive Chester Senior Cups. Their team manager was Mark Worrall, a former Christleton resident, whose father had played for the club in the 1930s. Brian Carman followed as manager and gained greater success. In the 1995–96 season the team won the Bill Weight Trophy, the Malpas Knockout Tournament, the Chester Senior Cup, and the Cheshire Amateur Cup. They later represented Cheshire in the Northern Counties Championship, narrowly losing 2-1 to the Northumberland side at Morpeth near Newcastle.

The success of the club will continue, especially if the junior teams continue to develop. The junior team, originally made up mainly of boys from Christleton High School, won the League and Cup double in 1995–96 and are now providing a steady stream of players for the senior teams. After 103 years, Christleton Football Club continues to go from strength to strength.

Cricket Club

Rector Lionel Garnett formed the Cricket Club during the 1870s and matches were played on the Lawn at the back of the rectory. The High School building now stands on this land, with the old chestnut tree, overlooking the main hall, on the boundary edge. The wicket was guarded by a small fence to prevent damage from the animals grazing the field. The outfield was uneven with the additional hindrances of meadow flowers and cowpats. Canon Garnett was a very capable cricketer. He held the side together, regularly making the top score and sharing in the wicket taking. During the 1876 match against Tarporley Christleton won easily, scoring 146 runs and dismissing Tarporley twice for 73 and 42 runs. Canon Garnett scored 54 runs and his brother 44; the Rector also took four wickets, his brother Captain Garnett seven, and Mr E Jones eight during the match. Mr Jones and Lionel Garnett were the opening batsmen. Sam Earlam was the only other Christleton player mentioned on the scorecard with 8 runs. At times as many as five members of the Garnett family turned out for the village team, and on one occasion the village XI played against a team of Garnetts. Matches were usually played against local village sides, such as Tattenhall, Waverton, Malpas and Calveley. Christleton usually won their matches and, in 1879, won six out of eight played, with similar results in 1881. The Rector was a true sportsman, always content at the end of a season to step aside and let a lesser player win the Best Cricketer of the Season award. In the 1877 season he scored 249 runs, the next highest scorer managed 93 runs.

The club continued to prosper under the leadership of the Rector, and W G Grace is reputed to have played on the ground, although no conclusive evidence can be found. Lionel Garnett was well-connected enough to invite him and it is possible that the event took place. The death of Lionel Garnett followed by the First World War saw an end to the club's activities for many years. The war clearly took a toll of the younger men, for there is no record of the club until 1934.

The Cricket Club was revived in July 1934 'for the benefit of the village.' A season subscription was 4s for an adult, 2s 6d for the under-18s and 1s the under-16s. They continued to play in the Rectory Field, owned at that time by Major Porritt. The wicket was still on the old square and the protective barbed-wire fence had remained. The players included Geoff Johnson, Jack Selby, Les Basnett, Tony Addis and the Carman and Bennion brothers, under the captaincy of Boys' School headteacher, Tom Solloway. The teams shared a small shed as a pavilion, taking it in turns to change. Mr and Mrs Bill Price, who lived at nearby Smithy Cottage, provided teas between 4.30 and 5.00 pm at the boundary edge. Frank Fleet, the blacksmith, played for the team and often entertained the teams with tunes on his violin. The club continued playing there until the Second World War.

There was an attempt in 1946 to restart sporting activities in the village under the auspices of the Men's Institute; all football and cricket matches were played at Little Heath, but the teams would change at the Institute. At about the same time, there was a move by the Rector, A A Guest-Williams, and the Parish Council to establish a village playing field on a site owned by Mr Philip Hunter. This was successful and it was named the King George V Playing Field. The Cricket Club immediately started to prepare the ground for cricket and erected a small railway shed as a pavilion. However, it was so small that the cricket teas had to be served in a nearby tent. Matches soon took place on the new playing field and the club continued to use these basic facilities until 1958, when they decided to build a new pavilion. A report in the *Chester Courant* by Christleton journalist Ralph Houdley gives an insight into their work.

'It can hardly be termed elaborate, but it has the merit of being thoroughly utilitarian, and adequate for its purpose. On a solid concrete base has been erected a building 24ft in length with a covered veranda in front. The corrugated iron walls are to be lined with hardboard, and when painted the club will have a pavilion of which they are proud.

The pavilion provides sufficient accommodation for both teams to sit down for tea, and there is a kitchen equipped with calor gas for the ladies to provide refreshments. Mr Hunter has also kindly and generously arranged for water to be piped from one of his nearby cottages. The cost of the new pavilion is £100 raised by whist drives and rummage sales. The labour was provided by the members themselves under the direction of Mr Arthur Broster of Littleton. He himself a skilled man, employed by Mr Herbert Witter a local builder. Christleton Cricket Club are to be congratulated on their enterprise and also for the beautiful condition of the playing fields. I shudder to think what conditions would be like if it were not for the care of the ground by the club. They have a good wicket and a well mown outfield thanks to Tommy Addis.'

Christleton Cricket Club, circa 1950 Back row l to r: Peter Eardley, Gordon Price, Bill Fleet, Martin Wheeler, Ted Kirk (Captain), Brian Denton and Sid Dandy   Front row l to r: Alf Owen, Mike Reed, K Andrews, Tony Gulliver and Marion Kirk

The leading players at this stage of the club's development were: Ted Kirk (Captain), Peter Eardley, Gordon Price, Bill Fleet, Martin Wheeler, Brian Denton, Sid Dandy, Alf Owen, Mike Reed, K Andrews and Tony Gulliver. The scorer was Marion Kirk and Cliff Boddy was treasurer. They played a fixture list of more than 20 matches each season against teams in Cheshire and North Wales, and they played in the Boughton Hall and Tattenhall Knockout Cup Competitions. They fielded a 1st XI and a Sunday XI, but there was great opposition from within the village to them playing at Little Heath on Sundays. This soon abated and matches for a 2nd X1 were added in 1960. Frank Poston, the well-known village character, apparently captained the 2nd X1 around this time, and there are plenty of stories about him offering the team transport to away matches in his coal lorry. It has been reported that they did not play very good cricket but had a great time.

In the early 1970s enthusiastic cricketer, Gordon Williams, joined the club and brought with him his son Richard. Richard played for the second team when only 14 years of age and soon afterwards was included in the 1st X1, even after playing in a morning match for his school in Ellesmere Port. He was a hard-hitting batsman who regularly hit big scores. Cricket became headline news in the village. His displays soon brought him to the attention of the first-class game, and he joined Northamptonshire County Cricket Club straight from school. He played for Young England and the Marylebone Cricket Club, although he never quite made the England team. His career lasted more than 20 seasons, the highlights of which were scoring a century against the West Indies and a career best of 175 against Leicestershire. He obtained a hat trick bowling against Gloucestershire.

The increasing demand for space on the Little Heath playing field and the expanding membership fuelled the desire for a new ground. The club set about raising funds for a new ground and pavilion, and with support from the Football Club, a joint Sports Club was formed. With support from the Parish Council, a bid was made to the Lords' Taverners and the Sports Council for help with funding. The members of the Sports Club provided all the labour for the construction of the new pavilion, as well as for the preparation and maintenance of the new fields. The new ground was ready in time for the 1975–76 cricket season and was officially opened by David Steele, MBE, the Northamptonshire and England batsman and spin bowler. This field, on the eastern end of the King George V Playing Field and surrounded by oak saplings, remains an attractive village amenity.

Gordon Price captained the cricket team during the 1970s and 1980s, supported by such figures as Gordon Williams, Sid, Terry and Richard Dandy, and Ted and Richard Kirk. Jim Partington captained the 2nd X1 and the opposition included teams from Weaverham, Runcorn, Alvanley, ICI Widnes, and Bowden Vale.

There were many memorable matches played, including several in the National Village Knockout Competition. A match was played against a Northamptonshire XI in the early 1990s to celebrate Richard Williams' benefit. Christleton CC has always been a great supporter of junior cricket, allowing Chester and Cheshire Schools' matches to be played there. In 1999 the club were runners up in both 1st and 2nd XI team competitions and they won the aggregate Trophy for the Mellor Braggins Cheshire Cricket League for the second time in their history. They now play fixtures at places like Prestbury, Holmes Chapel, Weaverham, Mere and Bowden. They are continually trying to upgrade their ground and playing facilities at Little Heath. The current President is Jim Partington and their Chairman is Gareth Davies. The 1st XI Captain is Guy Newell and Richard Dandy captains the 2nd XI.

1st Christleton Scouts

As in many other villages around Chester during the First World War, it is believed that the boys of Christleton formed patrols and carried on the business of scouting without any adult leadership. Such groups were not, however, registered with the Scout Association in London. The 1st Christleton Scout troop was formed by Mr Fred Taylor, an architect, who lived at Berwyn View, Littleton. The troop was registered on 30th September 1921 and given the number 8750. At first there were 31 Scouts and they met on Friday evenings in the Girls' School. In 1923 Mr J Baden Bramall, one of the assistants, took over the leadership. The Cub Pack was formed on 25th November 1925; there were 12 boys and the first Akela was Mrs Annie Tarbuck from Rowton. At the same time her husband Richard Tarbuck, a retired Police Inspector from the Liverpool Force, became the Scout Leader-in-Charge (i/c) and took over the running of the Scout troop.

The Cubs and the Scouts continued to meet in the Girls' School until Major Townsend-Currie, who was the District Commissioner, gave the group a piece of land opposite the Trooper Inn. The Scouts then set about raising the necessary funds to build a headquarters on the site. They held concerts, dances, jumble sales, coffee mornings and they invited public subscriptions. Colonel Thompson CBE, JP, who was the District Commissioner for the Chester District, officially opened the completed 1st Christleton Scout Headquarters on Saturday 26th February 1927. Christleton has the distinction of being the first Scout group in the area to build its own headquarters.

Mr and Mrs Tarbuck retired from the group in December 1941. They were publicly thanked for their long and devoted service and were elected Honorary Scoutmasters in the Chester District. Mr Tarbuck was succeeded as Scout Leader i/c and later as Group Scout Leader (GSL) by Miss H M Smith, who was then Assistant Cubmaster. She remained with the group for a further 33 years and even after her retirement continued to help. Under her guidance the group grew and was very active, attracting boys from Christleton and other local villages. Miss Smith lived at the end of a lane at the bottom of Rowton Bridge Lane, which the Scouts referred to as *Skip's Lane*. In 1975 the Parish Council agreed that this should be its official name, and Skip's Lane is her permanent memorial.

In the early 1960s a larger building was needed to meet the demands of the growing group, and the fundraising exercises of the 1920s were repeated. The original hut was taken down and sold to the Kelsall Scouts where it is still in use. Lord Rochester, the President of the Cheshire Scouts, opened the new headquarters on 22nd June 1963.

The group has been served by many hardworking leaders. The Scout Association, in recognition of their dedicated service over many years, awarded Miss Smith, Miss D Rylance and Mrs E J Luxton the Silver Acorn and Medals of Merit.

The group neckerchief is red with a brown border and, although an *open* group, it has always had close connections with Christleton Church, where the old flags are kept. Many of the group's activities have been recorded in the parish magazine. During the latter half of the 20th century, eight boys have been selected to represent the Chester District at World Scout Jamborees and 18 have achieved the distinction of becoming Queen's Scouts.

The group in 1999 consisted of Venture Scouts (the Hatchmere Unit), Scouts, and Cub and Beaver Scouts. They are led by GSL, Mr N Onslow-Macaulay, and his Deputy GSL, Mr K Harding.

Scouting activities

In 1925 the Chester Scouts were involved in a road traffic census on all the roads leading into the city. The Christleton Scouts manned a post on the Whitchurch Road (A41) and recorded all the traffic going in and out of the city over a period of 24 hours. The exercise came to three conclusions: first that horse traffic was extinct; secondly, that there was a need for wider roads; and thirdly, that there was a surprising increase in the number of women drivers.

The first Cheshire (West) County Scout Rally was held, also in 1925, on the fields behind Christleton Hall during the weekend of 30th May–1st June. There were about 2500 Scouts and Rover Scouts from Birkenhead, Wirral, Runcorn, Frodsham, Northwich, Crewe and Chester in camp and the Camp Commandant was Major Townsend-Currie. The Boys' School was converted into a temporary hospital, which was manned by a local doctor and the British Red Cross Society. On Sunday morning all the Scouts marched to the Roodee in Chester to participate in a service taken by the Bishop of Chester. It is estimated that the congregation numbered 5,000 people, including the Lord Lieutenant of Cheshire.

During the Whitsun weekend in 1928 the Founder and Chief Scout, Lord Baden-Powell, visited a Cheshire Scout Rally being held at Eaton Park. Lord Baden-Powell arrived in Chester on Friday and was accompanied to Christleton by an escort of Scout cyclists. The 1st Christleton Scouts provided a guard of honour along both sides of the driveway to The Old Hall where Baden-Powell was staying as the guest of Major Townsend-Currie. (Major Townsend-Currie had been assistant District Commissioner for Scouts in the Chester District from 1920–1927 and he became District Commissioner in 1928, a post he held for 3 years.) A telephone was installed in case the Chief Scout needed to be contacted. Residents on the route in the village who had bunting or flags were asked to display it. The local employers were asked to release Scouts from work to enable them to attend, and it seems that the younger children were allowed out of school to watch the proceedings. Lord Baden-Powell went to Eaton Park the following day after inspecting the newly opened 1st Christleton Scout Hut.

Guiding In Christleton

Guiding in Christleton started in 1958 with the formation of the 1st Christleton Brownies. They met in the school hut at High Walls where they

Christleton Scouts and Guides in the 1950s

enjoyed many activities, especially in the garden and the surrounding countryside. As the Brownies became older demand grew for a Guide company, and the 1st Christleton Guide Company was formed in 1959, meeting at the Scout Hut on Whitchurch Road. Soon there were waiting lists for both Brownies and Guides, leading to the formation of the 2nd Christleton Brownies in 1974 and the 2nd Christleton Guides in 1976. Over the years numbers have fluctuated and at the moment (1999) there is one Guide Company and two Brownie Packs.

Both Guides and Brownies have been involved in village affairs. The Brownies used to organise the Bran Tub at the Church Christmas Fair and helped to organise the Fancy Dress Competition at the village Fete. They still take part in the Fete parade through the village.

The Guides have offered service to the community in many ways at different times, their main efforts being: running a stall at the Christmas Fair; organising a crèche and manning a left-luggage office at the Fete; carol singing for charity; bellringing; keeping the footpath alongside the church and graveyard free of litter; and helping in the project researching into the age of the oak trees in the village. The Guides have always been fond of outdoor activities and camping and are grateful to local farmers who have allowed them to use their land for practice camps. For three years running they won the Sherlock Shield for life-saving. One Guide won the North-West Regional Finals in the National Tennis Tournament and played in the finals at the Queen's Club in London.

Duty to God is an important part of Guide training and both Guides and Brownies take part in occasional services at both St James' Church and the Methodist Chapel.

Looking further afield, the Guides and Brownies have attended many county events, the most memorable of which was the County Rally held on the Oval at Port Sunlight in May 1966 when Lady Baden-Powell was present. In addition, in 1985 the Guides attended a Service of Thanksgiving and Dedication in Chester Cathedral addressed by the Bishop of Chester, the Right Reverend Michael Baughan, to commemorate 75 years of Guiding. The Guides also joined in an International Camp at Bolesworth Castle in July and August 1993 where there were many foreign visitors. This was a wonderful opportunity for the Guides to realise that Guiding really is a worldwide fellowship. The weather was kind and the organisation perfect, so everyone had lots of fun and brought home many happy memories. During the 1980s and early 1990s there was a strong Ranger Guide Unit in Christleton. These girls in their late teens, although overseen by adults, organised themselves most of the time and participated in many adventurous activities including camping. Much of this was linked to the Duke of Edinburgh's Award Scheme. They also helped at ceremonial occasions, forming many a Guard of Honour and were a great help at camps and holidays for the younger girls; two or three Rangers went to help at camps that were run especially for handicapped Guides.

On the 75th Anniversary of Guiding a lighted torch was taken all around the county. The Rangers made a chariot and ran to Chester to fetch the Light, which they then took to each unit in Christleton and Waverton. Several of the girls were given the opportunity to go abroad to represent Great Britain at International Scout and Guide Camps in Europe and America. Numbers went down, however, during the 1990s and eventually the unit closed. More girls were going to university and college, and others found being a Young Leader more fulfilling, helping with Rainbow, Brownie and Guide units. The nearest Rainbow unit is in Rowton. It is hoped that these girls will be the adult leaders of the future. Guide Companies and Brownie Packs have had to close nationwide through lack of leaders. Christleton has been fortunate to have several dedicated Guiders over the years, and some of the older Guides have joined with Waverton Guides on a leadership course.

Guiding has flourished in Christleton in the past, it is flourishing now, and it is hoped that it will continue to flourish in the future.

Guiding in Christleton in January 2000

For 7–10+ years, the 1st Christleton Brownies started in 1958, later closed, but reopened in 1995, and they currently meet on Mondays 6.15–7.45 pm in the Parish Hall. The 2nd Christleton Brownies started in 1974 and has just celebrated 25 years of continuous meetings; they meet on Thursdays 6.15–7.45 pm in the Methodist Church Schoolroom.

For 10+–14 years, the 1st Christleton Guides, began in 1959, and the 2nd Christleton Guides, who began in 1975, currently meet on Mondays 7–8.30pm at the Scout Hut, Whitchurch Road.

For girls aged 14+–18, there used to be a Ranger Unit in the 1980s and early 1990s. Now the older girls belong either to Brown Heath District Young Leaders group, which meets monthly in Waverton, or the Vicar's Cross Seniors, meeting fortnightly in Vicar's Cross.

A Trefoil Guild was formed in 1975 for retired Guiders.

Christleton Fetes

There are several references to fairs being held in Christleton when the marlers were in the village to dig marl (clay) from the village pits. This used to happen about every four years, and they would spend their evenings in the local inns where they would amuse the villagers with their traditional songs and dances. At some of the fairs in the village bull-baiting and cock-fighting were reported to have taken place, and pink and white striped candy was for sale. The fairs were held on Phoenix Park, which appears to have been adjacent to the Green or a name given to the Green itself.

There were celebrations every St James' Day and there are many reported occasions of Parish Teas being provided for the older citizens. There is also a sorry tale in the November 1888 magazine when Canon Garnett regrets that there had been four weddings in the previous month. He complained, 'No wonder the Ringers want new bell-ropes. And probably Mr Johnson has had to renew his stock of rice. But I do hope we shall not see again a beer barrel on the Village Green. It is a very false kindness to give away beer in such reckless fashion as to make little boys drunk and set grown men fighting. I am sure that the public opinion of the village is against this sort of thing, so I say no more about it.'

The first Village Fete was originally only meant to happen once in 1875 to raise money for the new church. However, subsequent Fetes were again held to raise money for the running of the schools. Although parents contributed a penny a week towards their child's schooling, the Fetes were the main source of regular funds, providing money for the running costs, teachers' salaries, books and equipment. The early Fetes were called A Grand Bazaar and Garden Party, and were held at the former Rectory on Village Road. They were sometimes sponsored by Lever Brothers of Port Sunlight and often attended by the Duke or Duchess of Westminster. Prizes included money, soaps, washing powder and tobacco.

The Fetes continued occasionally after that but seem to have become fully established by 1905. The Fetes were traditionally held in the grounds of the former Rectory, but were also held at The Old Hall, the Morris Field, Mr Cullimore's grounds, at the High School, and from 1978 at the Primary School. In 2000 a special Fete and Pageant will take place in the walled garden and grounds of Christleton Hall. The Fete committee is an ad hoc group representing all sections of village life. The members meet throughout the winter to plan the event, which is always held on the last Saturday in June. A different chairman is chosen each year and a theme is decided; the committee, stallholders and children in the fancy dress competition are encouraged to dress up in relation to the theme. One memorable occasion was provided by the Tudor theme in 1981. The Rose Queen and retinue are chosen by the Fete committee in early March, and each year a new style of dress is chosen by the parents of the children involved to give new colour and shape to the proceedings.

Janet Brown, Village Rose Queen in 1959

A Grand Bazaar and Garden Party

in aid of the Parish Schools

......will be held at......

Christleton Rectory

on Thursday, August 1st 1901.

The Bazaar will be opened by The

Countess Grosvenor

at 2.30 p.m

Dairy Stall	Tea and Refreshments
Miss Oft, Mrs Walley, Mrs Mosford	Miss Butler, Mrs Okell, Mrs Dodd
Fancy Stall	Fancy Stall
Mrs Garnett, Mrs Fleming, Mrs Hickey	Mrs Ambrose Dixon, Mrs Rolt, Mrs Giles
Pottery, Baskets, Flowers, Plants	Needlework
Mrs Roberts, Mrs Cullimore, Miss Macfie, The Misses Day	Mrs Earlam, Miss Phillips, Miss Lunt, Miss Taylor

Managerie Race.
Shooting Gallery. Sunlight Washing Competitions.
Hat Trimming Competitions for Men. Bran Pies.
Band and Dancing
Admission till 5.p.m., 1s...... Afterwards, 6d.
**Wagonettes will run to Christleton throughout the day from the Bars, Boughton.
Prizes are offered by Messrs. Lever Brothers Limited, Port Sunlight, Cheshire**

A typical programme for an early village Fete

On Fete Day everyone gathers around the Green and, led by the Band, the retiring Rose Queen heads the procession through to the venue where the arena has been prepared and stalls made ready. She is followed by the new Rose Queen, maypole dancers, children in the fancy dress parade, Scouts, Guides and other village organisations through the village and onto the field. The Fete programme varies each year with different attractions to entertain the large crowd that always gathers. However, there are always some traditional activities, such as the Crowning Ceremony of the new Rose Queen, the fancy dress parade, Punch & Judy, bouncy castle, Primary School maypole display, and the Scouts' barbecue. The proceeds each year go to the local charities decided by the Fete committee. Almost every village organisation has benefitted from this generosity over the years. The Chairman for the 2000 Fete is Steve Henson.

Christleton Village Shows

In 1871 an Annual Show of Cheese, Brood Mares, Foals, Horse Leaping and Turnouts was held on the Rectory field and seems to have been a well-organised event. This successful show was open to the residents of the Christleton Townships and the surrounding villages of Great Barrow, Guilden Sutton, Trafford, Picton, Upton, Wervin, Croughton, Plemstall, Tarvin, Stapleford, Hargrave, Huxley, Handley, Waverton, Saighton, Tattenhall, Huntington, Aldford, Hoole and Newton. The Honourable Secretary was Mr J

Christleton Playgroup dressed in their costumes at the Village Fete during the late 1980s

Terry Large giving a falconry display

H Salmon of Rowton and the vet was Mr James Storrar MRCVS. The committee also included Mr Beech, Sam Earlam (headteacher), Mr Heywood, Mr Lunt, Colonel Logan, and Mr H Witter; many of these families are well-known in the village today.

This agricultural show was the highlight of the village summer, and after being held for some years in the Morris field near Christleton Hall and the Rectory grounds, it transferred to a field along Birch Heath Lane and later to a field at Little Heath. A big marquee used to be erected to hold the displays of flowers, produce and cheese.

The first Fruit and Flower Show in Christleton was held in 1872, after which it was decided to hold one every September. There is no doubt that the instigator was Lionel Garnett, who had arrived in the village four years earlier and who was responsible for the revival of various festivals and shows to encourage people to show pride in their village. In the parish magazine of 1875, Lionel Garnett paints a picture of a self-contained community with its traditional activities and home-grown entertainment. One feature was the Parish Tea held every January, which was attended by 200 parishioners. Tickets were sold from Mr Johnson's shop and the school, and the tea began at 5.30 pm in the Boys' School. The entertainment included the choir, handbell ringers, solos, duets and trios in song, recitations and piano recitals. However, the major event was the Annual Fruit and Flower Show. One reference in the parish magazine informed the village that Rule 1 was to be changed. In future, 'all articles for contribution arriving after 11 o clock on the morning of Show day will be disqualified.' Another magazine article made a plea for more entries. 'Don't be afraid of entering. We have heard many on show day express their regret at not having entered and their confidence that they

Christleton Show in the early 1900s

had stuff at home fully equal to that exhibited.' A new event, a Rose Show, was introduced during 1876 to raise funds for the new church building. It took place on Sunday afternoon, 25th July, after the St James' Day Festival Service. 'The show was deemed a great success, indeed judges were perfectly astonished with symmetry and general healthiness of the exhibits.' In Class 1 the competition was open to all and cash prizes of £1, 15s and 10s were awarded. In Class 2 the competition was open to all cottagers paying less than £10 rent per annum, and smaller cash prizes were awarded to the winners. Class 3 was an open class for roses. In Class 4 the prize for the best bouquet was won by Mrs Lucy Anne Ince of Christleton Hall, who also won the class for an épergne dressed with flowers. The Band of the 1st Royal Cheshire Militia played for dancing until dusk, and there was a large, well-patronised tea tent. This show was held in the Morris field (between Christleton Hall and Butler's Mill, adjacent to the old quarry. Lionel Garnett had put up a *No Smoking* sign at the entrance to the exhibit tent. 'The sweet smell of flowers is much marred by frequent puffs of tobacco smoke. I would recommend those parties who are so much wedded to the fragrant weed to cultivate the taste in another form, and grow for the next show the *Nicotiana*, which sends up a sweet and pretty white flower and is easily grown.'

Another event was arranged later that year also to raise funds for the rebuilding of the church. A Grand Fete took place on Bank Holiday Monday, 7th August, and the competitions included athletic sports, pigeon shooting, archery, skittles, Aunt Sally and quoits. The Band of the 1st Royal Cheshire Militia again played for the dancing.

Admission was 1s to the Rose Show of 1882. The cost of the teas was also 1s. Transport to the show was organised by a Mrs Barnes, who ran the Favourite Omnibus and Brakes from the Bars in Chester to Christleton every hour beginning at 2 pm. The fare was 4d each.

The following year, a bee tent was introduced to the Show in 1883 and a new category of farm produce in 1891. In 1893 a new rule gave the committee the power to inspect the gardens of the intending exhibitors, but no reason was given.

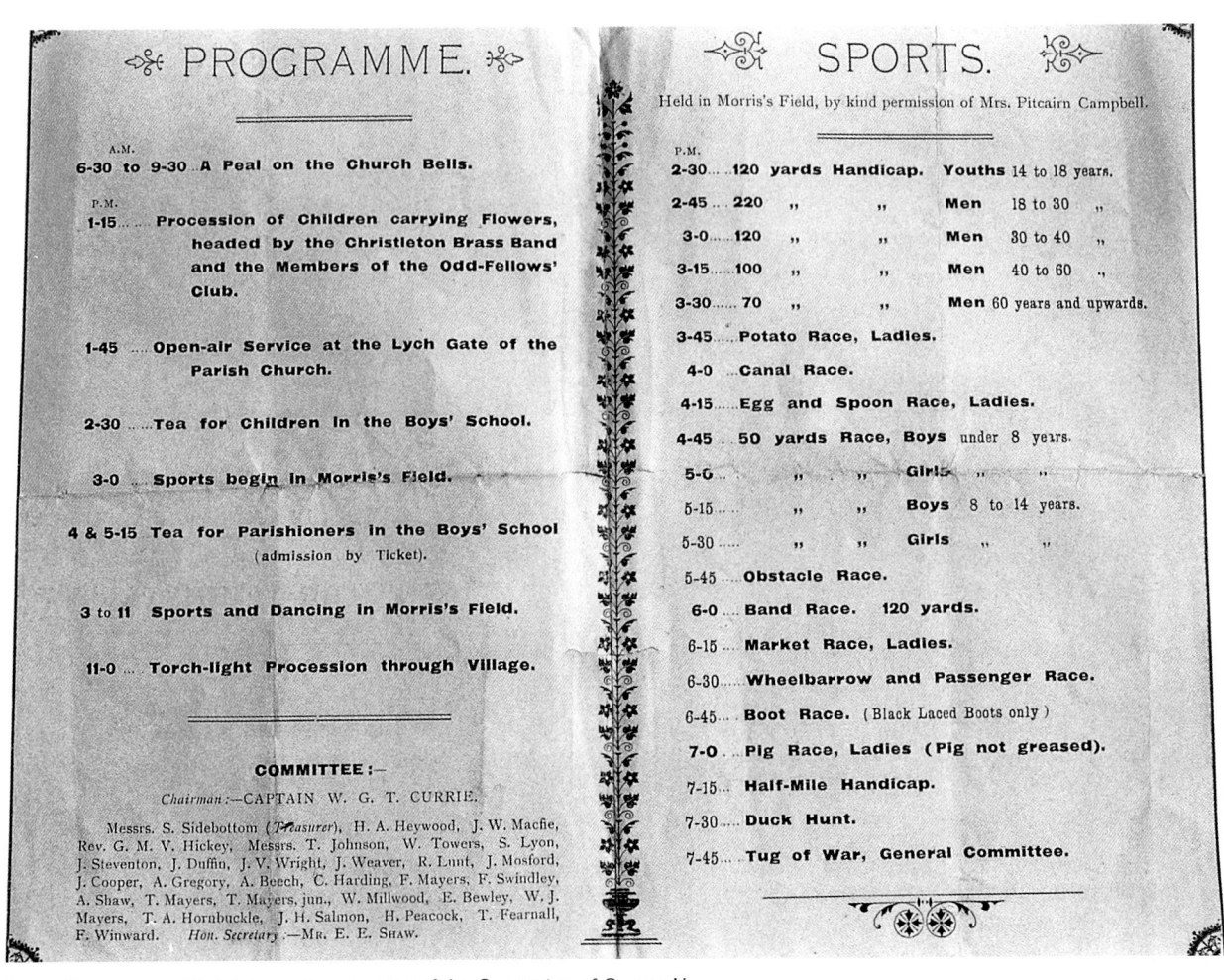

PROGRAMME.

A.M.
6-30 to 9-30 ..A Peal on the Church Bells.

P.M.
1-15 ... Procession of Children carrying Flowers, headed by the Christleton Brass Band and the Members of the Odd-Fellows' Club.

1-45 ... Open-air Service at the Lych Gate of the Parish Church.

2-30 .....Tea for Children in the Boys' School.

3-0 ... Sports begin in Morris's Field.

4 & 5-15 Tea for Parishioners in the Boys' School (admission by Ticket).

3 to 11 Sports and Dancing in Morris's Field.

11-0 ... Torch-light Procession through Village.

COMMITTEE :—
Chairman :—CAPTAIN W. G. T. CURRIE.

Messrs. S. Sidebottom (*Treasurer*), H. A. Heywood, J. W. Macfie, Rev. G. M. V. Hickey, Messrs. T. Johnson, W. Towers, S. Lyon, J. Steventon, J. Duffin, J. V. Wright, J. Weaver, R. Lunt, J. Mosford, J. Cooper, A. Gregory, A. Beech, C. Harding, F. Mayers, F. Swindley, A. Shaw, T. Mayers, T. Mayers, jun., W. Millwood, E. Bewley, W. J. Mayers, T. A. Hornbuckle, J. H. Salmon, H. Peacock, T. Fearnall, F. Winward. Hon. Secretary :—MR. E. E. SHAW.

SPORTS.

Held in Morris's Field, by kind permission of Mrs. Pitcairn Campbell.

P.M.
2-30....120 yards Handicap. Youths 14 to 18 years.
2-45 .. 220 ,, ,, Men 18 to 30 ,,
3-0....120 ,, ,, Men 30 to 40 ,,
3-15.....100 ,, ,, Men 40 to 60 ,,
3-30...... 70 ,, ,, Men 60 years and upwards.
3-45....Potato Race, Ladies.
4-0 ..Canal Race.
4-15.....Egg and Spoon Race, Ladies.
4-45 . 50 yards Race, Boys under 8 years.
5-0 .. ,, ,, Girls ,, ,,
5-15 .... ,, ,, Boys 8 to 14 years.
5-30 ..... ,, ,, Girls ,, ,,
5-45 ....Obstacle Race.
6-0 ... Band Race. 120 yards.
6-15 ... Market Race, Ladies.
6-30.....Wheelbarrow and Passenger Race.
6-45 ... Boot Race. (Black Laced Boots only)
7-0 ... Pig Race, Ladies (Pig not greased).
7-15... Half-Mile Handicap.
7-30....Duck Hunt.
7-45 ... Tug of War, General Committee.

Sports Programme, 1911 held on the occasion of the Coronation of George V

Christleton Tennis Club in the 1920s

By August 1904 the Show was fully established in the village calendar, and although 'drowned' by the weather, provided a variety of competitions to enter: washing (men), nail-driving (ladies), hat trimming, decorated perambulators and blindfold pictures. In 1925 it seems that the W I was organising the Show and serious disagreements arose over the distribution of the profits. The Rector, Mr Hickey, fell out with them over their running of a number of affairs, including the Show, and in the parish magazine he expressed the sentiment, 'it is not easy to argue with a body of women.'

After coming to a halt during the war years, the Show was revived on Bank Holiday Monday, 7th August 1946, at Littleton Old Hall, with all proceeds in aid of the building fund of the British Legion Christleton Branch. It was directed by Philip Hunter and John Kirk was the chairman, and a profit of £945 13s 9d was made. The total prize money on offer was more than £250. The Show continued for three more years on this site, but it seems to have folded in the early 1950s with the demise of farming as the main occupation in the village. Several years ago Christleton Parish Council, in association with Littleton and Rowton Parish Councils, decided to revive the Show in its present form. The Show continues to go from strength to strength and is now a focal point of village life each July. With emphasis given to arts and crafts as well as the display of locally-grown flowers and produce, the show enables many people to display their individual skills and creative talent.

A new competitive class for decorative hanging baskets was introduced in 1998 and it was hoped that both local businesses and individuals would enter. The committee wished to encourage people to display flowers and decorate their houses to make the village a real *Ville Fleurie* in preparation for a village floral display during Millennium year. As part of this development the committee sponsored and placed new hanging baskets around the village Pump House. 1999 also saw the introduction of a Garden Trail around 12 village gardens of all shapes and sizes, which raised a considerable sum of money for the National Children's Homes. In 2000 two new classes were added: designing a village website and designing and making a scarecrow.

Chester Flower Club

Chester Flower Club was formed 42 years ago and is affiliated to the Cheshire area of the National Association of Flower Arrangement Societies. The aim of the club is to encourage the love of plant material and to demonstrate their decorative value. The members support many causes and charities by organising exhibitions and competitions and they also encourage the conservation of rare species and plants.

The Flower Club meets at the Parish Hall, Christleton on the third Wednesday afternoon of the month except August and December, at which experts give flower demonstrations. The members visit shows and festivals to expand their gardening interests. During the years the club has arranged flowers at Chester Town Hall, Chester Cathedral, Westminster Abbey, the Cheshire Show and the Royal Horticultural Society Shows in London and Cheshire, as well as flowers in local churches. New members are welcome and during the Millennium year the members of Chester Flower Club are proud to be involved with the flower displays at St James' Church, Christleton during the Millennium Festival in July.

The Pit Group

In 1988 the Pit Group was formed under the chairmanship of John Salter; the other committee members were Eric Kenyon, Ian Gorst, Derek Bell, Tony Gardner, Phil Haywood, Gerry Crees, Charles Smeatham and David Cummings. The first working parties met in October that year with the intention of ensuring that the Pit was restored for the future enjoyment of the village community. The Parish Council offered financial and practical support.

Plans for the long-term future of the Pit were drawn up, based on the limited knowledge that had been acquired over the years. Advice was sought from organisations such as the Conservation Trusts and the then Nature Conservancy Council, but no-one had tackled such a large area of water (more than two acres). One of the committee's first resolutions was to decide what the problem really was. Did the geology of the area affect the water level? Could an additional source of water be obtained from nearby? Geoff Clifton of Gifford & Partners offered his company's services to provide a borehole survey that indicated the various depths of clay, silt and sand in the Pit area. From this the group devised their action plan.

The main aims of the group were: to clear areas of vegetation to enable a large water surface area to be seen by the public, and used by wildlife; to retain the area at the back of the Pit as a secluded wildlife reserve; to remove some of the accumulated silt and mud; to create a new and safe pond edge to prevent erosion and act as a natural barrier; and to create additional seating areas for the public.

Since then many other challenges have emerged, but the group has always kept to its basic principle that the Pit has to be a place of importance for wildlife and a valued amenity for the community. Since 1988 fishing and pond dipping platforms have been built, seating provided, a sandstone buffer built to prevent erosion of the banks, a silt trap installed to prevent surface oil from the road reaching the water and, more recently, a swans' nest site has been erected. All these objectives have been met, often using recycled materials including old telegraph poles, discarded kerbstones and slabs of unwanted paving stone. The team members have had to learn new skills but have always been enthusiastic and committed. Each year working parties are organised to clear or maintain certain aspects of the Pit, and all the improvements have helped to create a balance between the needs of the natural world and the community.

Many other members of the community have provided financial support, vehicles, tools and equipment. The Arden family regularly loans equipment, and help from the Dandy family of Littleton has also benefitted the project. Shell UK lent the group workshop space for the development of equipment, especially the *drag queen*, as well as loaning expensive cranes and lifting tackle. Shell also arranged the loan of an enormous crane from Ainscoughs that lifted complete trees out of the Pit. (Shell's contribution is recognised by the use of the company's logo on the top of the water depth posts at either side of the Pit.)

The *drag queen* was an ingenious device for dragging along the bottom of the pond, removing unwanted rhizomes and reeds without damaging the pond's base. It looked like a supermarket trolley mounted on a sledge, which was attached to a long hawser and towed through the water and pulled by

Children working at the Pit in the early 1980s

the long jib of a crane. This guided device was instrumental in clearing the heavy matting of material that had accumulated in the central area of the Pit between 1976 and 1986. The material was removed by boat and canoe and taken to the side of the Pit from where it was taken away and deposited on areas of farmland or burned.

When the conservation work started the group received little advice and, perhaps in hindsight, did some things that might have caused more harm than good. The removal of large stands of bulrush combined with the introduction (unknown to the group at the time) of fluoridated tap water killed off virtually the whole community of plants and thousands of pond creatures. This created a beautiful pond but it was devoid of important elements, such as the plants vital for the growth of insects and home to many aquatic creatures. Although there was little advice forthcoming from national organisations in the early days, thanks to the Heritage Ponds Project and research work at Oxford Brookes University, there is now a bank of knowledge available to pond rescuers in the future. The group also benefits from the skills and knowledge of committee member Eric Kenyon. Eric provides the drawings and plans and has been recognised as an expert in pond conservation by the Heritage Ponds Group. Future work will only be undertaken when absolutely necessary, so as not to disturb the pond, plant and wildlife community.

The Pit Project was nominated by Dr Andrew Hull of John Moores University, Liverpool as a Heritage Pond for the North of England for the Millennium Pond Project. This project has now achieved national status, and Christleton pond is one of 10 ponds chosen from across the nation to illustrate the conservation value of ponds to local communities. The strength of the Christleton Pit Project is that it is community based, receiving almost no outside assistance from bodies such as the World Wildlife Fund or English Nature. The illustrated plaque standing at the edge of the Pit was designed by Eric Kenyon to commemorate the event.

Millennium Group

The Christleton Millennium Group exists to help the whole community celebrate Millennium year. Events took place from Christmas 1999 and the build-up to the year change, and more events were planned for a three-week Millennium Festival during the summer. The project was funded by the group, together with a grant from the Millennium Commission's *Awards for All* scheme. These events celebrate the 2000th birthday of Christ and were led by Churches Together in Christleton and the Millennium Group. The main event of the summer Festival was the village Fete, incorporating an historical pageant that reflected life in the village during the last 2000 years.

The programme of activities included a Procession of Light and carols around the village Green; a village Millennium service with Churches Together in Christleton; the bellringers' national peal; a series of Lent lectures in the Parish Hall; a 1960s dance; the Beating of the Bounds walk; Fun Days at Rowton and Littleton; the Wednesday Group Millennium lunch; an Open Morning at Christleton Pit; an Exhibition of Talents at the Methodist Church; a Youth Pilgrimage by High School Students; a Celebration of Youth Music at St James' Church; the launch of the history books; guided trails around the church and village; and choral works at St James' including Vivaldi's *Gloria* and Fauré's *Requiem*; a Teddy Bears' Picnic for the youngest children; a Senior Citizens Street Party; a Christleton WI Open Evening; the Village Show and Garden Trail; an Open Morning at Christleton Primary School; an evening of music with the Dee & Alyn Gilbert and Sullivan Society; and a festival Songs of Praise at the Pit.

Legacies left for future generations will be: 50 oak trees planted around the village; a Millennium yew tree in the churchyard; a time capsule buried at the Primary School; a stained glass village window at St James' Church; children's play equipment at the Primary School; a village photographic album for the year together with a village diary; and various publications: *Christleton Pit, An Illustrated Village Trail, A Child's History of the Village* as well as this book.

A number of items were also provided for the developing world. These were a pump and equipment for a well for a village in Africa, and solar panels and water storage heaters for a family in Ghana and for St James' School, Shey in Ladakh.

The Millennium Group logo

7 Natural History

Christleton Pit

Early evidence of the Pit
The origins of the Pit at Little Heath date back to at least 1710 when Gerard Townsend, owner of The Old Hall, built 'a pond for fish', enlarging a pond on land belonging to the then Lord of the Manor, Sir Henry Harpur of Calke Abbey in Derbyshire. Evidence for this comes from a case at Chester Assizes in 1772 when Robert Townsend, Gerard's son, was prosecuted for not having paid tax to the Lord of the Manor of Christleton for the pond on his land. Robert was Recorder of Chester and it was an important court case with opinion being sought from lawyers nationwide, including Grey's Inn in London. The case was a very long drawn out affair, but it appears that Robert Townsend won the argument. The pond was on an area of common land that the people of Christleton had a right to use for grazing and watering their animals.

The geology
The area around Little Heath was the source of a number of minerals suitable for extraction, and used in many ways in village life. The village of Christleton is built on top of old red sandstone rock beds dating from about 300 million years ago, and there are several places in the village where this sandstone can be seen. The Old Surgery in Village Road is built directly onto the stone. The centre of Christleton is built on an island of sandstone projecting above a sea of clay and soft sand, which is very deep in many places.

During the last great ice age, glaciers covered the area and brought with them thousands of tons of boulder clay and debris of volcanic rocks from the Lake District and North Wales. The Cheshire Plain itself was carved out by these glaciers and evidence of this can be seen from any high point overlooking the area. The best place to see both boulder clay and the granite type erratic boulders is along the beach and on the cliffs at Thurstaston Country Park on the Wirral. However, most farmland in and around Christleton contains evidence of both deposits. The boulder clay now lies in various depths across the parish, and is best seen at Little Heath Pit.

In the early 1980s a borehole survey carried out at the Pit by engineers, Gifford & Partners, showed that typically the ground appears to be 1m of fill (silt and clay) over a thin lens of sand, below which is 1m of clay, and below that 75cm of dry sand all lying on top of the sandstone bedrock.

Extraction of minerals from the Pit
Villagers from early times used the sand for building, the gravel and rough stones for road making, the deep red clay to make bricks, and the grey clay (marl) as a soil conditioner and fertiliser.

The Pit at Little Heath
There were probably five or six pits at Little Heath. Several of these pits were very extensive, and others were used to dump rubbish that accumulated in the village. When the commercial activities ceased, the pits rapidly filled with water, and by 1890 there were two large areas of water connected by a causeway. Photographs taken around the turn of the 20th century show the Pit as being one large area of water surrounded on the east side by a line of trees.

Little Heath Pit, 1907–8

Water supply
The only source of water for the Pit comes from rainwater, and it has dried up on a number of occasions. In 1896 the minutes of the new Parish Council state, 'that the Pit has dried up and something needs to be done about it.' Yet by 1900 photographic evidence shows cows drinking water from a well-filled Pit and this has occurred at least four times during the 20th century. The last two dry

periods were in 1969 and 1975–6. Little Heath Pit depends on sufficient rainfall to keep it full. However, the larger the area of open water the more evaporation that takes place, and emergent plants with roots in the water, such as bulrush and yellow flag, absorb considerable quantities of water. A single willow tree can absorb 4000 litres of water per year through its roots, and there are about 40 willow trees in the pit. The removal of some of the trees and cutting down the branch growth from time to time has been quite successful in helping to retain a good water level. Long spells of warm weather also cause problems, and in a very sunny week in summer 5 cm of water can be evaporated by the sun and be soaked up through plants.

It seems logical to link changes in pond life to the quality of the water supply, but there are fears that the many ducks and the vast quantity of fish may have also been responsible for many of the changes. Since 1990 a new regime of plants tolerant to the changes have taken over the Pit. Amphibious bistort, a floating plant with a delicate pink flower and yellow flag iris have become the dominant plants and have grown in profusion. The submerged pondweed has not yet returned. In the several years since a leak in a water main was sealed, reeds and in particular the reed mace (typha), have begun to re-establish themselves and the water has taken on a murkier appearance typical of clay based ponds.

Fish
Roach, rudd, perch, tench, crucian and common carp can all be found in good numbers at the Pit and may derive from the earlier populations kept for food there. The recent release of a large orange fan tailed fish has crossed with a crucian carp, giving a new species of fish for the British Isles, one which appears to be able to breed much more quickly than native species. Fishing at the Pit is restricted to young people from the parish, who are allowed to fish from specially constructed platforms on the north side during the fishing season, so protecting the fish stocks but also ensuring the surrounding environment of the Pit is not damaged and can be used for other purposes by the local community.

Ponds in the landscape
Cheshire is still known as the pond capital of Britain with the highest density of ponds. In 1973 a botanical survey of Christleton by Barbara Redwood and Anthea Brian found that there were 181 ponds, a proportion of 14 ponds per square kilometre. These ponds, many of which are out of the public eye, remain as a rich habitat for wildlife. Pascale Nicolet, a Swiss student working for the Heritage Ponds Project, revisited many of the ponds in 1998 and concluded that 25% of Britain's wetland plant species can be found in the parish, a higher proportion than the national average.

Twenty-one ponds have been been lost since the 1973 survey, mostly to in-filling or drainage and two had been developed on. Fifty percent of the plant species found in the ponds in 1973 were present in 1998, whilst 90% of plant species in the parish were found in 1998. The major changes from 1973–1998 were: an increase in alien species (two to six species); a decline in conservation value; decline of some rare species; the loss of frogbit community, a pollution sensitive plant species; and a loss of pondweed community, particularly at the Pit. Pascale showed that changes in land use were the main cause of the loss of ponds between these years. There was a decline in grazed grassland, a decline of species needing grazing, for example frogbit, an increase in species intolerant of grazing, for example bulrush, and a decline of species sensitive to nutrient enrichment, such as pondweeds and frogbit. Her conclusion was that there are many high quality ponds, but everyone needs to work hard to protect the ones that remain for the benefit of both people and the countryside.

Wildlife
Ponds are a rich oasis for wildlife and play an important role in providing valuable breathing spaces. About 3,500 invertebrate species live in freshwater, over half of which can be found in ponds, and over 300 species of wetland plants can be found in and around Christleton ponds, including over half of Britain's rarest wetland species.

Ponds are packed with insects, the various species occurring in the many different zones around the water's edge, in the open water and on the muddy floor. Brightly coloured dragon and damselflies, which emerge on vegetation at the edge of a pit, can be seen hunting for caddisflies, mayflies and mosquitoes. On the surface film, pond skaters move jerkily around looking for aphids that have fallen onto the water. In the water great diving beetles, water boatmen and water scorpion hunt for their prey. On the muddy floor there are dragonfly nymphs, caddis fly larvae and several species of slimy black leeches.

Amphibians, including frogs, great crested newts, and toads rely on the ponds for breeding purposes, as do grass snakes and water voles. Christleton Pit and the surrounding land has a good population of newts, but frogs and toads are much less common than they used to be despite efforts to build up the population with the intake each spring of frogspawn from other village ponds. Ponds are also increasingly important for otters and water shrews, and at Christleton the pond and its surroundings are a vital source of building materials for the decreasing population of swallows and house martins, and a source of food for swifts and bats. It also provides a habitat for swans, ducks, coots, moorhens and visiting gulls, herons and cormorants. Many smaller birds benefit from the food supplies found in the vegetation and the trees surrounding the area. Native garden species such as robin, wren, dunnock, sparrow, song thrush, blue tit, great tit, long tail tit, coal tit, tree creeper, nuthatch, great spotted woodpecker, chaffinch, and goldfinch are joined by migrants like the chiff chaff, black cap, willow and garden warbler. The occasional tawny owl can also be spotted roosting there.

Christleton swans

There is a very long tradition of there being a family of swans at the Pit. However it is in more recent times that swans have been known to nest at the Pit. Photographs from the 1960s and early 1970s show the nest sited at the back of the Pit in an area of thick reeds and bulrush. However, following the illegal shooting of the female on the nest site in 1973, the male left the area and swans did not return to the nest site until the winter of 1989.

This followed the successful restoration of the Pit, and the return of a good water level. The pair of swans concerned were ringed as part of a national project and given the references 2SD

Swans at Christleton Pit, 1997

and 2SL. Over the next seven years they produced 49 eggs and successfully hatched 44 cygnets. After the death of the cob 2SL in 1996, a new pair VZN and TOV (a cygnet of the original pair) took over the territory and in the last three years have produced 22 eggs and hatched 20 cygnets. However their rate of cygnet loss after six months has been greater, because they have taken their cygnets to the canal when they have been between six and twenty days old. In 1997 they lost six of their seven cygnets, five of these were probably due to predation by mink. The swans have brought great pleasure to people over the years, but everyone is disappointed to see them leave the Pit after such a short time.

The majority of the cygnets have been ringed over the years by members of the Cheshire Swan Study Group, and because of this, many sightings and recoveries of the birds have been made and their progress plotted throughout the country. In the early 1990s most of the birds seem to have flown south, following the canal system and the river Severn, before being seen in Kidderminster and Gloucester. They have also been seen visiting the Dee at Farndon and the lake at Ellesmere. In recent years cygnets have flown along the Dee and Welsh coast to Rhyl Marine Lake, Conway, Bangor, the Menai Straits and Caernarvon. In 1997 there were three Christleton cygnets on the Menai Straits at the same time. Other birds have been seen in Warrington, Widnes, and Southport.

Hockenhull Platts Nature Reserve

This unique piece of our countryside has been managed as a nature reserve by the Cheshire Wildlife Trust since the early 1970s. The area, which is part of the Grosvenor Estate, has been actively farmed for centuries. When the Cheshire Conservation Trust first became interested in the area as a nature reserve, the Greenway Family farmed it. Mr Greenway made a verbal agreement with the Trust for it to manage about 11 acres of the area adjacent to the River Gowy. However when he retired, the farm reverted to the day-to-day management by the Grosvenor Estate, and a formal agreement was then drawn up with their land agent for the management of the reserve. The construction of a storage reservoir in the early 1990s, on land to the south of the farm buildings, has been a great boost to the wildlife and the area is now regularly visited by a wide variety of ducks, swans, geese and other wildfowl. Water is extracted from the Gowy in winter and used on the land during spring and summer. The National Rivers Authority also clears vegetation from the river each autumn to enable the Gowy to flow freely and prevent flooding. In 1996 the NRA was invited to assist the Trust, by sponsoring the construction of an artificial otter holt on the northern side of the reserve area, which it is hoped will help attract otters back to the river. The digging of the holt and construction of the internal chambers and pipework to the river was completed by local volunteers.

The landscape
Hockenhull has four distinct areas: a wet meadow (or alder carr) consisting of mainly floating vegetation, a reed bed, a poplar plantation and a large meadow of grassland. It also has mature hedgerows lining a mediaeval roadway complete with three red sandstone pack-horse bridges dating from 1470. The river Gowy has dictated much of the habitat, because over the centuries the river has changed its course several times allowing areas of floating vegetation and submerged water courses to develop, which gives the area its distinctive character.

In the 1970s most of the farmland in the area was used for grazing dairy cattle and was quite wet in nature, consequently curlew and snipe were common. However, the change from dairy to an arable culture has also changed the very nature of the landscape. Almost all the surrounding farm land has since been drained and the reserve area at Hockenhull Platts is the only remaining piece of wet meadow landscape that stays wet even in the driest of summers.

The poplar plantation has now become mature and creates more shade and cover than existed before. Few, if any, flowers now appear on that part of the reserve. The reed bed on the north west of the reserve has largely remained unchanged as it has been protected by fencing and not grazed by farm animals. The main meadow, which is much drier than the rest of the site and contains mostly grasses, has been alternately grazed over the years by both cattle and horses and seems to have developed into an ideal habitat for all the owl species. Small mammals, mainly shrews and voles, breed in the cover provided by the hummocky, tufted nature of the vegetation. Brown hare are also seen frequently there, and signs of activity by badger, fox and weasel can often be found on the reserve. The otter holt looks to have provided a purpose built home for mink, as there have been many sightings both on the Gowy and the local canal, but there have also been two or three sightings of an otter on the reserve area in the last two years.

Flowers
The first flowers to appear each year are celandines, coltsfoot and beautiful marsh marigolds, followed by water marestail, branched burr reed, common rush, water forget-me-not, lady smock and ragged robin. As spring goes into summer many beautiful orchids appear, a small number of northern marsh and early purple orchids followed by thousands of the common spotted variety, and hybrids of the two which in good seasons grow to a height of over 75 cm.

By mid-summer marsh valarian, meadowsweet, milk parsley, pink campion, marsh thistle and figwort are the more dominant plants whilst many species of flowering grasses, sedges and reeds grow profusely. Other plants such as buttercup, silverweed, purple and kidney vetch, birds foot trefoil and greater and lesser stitchwort can been seen all over the site. Although the river is now cleared each autumn, floating water crowfoot still emerges each spring and is a good food source and resting site for damsel and dragonflies. The ancient hedgerows contain wild arum, herb robert, stitchwort, campion, elder, dog rose and hawthorn, all of which provide food for birds and insects alike.

Birds
The British Trust for Ornithology Common Bird Census has now been carried out at Hockenhull for over 25 years and is therefore a very good indicator of the changes to the bird population in a largely farmland habitat over that period. Farmland species like skylark, corn bunting, song thrush, lapwing, winchat, reed bunting, snipe, and curlew have declined dramatically. However, extremely wet weather during January and February 1999 saw the return of a number of common snipe.

Many opportunist bird species have found the reservoir a very suitable habitat. In spring swifts can been seen in huge numbers (150 plus) hunting for insects over the water, followed later in the season by swallows, sand and house martins. Teal, pochard, tufted duck, common and green sandpiper, snipe, coot, moorhen and mute swan have been seen.

Herons, cormorants, Canada and greylag geese are now often seen flying over the reserve and landing on the reservoir. A single oystercatcher also appeared for the first time in 1998. A kingfisher also appeared frequently on the reserve in 1998, although its probable nest site is about 2–3 km upstream near Stamford Bridge. However the reserve has become a special place because of its growing population of owls. There are tawny owls breeding on the site, with barn and little owls close by, with visiting short-eared owls present during winter months. A special feature at Hockenhull is that the tawny owls can often be seen roosting in trees on the wet meadow during the day in late May and early June, and are not just confined to night-time appearances. The pair reared three young in 1997 and at least two in 1998. During the 1990s there was an increase in visits by other birds of prey. For many years kestrels were the only regular bird of prey species on the site, however red kite, buzzard, peregrine falcon, merlin, and sparrowhawk have been recorded. The changes to key bird species mentioned above do not seem to have affected our local woodland birds. Tree creeper, greater spotted woodpecker, wren, robin, dunnock, blackbird, long tail, blue and great tits, bullfinch, chaffinch, greenfinch and yellow hammer are seen regularly.

The decline of the migrant warbler species, such as whitethroat, black cap, chiff chaff, willow, sedge and grasshopper warbler has been reversed, with some species of warblers actually increasing in numbers of late, with blackcap and whitethroat doing particularly well. However, the cuckoo is only just hanging on to its status at Hockenhull and in the area generally. This once common species is down from seven pairs in its best season to one pair in recent years, although three singing males were recorded in 1998. Meadow pipits and skylarks are now almost rarities, although seven singing male skylarks were plotted in the census taken on 4th April 1999, after four had been recorded at the same time in 1998. As the poplar plantation becomes more mature so there are more sightings of greater spotted woodpecker, nuthatch, treecreeper and goldcrest. The goldcrests probably bred for the first time in 1988.

In recent years the song thrush population has slightly increased, and mistle thrushes have now become established as a breeding species at Hockenhull. Surprisingly the most significant change of any bird species over the 25 years of recording at Hockenhull has been the decline of the house martin. These used to be numerous, feeding over the reserve each day and nesting nearby, but they are now a rarity.

The reserve is best visited for its birds in May and June and has now an impressive list of over 125 species visiting or breeding on the site. A new footpath and trail has been created by Mr Hill, the local farmer, which makes a very interesting circular walk, passing through the causeway to the Roman Bridges, going alongside the reserve and following the Gowy to the south, and then diagonally across farmland back to the lanes, passing the new reservoir. The walk takes about 45 minutes and can be combined with a visit to the reserve with excellent views from the footpath.

Butterflies, damsel and dragonflies

There was a very promising start to 1998 with good warm weather in May influencing the emergence of the first broods of these insects, but due to the subsequent wet weather very few were seen later in the season. There has been a decrease in the number of these species during the 25 years of observation. Food sources on the reserve have not changed much, but clearly the habitat in and around the reserve has, and could have affected the species seen. There have been occasional years when numbers have increased dramatically, as in 1997 when hundreds of migrating painted ladies were seen and in 1998 when many holly blues were spotted. Small numbers of orange wing tips were also seen in April and May, but the expected influx of wall browns, small tortoiseshell, speckled woods and small skippers never materialised and the area never came alive with butterflies at all that year. A visit from two brimstones during the summer was a highlight. Dragonflies have never been present in any great numbers, but the brown hawker and the blue emperor did well in 1998 and were seen together with the beautiful demoiselle, the large red damselfly and the common blue damselfly. In 1999 an influx of southern hawkers, broad bodied chasers, red darters and more than 100 branded arigon demoiselles was most welcome.

Acknowledgements and Bibliography

This book has drawn on a variety of sources. Those that have been used most frequently are listed below, others are referred to under the chapter headings. We acknowledge the help and assistance in particular of the Cheshire County Record Office, which has kindly given us permission to publish some of the A A Guest-Williams material.

The documents & papers of the Rev A A Guest-Williams, DGW 2067/2087/2111
Christleton Parish Records, P28.
Rev J. H. Davies, Llandudno, private papers on the Guest-Williams family.
Christleton Parish Magazines (1871–2000).
F Latham and Christleton Local History Group, *Christleton. The History of a Cheshire Village* (1979)
Ecton Appraisal Group, *Ecton. A Northamptonshire Parish.*

Photographs
Most of the photographs are from the Christleton Local History Group Collection and were loaned by members of the community. In particular for this publication, the group would like to thank the Morgan family, Pamela Johnson, Ethel Witter, Sue Massey, Rene Stalker, Dot Sproston, David and Roy Fisher, Jim Partington, Jim Salmon, Ted Kirk, David Wain, Peter Langmead and Mr and Mrs Kidd.
They were taken by Reg Morgan, Ernest Hall, Gerry Lockley (*Chester Chronicle*), David Wain and David Cummings.

Drawings of Roman Artefacts
The Samian ware cup, drawn from *J of Chester Archaeol Soc* **62**, (1980 for 1979) fig2, Do27.
For a stamp by the 1st Century potter no 30. Secumdus ii., W F Grimes, *Holt*, (1930) p124, no 30.
Roman enclosures on Stamford Heath adapted from Ainsworth et al., (1990) fig 2
Roman coin adapted from Casey p124.
Thanks are owed to David Shotter of Lancaster University for his comments on the coins in the Christleton area.

Chapter 1
Thanks for helpful information are owed to Dr Jill Collens (Cheshire County Council, SMR),
Dr Rob Philpott (Liverpool Museum) and Dr David Shotter (Lancaster University).
CAB   *Cheshire Archaeological Bulletin*
JCAS   *Journal of the Chester Archaeological Society*
VCH   *The Victoria History of the County of Chester*, **1**, eds Harris B E &
       Thacker A T, (Oxford University Press, 1987).
Ainsworth S, Everson P & Wilson-North W R, 'Two rectangular enclosures on Stamford Heath, Christleton, near Chester,' *JCAS* **70**, 81–85 (1990 for 1987–8).
Bu'lock J D, *Pre-Conquest Cheshire* History of Cheshire, **3**, (1972, Chester).
Carrington P, ed. *English Heritage Book of Chester* (1994, London).
Dodgson J McN, *The place-names of Cheshire* **3, 4, 5 ii**. (1971, 1972 , 1997 Cambridge University Press for English Place-Name Society).
Gelling M, *Signposts to the past. Place-names and the history of England* (1978, London).
Grimes W F, *Holt, Denbighshire. The twentieth legion at Castle Lyons* (1930, London).
Margary I D, *Roman roads in Britain*, **II** (1957, London).
Mason D J P, 'The *prata legionis* at Chester,' *JCAS* **69**, 19–43 (for 1957, 1986).
Nevell M, ed., *Living on the edge of empire: models, methodology & marginality*, CBA North West (1999, University of Manchester and Chester Archaeology).
Philpott R A, 'New evidence from aerial reconnaissance for Roman military sites in Cheshire,' *Britannia* **29**, 341–352 (1998).
Stephens G R, 'The Roman aqueduct at Chester,' *JCAS* **68**, 59–69 (1986 for 1985).
Thompson F H, *Roman Cheshire*, History of Cheshire 2 (1965, Chester)
Ward S W, *Excavations at Chester. Saxon occupation within the Roman fortress: sites excavated 1971–1981* (1994, Chester City Council), Report No 7.
Ward M, 'A collection of samian from the legionary works-depot at Holt,' in Bird J, ed. *Form and Fabric. Studies in Rome's material past* (1998, Oxford) pp133–143.
Ward M, 'Some finds from the Roman works-depot at Holt,' *Studia Celtica* **32**, 43–84 (1998).
Williams S R, *West Cheshire from the air* (1997, Chester City Council) Occasional Paper No 4.
A A Guest-Williams, *Cheshire Life* **4** (1948).
Hazel Warhurst, 'Pew Dispute & The Glasshouse Inn' paper, Nottingham.

Ordnance Survey Maps.
National Monuments Records Centre, Swindon for aerial photographs.
Cheshire County Council Records aerial photographs.
Cheshire County Records Office, *Christleton Tithe Award 1844, Inclosure Award 1794.*
Oxford Companion to Local History.
C S Davies, *Agricultural History of Cheshire 1750–1850.*
G E Fussell, *Four Centuries of Cheshire Farming Systems.1500–1900.*
G M Trevelyan, *Illustrated English Social History.*
Thompson, McKenna & Mackillings, *Ploughlands & Pastures* (CCC).
Oliver Rackham, *Illustrated History of the Countryside.*
W G Hoskins, *The Makings of the English Landscape.*
Margaret Croston & John Lodge, *The History of Christleton Parish Council.*

Chapter 2
David Cummings, *The History of St James' Christleton.*
Rev David Fisher, *The Bells of St James' Church Christleton.*
Charles Smeatham and Eric Kenyon, *Christleton Methodist Church.*
Humphrey Broad-Davies, *Life at the Salvatorian College.*

Chapter 3
David Cummings, *Hockenhull Platts Nature Reserve* (Christleton Local History Group).
'The Cheshire Remonstrance of 1642,' *Cheshire Sheaf*, 10102, **51**, 10–11 (1956).
'The Armour of the Clergy 1625 AD,' *Cheshire Sheaf*, 10857, **56**, 75–7 (1961).
'Terrier for Christleton 1663,' *Cheshire Sheaf*, 11315, **60**, 24 (1965).
Dore R N, *The Civil Wars in Cheshire*, Cheshire Community Council, (1966, Chester)
Dore R N, 'The Letter Books of Sir William Brereton vol I, January 31st–May 29th 1645,' *Record Soc. of Lancs. and Chesh.*, **123** (1984).
Malbon T, 'Memorials of the Civil War in Cheshire,' in J Hall, ed. *Record Soc. of Lancs. and Chesh.* **19** (1889).
Morris R H,'The Siege of Chester 1643-1646,' in P H Lawson, ed. *J Chester Archaeol Soc* **25**, 1–279 (1923).
Ormerod G, *History of Cheshire*, T Helsby, ed. vol. **II** (1882).
The Diary of Henry Prescott, Record Soc. of Lancs. and Chesh.
1851 Village Census.

Chapter 4
Chester City Record Office for various papers relating to Thomas Dixon and family.
National Westminster Bank Archives and Brian Roberts for papers about the Dixon Bank.
Peter McCready of the Littleton History Group.
Daily Telegraph and *The Times* for obituaries of Jas Storrar.

Chapter 5
John Sellers' Trust Minute Book.
The College of Law Opening Ceremony, Mr Les George.
The College of Law Prospectus 2000
Christleton School Entry & Log Books.

Chapter 6
The Minute books of Christleton Players, courtesy of Mr Peter Jackson.
Photographs, programmes and articles about Christleton Players, courtesy of Mr and Mrs Stan Jones, Rene Stalker, David and Nora Wain and Peter Langmead.
'Christleton Football Club Centenary. 1897–1997,' *Evening Leader.*
The Story of Guiding in Christleton from Beryl Dimmer and Anne Stockdale.
The Story of Scouting in Christleton from Roy Fisher.

Chapter 7
David Cummings, *Christleton Pit and the Story of Ponds* (Christleton Local History Group).
David Cummings, *Hockenhull Platts Nature Reserve.*